Action,
Art,
History

Columbia Themes in Philosophy

Columbia Themes in Philosophy

Series Editor: Akeel Bilgrami,
Johnsonian Professor of Philosophy, Columbia University

Columbia Themes in Philosophy is a new series with a broad
and accommodating thematic reach as well as an ecumenical
approach to the outdated disjunction between analytical
and European philosophy. It is committed to an examination
of key themes in new and startling ways and to the
exploration of new topics in philosophy.

Edward Said, *Humanism and Democratic Criticism*
Michael Dummett, *Truth and the Past*
John Searle, *Freedom and Neurobiology: Reflections on Free Will,
Language, and Political Power*

B+T   WR/BA

Action,
Art,
History

Engagements with

Arthur C. Danto

Edited by

Daniel Herwitz and Michael Kelly

Columbia University Press

New York

Columbia University Press

Publishers Since 1893

New York   Chichester, West Sussex

Copyright © 2007 Columbia University Press

All rights reserved

Library of Congress Cataloging-in-Publication Data

Action, art, history : engagements with Arthur C. Danto /
    edited by Daniel Herwitz and Michael Kelly.
    p.   cm. — (Columbia themes in philosophy)
ISBN-13: 978-0-231-13796-6 (cloth : alk. paper)
ISBN-10: 0-231-13796-6 (cloth : alk. paper)
ISBN-13: 978-0-231-51084-4 (electronic)
ISBN-10: 0-231-51084-5 (electronic)
1. Danto, Arthur Coleman, 1924– I. Herwitz, Daniel Alan, 1955– II. Kelly,
    Michael, 1953– III. Series.
B945.D364A63   2007
220.5′208—dc22
                                                    2006013638

⬭

Columbia University Press books are printed on permanent
    and durable acid-free paper.
This book was printed on paper with recycled content.
Printed in the United States of America
c 10 9 8 7 6 5 4 3 2 1

Designed by Lisa Hamm

References to Internet Web sites (URLs) were accurate at the time of writing.
Neither the author nor Columbia University Press is responsible for URLs
that may have expired or changed since the articles were prepared.

Contents

Introduction

Daniel Herwitz and Michael Kelly

There are few today who have attained the kind of public status and recognition of Arthur C. Danto. In 2003 his book *The Madonna of the Future*
won the prestigious French Prix Philosophie: he became the first American to win that honor for philosophy applied to contemporary issues. An
earlier volume of his, *Encounters and Reflections*, won the National Book
Critics Circle award (1990). His concepts of postmodern art and culture
are virtual road maps of the present art world, powered by philosophical
depth and capacious inclusiveness. Past president of the American Philosophical Association and of the American Society for Aesthetics, Danto
is a leader in philosophy and art criticism. His work has done nothing
less than redefine those fields. Art critic for *The Nation* magazine, former
Johnsonian Professor of Philosophy at Columbia University, Danto is a
Spinoza of the (New York) marketplace, a denizen of the museum, the gallery, and the lecture hall beloved by three generations of philosophers, art
critics, artists, and New York *bricoleurs*.

This volume is a tribute to him that robustly carries on debate over his
work in various aspects of philosophy, art history, and art criticism. Its
authors—Stanley Cavell, Hans Belting, Lydia Goehr, Philip Kitcher (with
Daniel Immerwahr), Frank Ankersmit, Gregg Horowitz, and the late Donald Davidson—testify to the quality of response his achievements have
elicited. (The two editors of this volume are pleased to be among the con-

tributors.) Their essays engage Danto's philosophies of art, action, and history, along with his art criticism and his cultural role. The volume owes its origin to a celebratory conference on Danto's work organized by the *Journal of Philosophy* at Columbia University and cosponsored by the Columbia University School of Fine Arts (Bruce Ferguson, dean) and Department of Philosophy (Haim Gaifman, then chair). Special thanks also go to Daniel Shapiro, a trustee of the *Journal*, for his supporting role. Michael Kelly, then editor of the *Journal of Philosophy*, was the central organizer of this conference.

Danto has provided a response to each of the papers included in this volume, which is characteristic of his insight and generosity. The book's organization is piecemeal: Danto's response appears directly after each piece of writing. Assembled together, his responses represent a lucid statement of his intellectual biography, as well as his way of continuing the philosophical conversations he has been engaged in for nearly half a century. We have also included Akeel Bilgrami's short piece, "Arthur Danto at Columbia and in New York," delivered at the opening of the Columbia conference, because we believe it captures certain aspects of Danto's character and philosophy. We have kept the essay in an informal mode.

In order to appreciate the originality of Danto's views, two things should be kept in mind: the state of Anglo-American philosophy during the 1960s and the state of avant-garde art. Anglo-American or analytical philosophy, carrying the inheritance of logicism and ordinary language philosophy, was during the 1960s intensely focused on a small number of topics, about which it believed genuine philosophical progress could be made. The topics had to do with mathematical and scientific truth, semantics for natural languages, and questions of cognitive value, probability and certainty, action and intention, and the nature of ethical statements. When W.V.O. Quine announced with satisfaction that "philosophy of science is philosophy enough," the remark raised a few eyebrows but resonated with the moment. Danto's first book was an edited volume in the philosophy of science (with Sydney Morgenbesser), and it was through that work that the former Ann Arbor–Detroit–born GI Joe turned abstract expressionist printmaker turned philosopher became known to the philosophical world. Danto continued to do cutting-edge work in such (then) canonical topics as the theory of action and the philosophy of belief and knowledge. But his broad and synoptic mind quickly led him into the philosophy of history, to a study of Nietzsche, and to the philosophy of art. Danto was unique at the time in viewing this wide range of enterprises as not only philosophically worthwhile, but worthwhile because deeply connected to their more canonical cousins. He brought to philosophy the artist's unfettered imagination, along with a rigorous commitment to discovering singular metaphysical structures that would link the various fields of philosophical study with which he was occupied into something like a philosophical system.

The avant-gardes were as crucial to the formation of Danto's philosophical outlook as his training in analytical philosophy. His insight was to realize that what was happening in avant-garde art paralleled what was happening in philosophy: they were in something like the same enterprise. Clement Greenberg had claimed that modernist art was about the clarification—and justification—of its own foundations, the discovery of its artistic essence (which he believed resided in the medium). Greenberg had once gone so far as to call that avant-garde enterprise "Kantian." However, no one in philosophy had thought to take his critical bravado beyond thought-provoking generality, nor focus on the next generation of artists after his Picasso, Mondrian, Pollock et al.—George Brecht, John Cage, Andy Warhol and company, none of whom Greenberg favored. Danto broke that ground in a vision of the avant-gardes that proved astonishing for all philosophy of art, and indeed philosophy of culture. His breakthrough was made possible by W.V.O. Quine's work in the philosophy of science, and Danto's own first forays there. Following Quine's investigations into radical interpretation—how meaning is grasped/generated by interpreters of distant languages—Danto began to consider the similarly radical objects made and put forward by the avant-gardes: objects as distant from ordinary works of art as the languages of the Khoi and San are from Russian or Chinese. Duchamp's hat racks, George Brecht's light switches turning on and off, John Cage's performance of four minutes and thirty-three seconds of silence, Rauschenberg's erasure of a De Kooning drawing: these could not help but raise the question of what is at stake in thinking of them as art—or not. Above all, it was Andy Warhol's *Brillo Box* (exhibited in 1964 at the Stable Gallery) that struck Danto with the force of a thunderbolt. Were not these gestures ways of laying bare the philosophical stakes of art in their baldest (most essential) form? Did not each, Danto surmised, cause the interpreter to reflect on the conditions of art making? Were these avant-gardes not therefore historically convergent with the philosophy of art, not to mention with the investigations into linguistic interpretation that focused on the most distant, impenetrable languages (to speakers of English)?

Warhol's *Brillo Box*, far from being a mere game played with consumer advertising, was, he surmised, a gesture that revisited Leibnitz's problem of the identity of indiscernibles. Man/homunculus, animal/machine, language/sound, event/action: each pairing presents two sides of the same coin, and their differences cannot be grasped apart from conceptual interpretation. No mere inspection of a hand moving or sound on tape will tell the interpreter whether an action or mere event (by reflex, say) has taken place, nor whether a language has been spoken. Such indiscernibles focus philosophy on the question of what constitutes *knowing*, or put the other way around, what constitutes a thing's being of a certain kind.

Warhol's *Brillo Box* is (to all intents and purposes) no different from the mass-produced box in the store, so if it is art (as Danto believes), then whatever makes it such cannot reside in any of its visual properties. For it is (to all intents and purposes) indiscernible from the ordinary store-bought variety. Warhol's genius, being (according to Danto) Leibnitzian, solicited an answer to the question: "What then makes Warhol's art? What spells out the difference?" Danto's philosophical answer, following Quine's work in the philosophy of language, is that it is an interpretive theory held by the relevant community of interpreters (the art world) that performs this coup de grace. Thus he invests the modern apparatus of the art world with the logic of art making. How many artists does it take to switch on a light bulb? The answer is: one, but only if there is an art world to deem it art. To think of Brecht's gesture as art *at all* was audacious enough (to perform it as art took even more chutzpah). But once it was so thought of, to pursue the philosophical invitation to Danto's conclusion was truly, in Nietzsche's sense, to live dangerously.

Danto's answer to the avant-garde question therefore came in the form of an essential definition of universal scope. What makes a mere thing, gesture, or otherwise ontological entity into a work of art is the theory held by the art world that deems it so. As the art world evolves, its theories change, thus canonizing new kinds of artworks. Only in the late modernist period, for example, could a light bulb switch on as a work of art. The answer was utterly contemporary, but the presumption of its universality was traditional and branded Danto a "pretty conservative kind of philosopher," in his own words. What followed was an even more bold thesis about art history. Appropriating Hegel's idea that culture is always driven by the project of (philosophical) self-knowing, Danto concluded that with the avant-gardes and their use of the identity of indiscernibles, art had finally gotten to the point where it could take its own project no further. Having raised the question of what art is, the avant-gardes could not find an answer within art practice but only in the medium of words, specifically of philosophical theory. Art history had paradoxically been brought to an end by the very avant-gardists who thought they'd opened up its new road. This idea that art was at an end was again Danto's philosophical spin on the tenor of the times. He looked around and intuited in the art of the 1980s a moment of liberation from the heavy burden of driving the project of art further, a moment of diversity and game playing, and called it "posthistorical." Having taken art to its historical conclusion, the avant-gardes had paradoxically freed it to be anything and everything, liberated it into the condition of postmodernism. Danto the critic can be fierce (if always insightful) about the pitfalls of some of this art. Always on the cusp of things, Danto voiced what many were feeling was in the air—a moment of realization, of freedom—and gave it an astonishing philosophical riff by incorporating the moment into his own grand narrative.

At the core of this "pretty conservative kind of philosopher"'s approach has always been the Leibnitzian problem. His theory of action is motivated by the question of what makes a hand moving an "action" as opposed to a mere reflex. His theory of history is motivated by the question of what makes time of significance to it, given that (to recall Bertrand Russell's quip) collapsing the history of the world into the last five minutes would make no difference to perception, to how we "look back" on the past from the present. This question is, Danto argued, about narrative sentences, about the way human and natural history get told/understood. Related, therefore, is the Kantian question: how does a story of natural causes (the story of events told as part of physics) get recast as a story about human history (about actions and consequences, society and economy)? The key to narrative sentences turns out to be their mutability, their liability to change over time, their truth conditions relativized, as it were, to time of utterance. As events unfold and assignment of temporality shifts, as the context of interpretation alters, narrative truth shifts (at least about human history). It was not possible to call the Civil War a "war of emancipation" until the Emancipation Proclamation was set forth. Nor (to refer to Danto's own philosophical practice) was it possible to describe the end of art as an "end" until Warhol and the diverse/playful art of the 1980s came about. Subsequent postmodernism has cast the end of art in a less decorous, certainly less utopian perspective, which Danto has himself pointed out in essays subsequent to those of the mid-1980s. What makes the description of history *historical* is its temporality, and the mark of temporality is descriptive change (about past, present, future), meaning subsequent revision. Danto's is a kind of Nietzschean perspectivism.

It is also a theory of action writ large, or a theory deriving from the theory of action. For all description of all action is historically datable, and hence revisable. The kind of thing that makes an event appear as an action is precisely the kind of thing that makes it part of history. Historical stories are simply descriptions of actions and their consequences in narrative form. Indeed, narration is central to action since actors are always self-describers (however implicit): people who take themselves to be doing things for a reason, in the light of a past and in the name of a future. From the moment action happens, it happens in the form of narrative representations. History is the remaking of these. And so Danto's work on action, on history, on Nietzsche, and on art becomes finally a single, vast, analytical text.

This book is a recounting of Danto's philosophical trajectory in its broadest and most controversial scope. It is also a map of his fluent capacity to move between philosophy and contemporary culture. Were Danto's writing more overtly political, he might be called the Diderot of his time— except that instead of an encyclopedic mentality, his is one that seeks to revel in its times and expand them. In an age when the humanities are all too often consumed by bitter complaint, Danto's work is that of a Nietzschean personality surprised and delighted by his times and ready to convert that surprise into an audacity worthy of them. Being surprised, he wishes to be philosophically surprising. Danto's is perhaps the philosophical personality Nietzsche wanted to have but couldn't. To take one's times and make of them something as rich as possible, that is a kind of philosophical goal. To speak for the future as it is crystallizing all around, to speak before the crystals of the future appear: this is something as critical for philosophy to do as anything. No one has succeeded more admirably than Danto, nor with as much graciousness and generosity of spirit. It is for this monumental ability that he is admired and loved.

Daniel Shapiro, Danto's friend and companion in art, generously joined Columbia University Press in making the production of this book possible. We all thank him.

Action,
Art,
History

1

Arthur Danto at Columbia and in New York

Akeel Bilgrami

In the places where Arthur Danto worked for many decades—Columbia's philosophy department and the *Journal of Philosophy*—which have come together now to celebrate his work, there has always been a general feeling that, as much as he loved and labored here, he found us too confining. Perversely, this is a source of pride rather than hurt. Actually, if I may take a moment to congratulate ourselves, it is even a measure of the modesty of our intellectual self-conception that we take so much pride in having among us someone whose talents and intellectual appetites far surpass the nourishment that a mere department or journal, or even a profession-alized discipline such as philosophy, can offer.

The larger space that Arthur occupies with such relish is, of course, the city of New York. In fact, his whole style is so supremely metropolitan that one gets no sense at all of where he was born and bred. One might easily conclude, looking at the style of the man and of his speech and writing, that everything about his life has been striking, even his birth, which was on New Year's Day of 1924—but we mustn't forget that it was, after all, Ann Arbor, Michigan where he was born and Detroit where he was bred. But like all good New Yorkers and good Columbia men and women, Ar-thur gives the impression, however wrong, that he really only began to flourish after he came to New York and to Columbia.

His early flourishing took the form of successive books on analytic philosophy, which contained original and substantial ideas on the nature of history and human action, ideas that have been widely discussed and assimilated into the tradition of thought on these subjects. Then there were books with invaluably clear and novel interpretations of the thought of philosophers outside the mainstream of analytic philosophy, Nietzsche and Sartre in particular, which brought him wider fame, and, as he likes to say, a summer home in the Hamptons. But it was not until he began a study of the nature of artworks and art worlds that he poised himself for a major defection, or "transfiguration," to use a word that he has almost made his own.

Premonitions of that defection were there for some years before, when in his editorial judgments and in his stray remarks he would betray a mild weariness with the way philosophy had gone: the tedium of some of its professional protocols, the barbarous idiom of some of its writing, the lack of chivalry in some of its argumentative combat, and the routines of its reinvention of familiar and tired ideas. It was not that he was nostalgic for some earlier way of doing it, and it was not that he failed to recognize that there *were* pockets of creative and exciting work; it's more, I believe, that he was just yearning for *himself*, for some more human and gallant creed. So the defection finally came when that great old fox and facilitator, Ben Sonnenberg of the old *Grand Street*, urged various commissions of essays about art upon him, to which he responded with the passion of long-simmering intellectual tendencies being released; and then it was Ben again, if I remember correctly, who persuaded *The Nation* and Arthur to come together in what has been an extraordinary career of art criticism, though "career" seems wholly the wrong word for what *The Nation* makes possible for its writers as well as for the attractive life Arthur has led in the last decade or more.

I say this was a defection, but I should by no means give the impression that it was something complete or dramatic, *away* from philosophy. All the great modern writers on art have an accent. Clement Greenberg's zeal for the modern had a distinct New York tone, Harold Rosenberg's shrewd insights had the cultivated chattiness of *The New Yorker* (when *The New Yorker* was cultivated), and even Meyer Shapiro's vast learning had many hints of his progressive politics and humanity—and the special quality of Arthur's reviews in *The Nation* is that they are unmistakably the writings of a *philosopher*, revealing often how a line, image, or stone was the stimulus or the station of some idea, even sometimes of an argument. *The Na-*

tion has, as a result of his essays, managed to become something of a philosophical magazine, and that is no bad thing.

And conversely, in philosophy, what he has managed to assert in public ways in these last twenty years is a personality that makes him quite unusual, if not unique, among analytic philosophers—a genuinely cultured man. Not just someone grabbing every week the offerings of a prodigious metropole, but someone whose ideas and perceptions are tuned by a daily awareness of how the city and its arts have come to be what they are, and how they stand among the productions of other cities in America and the world. Culture, in Arthur's thinking, is perhaps more important than anything else, and this emerges in ways that are sometimes amusing—and appalling. I remember once how Isaac Levi and I were struck dumb when we asked him, after his visit to Calcutta, how he had managed to cope with the awful condition of its suffering, and he replied in a trice: "Oh, that was nothing; you see, poverty is part of the *culture* of Calcutta."

Before closing, I just want to say one little thing about his quality as a leader, from which I and others, alas, learned little, and that is his gift, not so much of what is called, in that charmless phrase, "consensus building," which no department with character will attain, but rather, in the face of a lack of consensus, of nevertheless avoiding all conflict with a sort of genial deflection. Indeed, as his earlier appalling remark just cited suggests, he would have managed to deflect all conflict, were he even the mayor of Calcutta! Adversity never seemed to toughen him, it merely brought out his likeable humors. I don't know where Arthur learned these arts, which seem to come so naturally to him. I only know that I want to go to school there.

I have used words like "geniality" and "deflection," but they seem to only skim what I think goes very much deeper—down to depths of a touching kindness of temperament, which made him a most appealing colleague and is no doubt part of his appeal as a critic. I can't put it better than he himself does in a short essay that I recently read ("From Philosophy to Art Criticism," *American Art* 6, no. 1 [Spring 2002]: 14–17):

> There is a lot I like and a lot I don't like, but these preferences do not give me reason either to defend or attack. I must some time discover why art criticism and criticism generally is so savagely aggressive against its target, almost—as Chekhov once wrote—as if the writer or artist had committed some crime. When I first began to write, there was a certain amount of negativity in my pieces, but I increasingly believe that that is a form of cruelty, and that cruelty is never permissible.

Notice that even the condemnation of the cruel here is gentle and incomplete, for as he says only (and I especially like this): "I must some time discover" why we are like that. . . . That is Arthur Danto all over. Is it a wonder that people, even cruel people, love him—here, and in the art world, and everywhere else that he is known?

To no one, not even to those whom he knows well—even, I am sure, his wonderful wife and companion, Barbara—does he ever give the impression that he quite believes in the remarkableness of his achievements. It's not as if he thinks it's all a dream. He is just having too much fun to stop and take it in.

A Note on My Responses

ARTHUR C. DANTO

Michael Kelly was very much the organizing spirit behind the conference for which the papers in this volume were conceived and written, and I appreciate beyond measure the imagination, the judgment, and the energy with which he invested it. Though my philosophy was the occasion for the event, and often, though not entirely, the subject of most of the papers, I think it a matter of consensus that the conference itself was remarkable for the level of the contributions and for the generosity of the speakers, who took the time to prepare papers of such quality and to travel to New York to participate in three days of wonderful philosophical interchange. I am grateful to Akeel Bilgrami for recognizing this by proposing that as many as possible of the papers be published, and that I be given the opportunity to respond to them; and to Daniel Herwitz, who, together with Michael Kelly, convinced the other authors to allow their writing to be used for this purpose. The conference itself was made up of nothing but high points. It is sheer gluttony on my part to regret the absence of the papers that, for whatever reason, were unavailable for publication here. No one who experienced the conference will have forgotten the papers by Daniel Dennett, Rosalind Krauss, and Richard Wollheim, nor the marvelous panel on philosophy and art criticism, organized and moderated by Daniel Shapiro, that concluded it. But the nine papers that were made available are as rich and rare as anyone could wish, and I am exalted by their existence. It has been a joy and privilege to be able to think through the ingenious arguments, examples, and objections that have been offered me as gifts.

I had originally imagined writing a long essay, weaving my responses together into some integral summation. But each paper was so striking, each trailed so different a history and expressed so different a personality, that I felt it would somehow be unsuitable to dissolve them into some larger entity. I thought it better to respond to them singly, engage with them one on one, so that the reader could rethink the paper through my reaction to it and treat each exchange as a separate dialogue. I may perhaps be forgiven for noticing that the number of contributors maps exactly to the number of suitors in the bottom compartment of Marcel Duchamp's masterpiece, *La Mariée mise á nu par ses célebataires même,* with the bride isolated in the upper compartment. That had always emblematized for me a highly unsatisfactory arrangement—a depiction of unfulfillable yearning in both directions. A somewhat better matrimonial condition is projected in the *Mahabharata,* where Arjuna and his brothers return home with what they describe as a treasure—the princess bride won by Arjuna's prowess as an archer—and their mother tells them to share it equally. The ideal situation is simultaneous monogamy with nine partners, and while I know this is impossible, one must always try to live by the principle of having one's cake and eating it too. Only Duchamp could have pictured that, but alas, he didn't.

2

Danto's Action

Donald Davidson

When I was invited to participate in this fine Dantoesque orgy I thought I could write, if I wanted, about Danto on art. I rushed out and bought a beautiful pile of books from Amazon.com and started to read about Brillo boxes. What fun! I had in mind for a title "Art on Art." But then I was told I should talk about Danto on action. Long ago I had read some of Arthur's seminal essays on action and had acquired *The Analytic Philosophy of Action*. I should not have worried that I would be entirely starved of Arthur's take on art. The first paragraph of the book asks us to remember six panels among that galaxy of Giotto's frescos in the Arena Chapel in Padua. Each panel depicts Christ doing something by raising his arm, for example, blessing people at the Jerusalem gate, admonishing the elders, or expelling the lenders from the temple. As I went on, I discovered there were about as many allusions to art in this book on action as there were pages. Cruising through Arthur's encyclopedic output, I could not help noticing the extraordinary way everything fit into a grand pattern. Epistemology, philosophy of history, philosophy of art, and theory of action illuminate one another, patterns recur, and themes have variations. Not only were there many artistically animated books on philosophy but there was also a book on art as philosophy. Arthur has many arts. Now I had my title: "Art's Arts." Much better than "Arthur's Actions."

I learned from *The Body/Body Problem* that when Arthur turned from art to philosophy (as he misleadingly puts it), he already had the ambition to write a number of books on various topics that would present an organized picture. Santayana's five-volumes *The Life of Reason* was the model. I find the purpose and skill with which Arthur has carried out his plan admirable. I also find it amazing, perhaps because my own trajectory through philosophy has been the precise opposite. (I have finally finished a small book.)

Given what I have just said, it is not surprising that Arthur begins his book on action by relating the structure of action to the structure of knowledge. The comparison is apt. In perception, which roots knowledge in the world, outside events cause such events within as the formation of beliefs. Some of these beliefs in turn become reasons for acting, thus changing the world. It is these points where thought affects the world and the world affects thought, where hard questions arise. It seems (at least to me) natural to say Christ in his infinite goodness knows it is his role to confer blessings, and that he can play this role on occasion by raising his arm. This explains why he acted as he is depicted as acting. If one tries, as I have, to spell this out much as Aristotle did, by saying that a positive attitude toward bestowing a blessing, plus a belief that raising an arm would effectuate the desired end, explains the action by revealing the light in which the agent viewed it and caused the action, then it is tempting to try to define an intentional action as one that can be explained in this way. But it is not always so simple. My favorite counterexample to the definition was invented by Daniel Bennett (wild pigs). One must at least add to the definition that the relevant reasons caused the desired end more or less as the agent intended. But this addition uses the notion of intention, which was to be defined. My conclusion is that there is no way to perfect the definition, and that part of the reason for this failure is that the definition tries to bridge the gap between states and events described in nonintentional terms and states and events described in intentional terms. ("He raised his arm in order to bring it about [cause it to be the case] that the crowd was blessed," "He moved his arm in order to cause the rock to be moved," or, to put it more nearly as Arthur does, "He brought it about that the rock was moved by moving his arm.") Perception raises the same problem in reverse: if I see that the sky is gray, the grayness of the sky brings it about (causes it to be the case) that I believe the sky is gray. But of course this leaves out something: my belief must be caused by the sky in the right way. But try to say what the right way is without begging the question. I think you can't.

Arthur sees the analogy between epistemology and action in a different, though not conflicting, light. He notes the standard way of defining knowledge as true belief for which one has adequate evidence, and Arthur knows, of course, that this won't quite do: someone may have a true belief, and that belief may be justified by things he knows, and yet the justifiers cause the true belief in such a way that the result is not a case of knowledge. In the book on action, Arthur compares the claim (with which he agrees) that nothing can be known by the appeal to further knowledge unless *something* is known without further knowledge with the claim that nothing can be done by doing something else unless some things can be done directly—that is, not by doing something else. Actions that are done directly Arthur calls basic actions, and much of his book is devoted to elaborating, defending, and exploiting the distinction between basic actions and all the other actions that depend on, that are done by performing, basic actions.

I once criticized several earlier articles by Arthur in which he seemed to say that if one moves a stone by moving one's arm, then the act of moving one's arm causes the action of moving the stone. I was not alone in criticizing this view. But did Arthur actually hold it? I wonder, because the book does not seem to say this, but rather that by moving one's arm one causes it to be the case that one has moved the stone, which is different, and no longer sounds as if, when a nonbasic action has been performed, it must always be correct for the agent to say, "I made me do it."

In any case, the question I will concentrate on is whether there really is a distinction to be made between basic actions and the further actions that are done by performing them. The issue is one of identity: Arthur says that if a man moves a stone by moving his arm, he performs two different actions; I say he performs one.

A theme that runs through Arthur's work and relates his views on actions, epistemology, language, and ontology to his interest in art is the importance of the notion of representation. Thinking, like art, is representational. This fact can infect the concept of identity. Arthur grants that Frege was right that although "the morning star" and "the evening star" are one and the same thing—the planet Venus—the descriptive phrases represent Venus in such different ways that someone may consistently believe the morning star is not the evening star. But he thinks that being thought by someone to be the morning star is not a property of Venus: "Certain things, then, may be true of something without being a property of it" (67). His argument is brief: if so much as one person thinks the morning star is not the evening star, and being thought to be something were a property of the thing thought about, then the morning star and the evening star could not be identical objects, for one would have a property the other does not. I'm afraid this is not a good argument. The identity of the morning star and the evening star will not suffer if we take someone's faulty thinking that they are not identical to be an objective property of a single object.

Arthur's conception of causality falls prey to a similar mistake. He apparently accepts that events are entities, and that actions are events of some kind. But he thinks the verb "caused" in a sentence like "His moving his arm caused the motion of the rock" is not, as it appears to be, a two-place predicate true of pairs of events, but a three- ("or more") place predicate. The reason the third place is needed, he says, is that if two events are causally related, there must be a law that covers the case. I agree that if c caused e, there must be a law. However, it seems to me there is no way to make this a *semantic* feature of singular causal claims. If c caused e, then according to Arthur, there exist descriptions of c and e, for example d and f, such that the statement "If d then f" instantiates a law. I agree. But this is a much-debated metaphysical claim, and it does not follow that "c caused e" *says* something about descriptions and language or that it refers to a law (97). Quoth Arthur: "Only under certain of its descriptions is e causally dependent on c." Surely what he means is that only under certain descriptions of two events does a singular causal claim follow from a law, for nature does not care how we describe it. Causal dependence is not up to us. How we describe and explain is our work, but having described and explained, whether what we say or think is true is up to nature. Long before there were languages in which to describe anything, the presence of oxygen was necessary for combustion. This is not to deny that when we ask for the cause of some event we usually want more than any old description of the cause; we want a causal *explanation*, and explanations are intentional. But we can understand a singular causal statement although it instantiates no law, and even though it fails to explain.

Let's get back to basic actions, those actions Arthur defines as not being done by doing something else. What should we count? Raising one's arm is a favored example, as long as one does not do it by using a block and tackle. But doesn't one have to move the muscles in the shoulder and arm in order to raise it? Why isn't moving one's muscles in the right way the basic action? Arthur says it is not because in the normal case we do not know how to flex our muscles in the right way—except by raising our arm. I'm not sure I understand exactly why this rules out saying we raise our arm by flexing our muscles in the right way, but it certainly does not rule out our saying that flexing our muscles that way *is* raising our arm, so flexing our muscles couldn't be an action *separate* from raising our arm.

We would just have two ways of describing the same action. Arthur doesn't say this, however. He allows that when we raise our arm intentionally, some events take place in our brain that cause our muscles to flex in the right way, which causes our arm to go up. This series of events as a complex whole is the action, but no proper part of the whole is an action. I think this is a perfectly plausible position, and I have no better. In fact, I have written, in agreement with Arthur, that basic actions are bodily motions. The trouble is, I have also argued that *all* our actions are basic, and so there is no ontological distinction to be made between basic actions and other actions.

One of the first things I read when I became interested in the philosophy of action was Elizabeth Anscombe's wonderful little book *Intention*. In it she asks, "Is there any description which is *the* description of an intentional action, given that an intentional action occurs?" and she gives the following example: a man is moving his arm up and down in order to pump water into the cistern that supplies the drinking water of a house in order to poison the inhabitants of the house (for he knows the water is poisoned) in order to kill the inhabitants in order to rid the world of some evil people, etc. "What," she says, "is *the* description of what he is doing?" First, she says, any description of what is going on: he is earning wages, he is wearing away his shoe soles, he is sweating, he is poisoning the inhabitants of the house. But we can narrow down the list by considering only what he is doing intentionally, and thus draw the "in order to" list of the sort I just gave, provided the man is succeeding in his purposes. So if he is poisoning the inhabitants of the house, for example, and this is his intention in pumping the water, then "he is poisoning the inhabitants" is one way of describing what he is doing. Anscombe's opinion is that we have here just one action "under many different descriptions." The man's moving his arm (on that occasion) was identical with his pumping the water, poisoning the inhabitants, and so on. The action Arthur calls "basic," the man moving his arm, *is identical with* his further actions, which Arthur calls "mediated" and believes are numerically distinct actions. If Anscombe is right, there is no *ontological* distinction between basic actions and the rest, though of course there remain many distinctions among the *descriptions*. Once more it is a question of identity that is at stake. To make the issue clear: according to Arthur, if a man poisons the inhabitants of a house by moving his arm, there are (at least) two actions, moving the arm and poisoning the inhabitants; according to Anscombe and me, there is just one action twice described. Arthur's view, as I understand it, is that the action of the man moving his arm is a proper part of his action of poisoning the inhabitants of the house. There cannot be any objection to the idea that one action can contain many others. Playing a game of tennis is an action that clearly contains many other actions. The question is whether, when a man poisons the inhabitants by moving his arm, moving his arm is contained in the action of poisoning, or is there is only one action twice described.

I have always thought Anscombe's view was right. One thing puzzled me, though: if there are many descriptions of an entity, there must be an entity to describe. Yet sentences like "he moved his arm" mention only a man and his arm, and these are certainly not what is mentioned in a sentence like "he poisoned the inhabitants," which mentions the man again and now the inhabitants, but says nothing about the arm. There seems to be nothing in the grammar of these sentences that justifies the claim that they describe some one thing in different ways. I dealt with this problem by proposing that such sentences do not wear their logical form on the surface: there is a reference to one or more events, and these events are the entities—actions, in the cases we are interested in here—that are variously described. The introduction of events is also essential to straightening out our talk about causality. As we shall see, here the issue of identity of events and the concepts of agency and causality come together.

My position, that the man's moving his arm and his poisoning the inhabitants of the house are one and the same action, seems odd, if not plain absurd, while Arthur's counting two actions here is attractive. It is obvious that moving one's arm, or even pumping water, is not generally intended to kill people, and doesn't generally result in deaths. Moving an arm, pumping water, and poisoning people are different *sorts* of action. Yes, but any entity has endless properties and so belongs to many different sorts. As types or classes of actions, we have here three. Yet single objects or actions always fall into many different classes. (The class of people in America is not identical with the class of people in this room, but all of you belong to both classes.) The thesis isn't that every pumping is a poisoning, but that in the story a particular action is both. And, come to think of it, doesn't it sound odd to say that if a man moves his arm for a few minutes, thus intentionally pumping water, poisoning the drinking water, killing the inhabitants of a house, and saving the world from despotism, he has performed at least five actions? Wasn't his action over when he stopped moving his arm?

One issue I think we can set aside concerns the relations between what a person intends to do and what he actually does. There are of course many times that we intend to do something by acting in a certain way and we fail;

we sign the check, put it in an envelope and then in the mail with the intention of paying a bill, and it never gets there. It is not such cases that pose a problem. But there clearly is a difficulty in a case like the one I described earlier of the faulty marksman who nevertheless causes the death of his victim through an utterly unexpected turn of events: a stampede of wild pigs. Should we say the marksman killed the victim? Did he murder him? He intended to, and what he did with that intention—shoot his gun—caused the desired death. How devious or unexpected should the series of events that intervene between the shooting and the death be for the marksman to escape blame, or the law? Here is an actual legal case (I think I read it in Hart and Honoré's *Causation in the Law*): the scene is a West African country when it was still a colony of Great Britain. A man (the "agent") hits another man (the "victim") over the head with the intention of killing him. The agent then disposes of the body by stuffing it in an anthill. The law that applied defined murder as doing something with the intention of killing someone, where that very act kills the victim. But in the case at hand, these conditions were not satisfied. The blow to the head, which was intended to kill the victim, merely knocked the victim out—unbeknownst to the agent, who then stuffed his live victim in an anthill, which did kill him, though he did not intend it to, thinking the victim already dead. I do not know what the court decided. It is clear that what we say an agent did depends not only on what the agent caused but also on how the causal chain evolved. Unintended consequences are different in important ways from intended consequences, but the same issue arises. I recently read in a newspaper that the inhabitants of a village were firing their guns in the air to celebrate some occasion and a bullet from one of the shots injured a child in the next village. If we knew who fired the unlucky shot, should we say *he* injured the child?

These borderline or puzzling cases raise questions about the interrelations between the notions of causality, action, responsibility, and blame, and they are puzzling whether you think there are one, two, or many actions performed. So let us suppose such questions settled one way or another, and limit ourselves to the plain cases where the outcome of an action was intended and where we have no doubt that the agent brought about the intended result by acting as he did. The last scene of *Hamlet* provides enough homicide to keep us busy. In what is supposed to be a friendly joust, Laertes intentionally takes up a poisoned rapier and wounds Hamlet. Hamlet dies; Laertes has murdered him. Laertes killed Hamlet by stabbing him. There are two events: the stabbing by Laertes and the death of Hamlet. These two events are clearly discrete; the first caused the second, but the first was finished enough before the second to allow for some conversation and a few other events, such as the death of the queen, then of the king, and the fatal stabbing of Laertes by Hamlet. There are about sixty intervening lines of the play.

So, two discrete events, Laertes' stabbing of Hamlet and Hamlet's consequent death. Where should we place Laertes' act of killing Hamlet? Arthur says it is a *third* event (and second action), which begins with the stabbing and ends with the death. I say there is no such third event because Laertes' act of stabbing is identical with his killing Hamlet. You can see that there is something to be said for each answer. Arthur will say it is absurd to suppose Laertes has killed Hamlet until Hamlet is dead; I will say that after he did his stabbing, Laertes did nothing more to kill Hamlet.

Arthur will point out that if Laertes' stabbing of Hamlet was identical with his killing Hamlet, then Hamlet must have been dead before he killed Laertes and made his final speech, "—the rest is silence." Curiously, Hamlet and Laertes are both on my side. Well before he dies, though he has already been fatally stabbed, Laertes says, "I am justly killed," and adds for good measure, "Hamlet, thou art slain." Hamlet agrees:

I am dead, Horatio. Wretched queen, adieu!
You that look pale and tremble at this chance,
That are but mutes or audience to this act, [note the singular]
Had I but time—as this fell sergeant, Death,
Is strict in his arrest—O, I could tell you—
But let it be. Horatio, I am dead. . . . (V.2.333–38)

When I first confronted this puzzle, which became known as The Time of the Killing, I bit the bullet and decided that when Laertes had stabbed Hamlet he had already killed him (after all, Hamlet said so), but I was correctly jeered at. People talk that way only in the movies and in Shakespeare. There is a better way to defend the view that the stabbing and the killing were one and the same action. Here is an analogy: my father's father was a bit of a scoundrel, but he was just one person. At one time he was not even a father, then he became one; later his son became a father; later still that son became my father. By this time my great-great-grandfather had become describable as such. So with actions: Laertes' stabbing became a killing when Hamlet died. Events collect a history as time goes by, just as people do. At the time of the stabbing, Laertes had not killed Hamlet. Shortly thereafter, his single act acquired a son, and the act became a killing. In Arthur's terms, Laertes' basic action was, perhaps, his moving his body; this begot a movement of his rapier, which begot Hamlet's wound, which begot Hamlet's death. He did not perform another action with each begetting; his one action just accrued intended along with unintended consequences, as did my grandfather. I am one of the latter.

As Arthur notes, many verbs are causal. The verb "to break," when transitive, is an example. "The stone broke the window" must mean something like "There was a motion of the stone and a breaking of the window, and the first event caused the second." It must mean this because we infer from "The stone broke the window" that the window broke. Similarly, if Paul broke the window, Paul must have done something that caused the window to break. We then call whatever he did his action of breaking the window: a new description for what he did. Notice that it is not true that Paul broke the window until the window was broken, just as it was not true to say that Herbert Clarence Davidson was my grandfather until I was born.

There is an interesting variant on this theme. Just as there at first seems to be a puzzle when we ask of some actions *when* they were performed, so we can ask *where*. This was a legal case: a man in Massachusetts shot dead a man in Rhode Island. Where did the killing take place? It mattered because the answer to this question would determine the state in which the case was heard, and the laws differed. Or another true story (which also may be from Hart and Honoré): Two seamen on a ship had a fight, in the course of which one man pushed the other overboard with the intention of drowning him. He succeeded. Once again there was a legal dispute about where the murder took place, on the ship or in the sea. Once again it mattered, for if the murder took place on the ship, the case would be decided by an Irish court, since the ship was Irish, but if it took place in the ocean, then the crime occurred in international waters and would be tried under a different jurisdiction.

No one asked me to decide these cases; if they had, I would have explained that the first murderer performed the act of killing in Massachusetts, and the second murderer did the deed on board the ship. Arthur would, I think, say the first crime was in both Massachusetts and Rhode Island, and the second on board the ship and in the water. I do not know whether he would say it also took place in the areas in between shooting or pushing and death. But surely in both cases the assailant intended all that came between the original action and the resulting death.

Perhaps this is enough homicide. Here is a difficulty for the monistic view of action I have been touting. It centers on Arthur's key word "by," as in "He turned on the light by flipping the switch." The critic remarks that if flipping the switch and turning on the light are one and the same action, why do we say he turned on the light by flipping the switch but not say he flipped the switch by turning on the light? The reply should, I think, be much the same as before. Two events (at least) must have occurred if he turned on the light by flipping the switch: an action of flipping the switch and the light coming on. The relation between these events is not symmetrical, since it is causal; the first event, the flipping, caused the second, the light coming on, not vice versa.

There are cases where it may seem harder to spot the asymmetry of events that the word "by" suggests. If I sign a check by writing my name in the right place, writing my name and signing the check are not two actions, though of course they are different types of action. So one cannot be the cause of the other. Yet I cannot say I wrote my name there by signing the check. The same issue arises if someone signals to another by raising her arm (but doesn't raise her arm by signaling). In these two cases, I imagine—hope—that Arthur agrees that there is only one action: in the first case, writing my name (under the appropriate circumstances) and signing the check are the same; in the second case, her raising her arm (in appropriate circumstances) and signaling are the same action. In both cases there is an end state that has been produced (caused) by the action (the name is there, the check is signed, the arm is up, the signal made). But this seems no help in explaining the asymmetry of "by" in such cases. However, I do cause the check to be signed by writing my name there. Of course, I also cause my name to be written there if I write it there. But it is a trivial truth that if I write my name there, I have caused my name to be written there; it is not trivial that if I have caused my name to be written there, I have caused it to be the case that I have signed a check. This logical difference echoes the fact that I wrote my name in order to (with the intention to) sign the check, and not vice versa, and explains the asymmetry of the "by."

Samuel Guttenplan has suggested that when we add to a bald statement that someone has done something that he has done it by doing something—for example, adding to the statement that I signed the check that I did so by writing my name there, or to the statement that someone went around the world without making use of a propelling engine that they did so by getting in a balloon and making use of the winds—we are amplifying and making more precise what we add. We are also, in part, explaining it. In most cases the explanation has two aspects: it is psychological, because it tells us more about the motives of the agent, and it is causal. Our normal descriptions of actions thus look to the past, to the mental workings and states that prompted our actions, and to their consequences. Adding to such descriptions further descriptions that are answers to the question "Why did you (or he) do that?" we don't add further actions, but place the original action in a larger psychological and historical setting.

Placing an action in its psychological and historical setting is just what the opening paragraph of Arthur's book on action was about. No other book does this so comprehensively, wittily, imaginatively, and, well, artfully.

╫ ╫ ╫ ╫ ╫

Response

Whether, in turning on the light by flipping the switch, one action or two is involved, is Donald Davidson's way of framing a question that divided us in the 1960s, when action theory flourished, and still divided us when he presented an earlier version of this paper at our conference at Columbia in 2002. Something evidently came out of our exchange after the presentation, however, since the written text differs from the one presented, so far as my memory of it can be trusted, and I am moved by the fact that the paper incorporates what turns out to be the final exchange between us on an issue we had both written about forty years earlier, when the analytical theory of action was on the cutting edge of philosophy. But I wondered whether the question was really any more alive for him that it was for me. Donald had hoped to write on art when he agreed to participate in the conference, and had ordered some of my books from Amazon in preparation for what he obviously thought would be fun to do. But Akeel Bilgrami told him that he was to speak instead on the theory of action, so he went back to my *Analytical Philosophy of Action,* and to the unresolved—I would say irresolvable—division between us. And though this is simply a guess, I take that as evidence that he, as I, would have had to dig through a fairly thick bed of ashes in search of some living ember in a body of thought that at one time had excited the two of us greatly.

I was glad to be reminded—as he was glad to discover—that *Analytical Philosophy of Action* begins with an extended example from the history of art. When I was writing the preface, I had been reading about Giotto's Arena frescoes in Padua, which had something like the impact on me that they had had on the character of Charles Swann in Proust's great novel— as a visual encyclopedia of how human beings express moral feelings. I had been struck by the fact that in a whole band of paintings in the middle register of Giotto's narrative of the life of Christ, Jesus is shown with one arm raised, performing what I called a "basic action." My aim in the book, I told the reader, was to "erase" the various contextual cultural factors that make one raised arm a blessing and another a driving of money lenders forth from the temple, and to just immerse myself in this issue: in virtue of what is a raised arm an action at all? This was what had primarily engaged me when I first got involved with the theory of action. Wittgenstein had famously asked what remains if, from the fact that I raise my arm, I subtract the fact that my arm goes up. I think we both learned from Elizabeth Anscombe's powerful little book, *Intention,* that Wittgenstein's answer would have been: nothing. Nothing remains over. For a man with such a rich interior life, he seemed eager in effect to empty the head of anything mental and explain the response by external differences of language or, in Anscombe's view, to descriptions. Thus "blessing" and "expelling the money lenders" are the same kind of event—raising an arm— "under . . . different descriptions." Donald, not as intimidated by the mental, would have said that what made the difference were reasons that explained the raised arm. That was the gist of his celebrated Presidential Address to the American Philosophical Association. My interest in the book lay elsewhere. I thought there was a deep difference between an action like raising an arm and what need not be an action at all, like my arm going up without my intending it, say as a kind of tic. I thought there are two kinds of event that might outwardly appear the same.

And that is what I meant by erasing everything external and cultural. All the paintings, I felt, were of Christ performing a basic action. What accounted for the differences between blessing and expelling—or greeting— began further up the line, when the question of what made any of them actions in the first place was answered. I was interested in basic actions versus mere bodily movements, just as, later, I was to be interested in the difference between a work of art and a mere real thing, when nothing outward marked the difference between them. Driving the money lenders forth was a bit more complex than turning on the lights, but it gave me a certain pleasure to use an example from high art to raise an issue in the philosophy of action. Had I known at the time more about contemporary art, I could have cited a work by the composer George Brecht, a member of Fluxus, to much the same end. Around the same time that Donald and I were opening up the theory of action, Brecht made of turning on the lights by flipping a switch a work of art, overcoming thereby the gap between art and life and closing the gap between art and action. George Maciunas, the founder of Fluxus, felt that Brecht had gone beyond Duchamp with this piece. "That's the piece," he said in a 1978 interview with Larry Miller. "Turn the light on and then off. Now you do that every day, right? Without even knowing you're performing Brecht." I mention the matter to emphasize at the outset that the method of indiscernibles was the way I always did philosophy. Find two things that are outwardly alike but momentously different, and then account for the differences.

This explains, I think, why I never tried to deal with Donald's question, which applied pressure at a point beyond anything that concerned me fundamentally. Consider a subsidiary question that Donald draws from Hart and Honoré's book on causation and the law: where does a killing occur? If someone, as the result of a murderous action, dies on board a ship, that falls under one jurisdiction; if he dies overboard, it falls under a different jurisdiction. Those are fascinating issues, but what was of concern to me could not be a matter of jurisdiction. The difference between a basic action and a bodily movement was never a matter of convention and legal negotiation, but of how the universe is made up. It does not depend upon mere law. I was in that way a pretty old-fashioned philosopher. How many actions take place in turning on the lights? That is likely to strike the unphilosophical reader—or the philosophical reader who came of age after the era in which the analytical philosophy of action was ascendant—as almost frivolous, like the chestnut about how many angels dance on the point of a pin. It could hardly matter greatly whether the answer might be "one" (Davidson) or "two" (Danto)—and if it did matter, how long, really, would it take to decide the issue?

I don't think either Donald or I ever bothered to define "action." I somehow remember Donald saying that it was a primitive concept, but we both more or less felt that what we meant by the term was too familiar for anyone to be in doubt as to what we were talking about—that anyone with a normal body had examples available whenever one might be needed. Unlike "art," where the issue of definition was made necessary by the internal evolution of the concept, with action one was dealing with something too familiar for analysis. My interest was in any case less in the analysis of the concept than in drawing attention to the difference, immediately available to experience, between a certain class of actions and a certain class of mere bodily movements. Winking an eye would be a good example of a simple action, as over and against an eye involuntarily closing, as in a certain nervous tic. My sense was that winking an eye was an action if done by the agent, whereas the same movement—an eyelid shutting and then opening again—would not be an action if *not* done by him. I had a piece of notation

I used: an event *a* is an action when *m*D*a* is true. In my early papers on the subject, *m* was read as "man" and D was a kind of operator and *a* was an event that was an action when *m*D*a* was true. When (*a* and not-*m*D*a*) was true, *a* was an action of *m*'s. I'll talk about the notation in a moment, but *m* calls for some comment. It is somewhat shocking to read those early papers and see "man" written brazenly out, as if action was, as we say today, a "guy thing." My stern prose of the time seems retroactively sexist, but it was, for better or worse, commonplace practice, not just in philosophy, to employ the word "man" without qualification. Thus the painter Barnett Newman, in an interview with David Sylvester in 1965, said, "One thing I am involved in about painting is that the painting should give a man a sense of place: that he knows he's there, so that he's aware of himself" (*Interviews with American Artists*, 1965). I don't think anyone would have found it odd or biased that people expressed themselves this way—even women, like Elizabeth Anscombe did. Already by the end of the decade there were pressures in the culture to say "man or woman" and to find ways around gendered pronouns. Or even, as in current journal usage, to use the pronoun "she" as a matter of principle. As a feminist I go along with this, though it is not a practice I especially follow.

But in fact I often had the male body in mind, and in this I suppose I was a bit ahead of my time in thinking of embodiment as a gendered fact: human beings are sexed. And the example I made central in discussing the issue was penile erection—a bodily event of immense significance in intimate relationships and human happiness. Like many of my philosophical views, my philosophy of action arose directly from life. I was struck, as only a male could be, that a bodily event that resembled the raising of an arm, namely the erection, was something one had very little control over—it happened when one didn't want it to, and didn't happen when one wanted it to. The comedy of the sexed body is part of being male. In the *Salon* of 1767, Diderot narrates a sweet episode between himself and Madame Therbouche, a painter. It is well known that historical painting was the highest category recognized by the Academy in France, which meant that women were excluded from the highest commissions and prizes, since they were not allowed to study the male nude. Diderot offered to pose for Madame Therbouche in the buff. But "Since the first sin of Adam," he writes, "we no longer have as much control over all our body parts as we do over our arms, seeing that there are some that will do one thing when the sons of Adam will it to do another, and that sometimes fail to respond to the bidding of the sons of Adam." Though fearful that he might involuntarily stiffen, Diderot stripped. "I was nude, completely nude. She painted me and we conversed with a simplicity and innocence worthy of the first centuries." Obviously there are limits to the use of "she" in academic journalese: "his or her erection" is a joke of political correctness.

I thought the mark of the kind of action that concerned me was that one does it without there being an answer to how: one simply raises the arm. I called such actions basic actions, and defined a basic action as one we perform without performing another action through which it happens—"Non hay reglas," as Goya said about painting. It is easy to see what a nonbasic action would be—an action we perform through performing another one. We crack an egg by knocking it against a hard surface—but knocking, I thought, would be something we learn to do by moving a hand. To be sure, there are recipes of sorts. Grasp the egg firmly in one's fingers, and hit the egg against a hard surface. But sooner or later there are things we do for which there are no recipes. There *have* to be, on penalty of infinite regression. So unless there are basic actions, there are no actions. The nonbasic action is what bothered Donald Davidson in my writing, and what continued to bother him in this last paper. To say there are actions we perform by doing something else suggested that in such simple performances as cracking an egg, I am performing (at least) two actions. Since that seemed excessive, he claimed there are no nonbasic actions. And there the matter stood.

The "D" operator I more or less borrowed from Jaakko Hintikka's use of "K" as standing in for "knows" in a notation he developed for talking about knowledge: mKs would in effect assert of somebody that he knows that s. I guess it is worth reflecting on the fact that there is a feminist position that there are certain things women alone know—or there are ways of knowing uniquely available to women. So gender would have to be taken into consideration in epistemic logic as well as the logic of action sentences—a consideration that lay over the horizon in the middle '6os. In any case, the idea of basic action was suggested to me by the use of the term "basic sentence" in positivist epistemology. A basic sentence is one that would be known directly, without, that is, there being something *through* which it is known. The parallels between basic actions and basic cognitions excited me beyond measure, and the books I dedicated to the two concepts reflect an effort to exploit their structural parity. If there is only one kind of action, of course, the term "basic" loses its intended systematic meaning. But when I was presenting these ideas in talks for various departments, I felt my sense of parity was confirmed by the fact that when someone raised an objection to basic actions, I could pretty well predict that they would have a structurally parallel objection to a corresponding proposition in epistemology. And I gradually got the idea that I was dealing with parallel philosophical structures that defined a mode of thought—a kind of system wired into thinking philosophically. The reason I stress the systematicity with which I was working all this out is to make the point that whether there is one action or two cannot easily be answered, as if it were a question of simple counting. The concept of a basic action was too embedded in a system to detach it from the system. I grant that there would be awkwardnesses in passing from mDa into vernacular English.

I became obsessed with questions that objections against basic sentences on antiformalistic grounds never dealt with. I supposed there is a normal repertoire of modes of cognitive access to the world, viz "the five senses"—natural cognitive gifts most of us are born with. There are negative abnormalities—cognitive deficits, like blindness or deafness. And there are positive abnormalities—cognitive gifts, whereby someone knows immediately and, as we say, intuitively, what others at best can eke out indirectly. I imagined a world in which the sense of smell was something rarely conferred, but if someone possessed it and most did not, they would be capable of astonishing feats. They would know there was ham for supper by merely smelling that unmistakable aroma. Such a person could not answer, "How do you know that?" since presumably "smell" would not be in the language. So he or she would be able at most to say, "I simply do"—the way clairvoyants would when it turned out they "knew" what the rest of us could only guess at. Oddly, the idea came to me from an observation by Galileo, who says that we can know whatever God knows, with the difference that God knows everything through a sudden simple intuition, whereas we have to have science, and build our understanding of the world by means of evidence and inference.

It was a simple matter to develop the idea of a normal repertoire of actional gifts as well, like moving arms and opening mouths and maybe swallowing, but in any case opening our mouths and closing our eyes. There are positive abnormalities, like wiggling our ears and, I guess, erecting at will. There are negative abnormalities like paralyses and physiological impotence—though the fact that we cannot erect at will means that sexual potency is a gift of a different order. In his autobiography (*Killing Time*), Paul Feyerabend describes being sexually incapacitated because of a war wound, so he would have been unable to "know" a woman. But that did not keep him from finding ways around this (which he does not describe) and satisfying women sexually, even if, as he says, he had no way of knowing what it was like to be sexually satisfied (which I suppose meant that he was a virgin at the time of his wound, and did not have a history of masturbation). I got the idea for all this from Saint Augustine, who, noticing all the freaks in the world, inferred that in the Garden of Eden, Adam could have been in complete control of his body—which meant erecting at will, impregnating Eve as if planting a seed, rather than being "blinded by passion," which Augustine understood very well. And, to find a theological position parallel to the one Galileo describes, it was not difficult to consider that whatever God does is done as a basic action. Samuel Clarke advanced such a view in his correspondence with Leibniz. So when the Bible says, "God said, 'Let there be light,'" there was light. God did not, as it were, flip a switch. He just made it be that there was light as a basic action. Anyone can find ways of illuminating a room. But doing that as a basic action is a mystery, as any positive abnormality would be— like retracting our fingernails the ways cats retract claws.

I developed all this as far as I could, and more or less took it for granted in such subsequent writing as *Connections to the World*. The two connections were causation and truth. The basic model for knowing was having a given representation made true by what caused it, as I discuss in my response to Gregg Horowitz. My basic model for action was causing the world to underwrite my representation of it, counting intention as a representation. Two components—representation and reality—and two relations— causation and truth—served, I believed, as the armature for framing all the fundamental questions of traditional philosophy, East and West.

I don't know to what degree Donald Davidson had worked out in comparable detail his philosophy of action, but I think at the very least he had a tacit system different from mine. But that would have meant that any question between us consisted in the confrontation of, as Galileo would have put it, Two Chief Systems of Action and whatever else. I don't know if there would have been any extrasystematic way of settling the issue he raises in his paper. I believe in truth that there are two deeply different systems of philosophical thought, between which it is all but impossible to arbitrate without begging the question. But that is about as far as I know how to take the matter here. So let's say that from his system there is just one action and from mine there are two.

Donald was certainly a great philosopher, and among my contemporaries the one whose writing stimulated me the most. His discussion of primitive predicates and learnable languages put an end to a kind of irresponsible logicizing, and I know I could never have written the paper in which he laid all that out. But I do not need to proclaim his accomplishments here. I consider it an immense gesture of collegiality that he was willing to participate in the conference, and to have written—and rewritten—a paper. He had great humanity as well as great philosophical gifts, and I am grateful to have walked the same world with him.

3
Crossing Paths
Stanley Cavell

Celebrations inspire reminiscences, and those that follow are as much concerned with keeping similar paths from crossing as they are with recognizing the fact that different paths have crossed and keep crossing. Arthur Danto and I are perhaps the only American philosophers of our generation—I know of no others—about whom the following four descriptions can all be said to be true: first, our itineraries contain a period, beginning in our youth, in which our lives had been devoted to the practice of an art (painting and printmaking in Arthur's case, composing music in mine), and we discovered philosophy as if by accident, after moving to the East Coast for college, or postcollege. Second, on the basis of an education in analytical philosophy, and without ever forgoing an identification with the dispensation of American philosophy, we both came to spend extraordinary amounts of liberating, productive time writing, in ways whose philosophicality we had explicitly to insist upon (in the introduction to a collection of his articles as art critic for *The Nation*, Arthur calls this writing also a contribution to literature, and I sometimes describe some of what I do as calling for philosophy), in part for those beyond the world of professional philosophy who were invested in one or another of the arts, or to what we had to insist were arts, perhaps endeavors that revised the idea of art. Third, we each found ourselves in large part philosophizing in connection with work intimately related to the place we had moved eastward to and found also to be home (for Arthur, the exploding world of painting in the 1960s in New York; for me, the remote world of Emerson and Thoreau in Cambridge and Concord). And fourth, a recurrent motivation in Danto's writing about art after modernism, and in my writing about film, was to express both admiration for the achievement of Clement Greenberg as the dominant theorist of modernism, and a fundamental dissatisfaction, and break (in my case, building on conversations with, and in reading, Michael Fried), with Greenberg's idea of the essence of the medium of art, represented as painting, and most particularly with his identification of that essence with the use of paint on a two-dimensional flat surface—a dissatisfaction and break precipitated, however differently understood by us, by a kind of revelation of a break in the history of the arts that linked the fate of art with that of philosophy.

Yet for all the affinities suggested in these four descriptions, and in great measure because of different accents in our inheritances of the discourse of philosophy, we may not often have seemed to find helpful details in each other's writing. But Arthur had begun publishing books years earlier than I, and his example of independence of mind was a signal encouragement in my beginning years of a certain strife with the difficult and indispensable profession of philosophy. The spirit of my contributing to these days of celebration is to express my sense of gratitude for his achievement.

It pleases me, in that spirit, before noting certain differences in our work made interesting to me by those similarities—brought home in my recent weeks of renewed companionship with Danto's writing—to commemorate two early encounters in which our paths literally crossed, in 1964 and 1965, years decisive for each of us in determining the ensuing decades of our writing. They were the years in which Danto's *The Transfiguration of the Commonplace* was prepared, in which Andy Warhol's Brillo box revelation had played a defining role in demonstrating for Danto that there are no sensuous criteria for distinguishing art objects from what he called ordinary or mere real objects. They were also principal years of my writing or drafting the bulk of the essays making up my first book, *Must We Mean What We Say?*. In those essays, I confessed that the significance of the ordinary for philosophy was a revelation for me, especially in the work of J. L. Austin, and the problematizing of the ordinary (sometimes meaning the commonplace)—as it was made extraordinary in, for example, the writing of Samuel Beckett's *Endgame* and shown tragically unachievable in Shakespeare's *King Lear*—struck me as literature's taking on the condition of philosophy's self-criticism, and at the same time as philosophy's chance, or obligation, to face the return of the repressed (both in the form of literature's contesting of philosophy's early dominance, in Plato, in assessing the state of the soul, and of philosophy's contempt for, or impatience with, the everyday).

The first of the encounters I have in mind was the result of a phone call—I cannot remember whether it was from Arthur or from Sydney Morgenbesser—saying that they were both driving up to Cambridge in the company of a philosophy student of theirs who was a filmmaker and who wanted, as part of a film he was working on, to shoot a scene of philosophers having an informal philosophical exchange in a location in the countryside near Cambridge, and that they would all like me to join them. Moved by the idea of these teachers wanting to spend a vigorous weekend helping a student with a project that, while in an extended sense in service of philosophy, risked making fools of themselves, I found the invitation irresistible. The idea of the film, I vaguely recall, seemed to be, beginning on the West Coast, to follow a young man's spiritual adventures hitchhiking across the country, ending on Cape Cod; the late adventure, in or near Cambridge, consisted in being given a lift by three philosophers who were driving to a philosophy conference, and who would persist in pursuing an impassioned philosophical conversation regardless of their surroundings. It would turn out that virtually all of the footage shot that day was technically, unusably flawed. The screening of the film I attended, one midnight in Boston, did include ten or fifteen seconds of blurred red footage capturing three almost recognizable grown men inexplicably playing kick-the-can in a large meadow. So three careers as film stars vanished like a dream. But something else that remains from that day is my impression that each of the philosophers, in the exoticism of the event, had found pleasure in the sheer sound as well as in the fact of earnest and playful philosophical conversation, and were willing to go, by academic standards, to extravagant lengths to convey this to strangers. It seems to me that I have been finding an enviable, refined version of such a willingness, or say generosity, in the outpouring of Danto's work as a philosophical critic of art, and of the concept of art—the aspect of his work that I will confine myself to on this occasion.

This fluency relates to the second of our early encounters, again in a car, this time as Arthur was driving the two of us, the summer we both taught classes at the University of California at Santa Barbara, to a roundtable discussion on, as it happens, philosophy and film. Out of the blue, Arthur said, getting better acquainted: "You haven't published much, have you?" I admitted glumly that I had not. He persisted: "What's the matter, Stanley, don't you *like* to write?" This version of shock therapy, I have come to think, going over it more than once, had a beneficial effect upon me. I could not protest that I had written more than I had published, because I seemed to recognize that that might only prove the truth of Arthur's surmise—not that I hadn't in some sense written, but that what kept me from offering it to strangers was not simply my fear that it wasn't good enough but, compounded with that, the fear that my pleasure in it would show—which for some reason would constitute a worse exposure. I guess it is not news that philosophy is as forbidding as it is attractive.

Perhaps the central cause of difference, of paths parting, within the similarities I have described, can be articulated by taking the circumstance Danto describes in his later essay, "The Philosopher as Andy Warhol," in the following way:

> It is perhaps of some value to pause and reflect on some parallels between what Warhol was doing and what some of the advanced philosophers of the time were doing. The latter, largely under the influence of the late philosophy of Wittgenstein, were making a certain return to ordinary language the center of their thought; precisely, the language of the marketplace, the nursery, and the street, the language everybody knows how to use in the commonplace situations that define the common life. This requires some explanation.
>
> In the period up to and following World War II, philosophical attitudes toward common sense and common speech were by and large contemptuous. . . . The task of philosophy was to construct an impeccable ideal language suited to house the truths of science, and mathematical logic offered a magnificent tool for this rational reconstruction. . . .
>
> All this changed abruptly in the 1950's, in a shift as dramatic and as climactic as the shift later in that decade from abstract expressionism to pop. . . . There was nothing internal to either art or philosophy that explains the shift—it seems to have come from outside, from exactly "the spirit of the times." All at once the prospect of an ideal language seemed as preposterous as the claims of the New York School seemed pretentious. (*Philosophizing Art* 77–78)

Let's remember that there was a further element often playing a role in the characteristic reception of each of these two shifts, or turns, namely the sense of the ending of something—in the case of art, of the end, or inertia, of painting; in the case of the work of Wittgenstein and of Austin, of the end of philosophy. I did not share this quite widespread feeling about the significance of these philosophers, and if I did not find Danto's articulation of the subsequent course of art perfectly satisfying, I was less satisfied by what various of his philosophical critics were saying in response. Even if I had been moved, and free, to enter into that debate then, it would have been pointless (I felt) apart from living a New York life—I mean living with the work, and with conversations about the work—that Danto was responding to.

But in fact I was not free, since what was claiming my attention was that other half of the coincidence of developments in art and in philosophy that Danto had pointed to, namely the attempt to inherit what seemed to me right, and irreversibly innovative, in Wittgenstein's later work and in the work of my teacher Austin. (I am not relying on the report, and in fact I do not know what to make of it, in a volume of interviews of American philosophers done in the 1990s in which Danto and I both participated, of his saying, "The later Wittgenstein strikes me as hazy: it is beautifully written, marvelous thought, but philosophically of no significance whatsoever" [in G. Borradori, *The American Philosopher* (Chicago: University of Chicago Press, 1994), 90].)

Writing philosophy has not, I believe, presented itself as an open *problem* for Danto, philosophically or artistically, as making art has done; a new age of philosophy still to be articulated did not beckon to him as he felt drawn to articulate a new age of what he called pluralism in art, against, primarily, Greenberg's monism; a new language did not have to be invented in which to understand and participate in what one found new in philosophical thinking, as he found to be called for by the new art. (I think here of Danto's repeated expression of his devotion to analytical philosophy as expressed in the writing of it he most admires, principally that of Russell and of Quine.) It was essential to my attraction to the work of Wittgenstein that for him philosophy is an incessant problem, in a sense is the essential problem of philosophy, expressed in its quintessential human wish to escape the conditions of human knowing and speaking, to escape, as I sometimes put the matter, the human. (It is not science or art that Wittgenstein contrasts with the ordinary, but metaphysics, especially as an answer to skepticism.) Wittgenstein was not the first to see this predicament of human self-dissatisfaction. Kant built systematic bulwarks against it, perhaps increasing the temptations but at the same time diagnosing and locating the points at which human restlessness, let us say, makes its gravest assaults upon reason (in metaphysics, in skepticism, in magic, in fanaticism). Wittgenstein's innovation, to my mind, was to perceive this as a drama enacted in philosophy's dissatisfaction with or disappointment with ordinary language, one in which ordinary language both rejects itself and assumes the obligation to come to itself. In this way of looking at things, the "return" to ordinary language is rather seen as a return *of* it, not as to a place of stability, but as to a place of inevitable loss. In particular, it is not to a place of common sense or shared belief—the thing Emerson calls conformity—but is equally to be understood as an attack on settled beliefs. It is the possibility, or necessity, of this self-dissatisfaction, this battle of the human with itself, that creates the possibility, and necessity, in philosophy, of skepticism.

I express this in the first part of *The Claim of Reason*, in chapters adapted in a later decade from my doctoral dissertation, as the discovery of the absence of criteria for distinguishing the real from the imaginary—Descartes says from dreams, I say also from simulacra (though I did not use the word): characteristic examples I employ (taken from Wittgenstein and from Austin) were pretended pain and a painted goldfinch, which must exhibit the same criteria of identity as real pain and a real goldfinch, since otherwise it would not be *pain* that was pretended and not a *goldfinch* that was painted. The conclusion I drew from such cases was, unlike all other accounts of *Philosophical Investigations* that I knew of then, that Wittgenstein had not in fact or in intention provided a refutation of skepticism but had articulated a source of it. Human language is such that dissatisfaction with it can never be stilled; the question is not so much whether we can live within our finite means (which those who have respected skepticism, from the ancient Greeks to thinkers through Descartes and Hume to such as Bertrand Russell, have in different ways recommended) as whether we can become responsible for our infinite desires.

Danto somewhere uses the term "skepticism" once, as I recall, as an instance of what he calls the duplication that Warhol and Duchamp had introduced into art, making explicit the inherent philosophicality of art. I might ask: has Danto shown Warhol, first among others, to have made art, in linking its fate with philosophy, at the same time an illustration of a form of skepticism? Put another way: is the discovery that real things and their images (in perception or dream) are, in Bishop Berkeley's phrase, sensuously indistinguishable, a general version of the specific discovery that a real thing and a work of art are sensuously indistinguishable?

One difference is that in skepticism we discover that we know less than we thought we knew, indeed perhaps nothing; whereas in Danto's proposal we know, as it were, twice as much as everything we thought we knew, that any and every object (or artifact, any object that reflects the hand of man or woman) may be a work of art. This is a proposal whose power I do not question—Danto has, I believe, been convincing to others beyond any predicting in realizing his desire to show the postmodernist world of art accessible to philosophical criticism, that is, in his wish to do for postmodernism what Greenberg did for modernism, and to do it by turning art and the ordinary toward each other. I have said that I have never felt sufficiently experienced in the world of that development of art to debate his achievement, even if I had wanted to. A reason I might have wanted to is my sense of not sharing what I might call his taste for the objects he champions; but there again I cannot dismiss the doubt that the same lack of experience disqualifies this sense of mine from serious attention. (It is a lack magnified by the fact that my main experience of art has been with literature and music, in neither of which has modernism, however challenged, been thought to be eclipsed by a worldwide movement that tends to make, say, Schoenberg or Bartók or Proust or Joyce unlistenable or unreadable.)

Of course I have to take my lack, which is to say, my experience, seriously. So I notice the number of times, in response to Danto's assertion, or revelation, that there need be no sensuous mark distinguishing an art object from a real or mere object, that I have felt the question begged: his assertion would be true on the condition that there *is* an object of art here, which is just what is contested. Perhaps it will be replied that that is the point, to show that art now begs the question of art. But in this mood, Danto's suggested two criteria for the existence of art, namely that the object is "about" something and "embodies" what it is about, seem quite elastic enough to fit equally well how one is to take modernist, not alone postmodernist, works. The series of paintings called *Unfurled*, by the modernist Morris Louis, is for example about blankness and diagonals and corners, and embodies these. But at some stage I realize that Danto, or anyone I have read who follows his thought, never, or almost never, puts things as I have been doing, speaking of distinguishing an art object or a work of art from a real or mere object.

Danto speaks rather of the presence of an "artwork," sensuously indistinguishable from, for example, this box or this snow shovel or this bottle rack or, most lingeringly, this urinal. I do not know the provenance of this use of the English word "artwork" (which those born before a fairly recent date would have taken to mean the visual material, other than written copy, in a glossy magazine or on a printer's layout; or perhaps what Desdemona means by saying of the terrific handkerchief that she had thought to have the "work ta'en out," that is, its design or decoration copied), nor whether that revised use has been part of a familiar discussion that has passed me by. So—in any case—what? What could be more familiar than the introduction of a new word, or a new use of a word, into our language?

But is that what has happened—that "artwork" has taken on an additional use as what Quine calls an individuating noun in contrast with its established existence as a bulk or mass noun, so that in addition to speaking of needing or copying *some* or more artwork, we can speak of *an* artwork and hence of a *different* artwork? Such a use doesn't quite seem to capture Danto's sense that what happened—with a "Blam!"—when in the 1960s painting came to (something like) an end, but art continued, was that art was suddenly replaced by incidents of artwork, as though the visual world, so far as the hand of man or woman was discernible, and as far as the eye can see, had taken on the value of decoration. His idea, beyond this, is that things were still being made, or shown, that had the power to transform the beholder or participant, or the experience of the beholder or participant. Danto never tires of speaking of his own transformation in realizing this condition. But that leaves the matter of the kind of transformation in question.

While I seem unable in general to endow the realm of objects Danto has philosophically rescued for art with the interest or fascination he expresses (from which it perhaps follows that I am unable to allow them to transform my conception of the house of art), I think I may not altogether be a stranger to moments of intensity and gratitude in relation to them, which keeps their form of existence a question for me. I cite two instances, one in connection with an installation, the other in connection with a series of lecture/performances by John Cage, a composer Danto is not alone in associating with the art he champions. It is from such instances, or touchstones—I sometimes say "good encounters"—that I would attempt to test the extent to which I have been abandoned by history.

The installation I have in mind, which I encountered on a visit to the Museum of Fine Art in Caracas several years ago, was made by the Venezuelan performance artist Antonieta Sosa. I excerpt a few sentences here from notes I made the following day and read as a preface to one of the several lectures I gave in the museum during my week's stay.

Sosa's installation is a sort of representation or facsimile or simulacrum or abstraction of what some title card identified as her own apartment. It is a real space, with real, smallish rooms that one walks through. I asked myself what such a piece is doing in a museum in which, for instance, there are Chinese porcelain vases that take your breath away with their beauty; classically scaled sculptures set in gardens or on a terrace that overlooks the city; and suddenly, set in a niche at the turning of a ramp, ancient tiny gold and silver ornaments of fascination. Is an installation a beautiful or imposing or fascinating thing; is it an ignorable thing, or a thing about the ignorable? What is it about the space of the installation that questions whether it is out of place, or arbitrarily in place, in the space of a museum? Sosa's installation incorporated a window of the museum as a window within its installed, self-defined space. Is this some declaration that this installation of an apartment shows our dwellings, our houses as they are, to be museums themselves of some sort? Then what do they exhibit, or re-member, or collect? At the same time the installation questions the idea that what there is in a museum is collected, since the installation itself ob-viously cannot be collected—questions the idea, that is to say, *if* it turns out that it itself does indeed *belong* there, that is to say, if we accept its presence there in the right spirit, and it is not for some reason, for example, being stored there, which may or may not serve to discourage that spirit. Anto-nieta Sosa's bed is empty, but there are traces of someone's having lain on its sheets. The impressions are like prints left by something immaterial, as if some ghost had (or has) fallen asleep in that bed. Other traces strug-gle against the idea of the immaterial. At about eye level, or a bit higher, along the walls of the installation's opening room, there is a continuous horizontal line of dozens of small, tidy, transparent packets of dust, each with a meticulous label giving the date on which its portion of dust was collected in this apartment. In one packet there is a torn theater ticket, in another a broken hair clip. That theater ticket is the only thing that has color in the whole region of the wall, a red ticket that appeals to your atten-tion and to your imagination of the life beyond these walls. Dust, the very type of insignificance, worthlessness, triviality—ranking with Plato's mud, for which it is doubtful that there is a corresponding type or Platonic Form, rendering it fit for recognition, redeeming its imperfection—is here being granted lucid space to participate in our self-discovery. Sosa is of course not the first artist to elevate, or sublate, and incorporate the debris or leav-ings of life into a work of art. (For example, Chris Marker's film *Sans Soleil* takes as essential to its study of eternity and impermanence the impor-tance of respecting the residue, say the consequences, of what we do, as well as of what we have left undone, wastes of actions and of possibilities of actions; and I have no way of doubting that this film is a masterpiece of art.) Yet Thoreau's text about Walden, which Sosa's installation brought to mind, urges us to get rid of our debris, which he names dust, which for him includes the bulk of our possessions, on the ground that we fail to know what is of real interest and importance to us, what we live for. I phrase this so as to allude also to a moment of Wittgenstein's self-portrait in *Philosophical Investigations* as he lets himself inspire the question "Where does our investigation get its importance from, since it seems to destroy everything interesting, that is, all that is great and important?" (sec. 118). His answer is, in effect, that whatever we, after him, seem to destroy was already of the value of dust.

(I had a chance, the day after reading the lecture these remarks preface, to ask Antonieta Sosa if she had read Thoreau. She answered in excellent English that she had read enough to know that she was still too young to study it more thoroughly—though she was, even if her dancer's body made her seem younger, surely close to Thoreau's age when he died. I detected no grain of irony in anything she said or did.)

I am reminded that I have neglected a pervasive feature of moving through Antonieta Sosa's rooms. Because the walls of her rooms are apparently no different, in color and texture, from those of the museum, you enter them before you know you are there, I mean you expect (I expected) that what is exhibited there is *on* its walls, not that the walls *themselves* are on exhibit, along with everything they enclose, if anything. Then the recognition perhaps dawns that you are yourself enclosed there, hence exhibited while the music of your presence lasts, hence (since you are a human being) that you are a subject of interrogation. So the question why this installation is here becomes the question why you are here, what interests you here, hence perhaps exhibits your confusion. It is philosophy's invitation.

This brings me to the other of the good encounters I mentioned with the artwork world, namely John Cage's Charles Eliot Norton Lectures delivered at Harvard in 1988–89. The six lectures, so called—he titles them, for short, I through VI—were constructed by establishing (as what composers for a while called precompositional assumptions), a set of what Cage would use as source texts, namely ones from which, by various chance procedures, sentences and parts of sentences were extracted and joined together for the length of whatever length a lecture may be. The resulting lecture-texts consisted of chains sometimes of near gibberish, sometimes of what almost seemed sense, and sometimes with a whole English phrase or sentence (sometimes one perfectly familiar—Thoreau and Emerson and Wittgenstein, I am happy to report, were prominent among Cage's source texts). These constructions were read by Cage sitting before a table on the lit platform/stage of a dimmed Victorian quasi-amphitheater with a balcony running through a full semicircle, the hall

seating better than a thousand people, reading from what I recall as an ordinary notebook in a clear, fluent, rather sing-song tenor voice, at a steady
pace, never looking up from his text. I found myself charmed, my overall
mood as of hovering in a sort of active peacefulness, freed from the demands either of sense or of silence, punctuated from time to time by the
wonder whether something intelligible had found its way to speech, and
more rarely, but striking with the force of revelation, by a completely pure,
unmistakable sentence, after which I actively for a while held myself in
readiness for another such incredible gift. I became almost joyful as I took
in the joke (Danto asserts that a postmodern object works in the region of
metaphysical jokes) that, apart from the sensuous pleasure of the event, it
was almost mimetic, a simulacrum, of an ordinary lecture, of one of those
uncountable hours in which audiences have sat without effective complaint through an hour-long talk, so much of so many of which are recy-
clings of personal or cultural source texts, parts of which are unintelligible
and other parts almost intelligible, with here and there perhaps memorable leaps or slips of clarity. Cage's imperturbability seemed to question
how much of any of this is taken into the sum of one's happiness, and
whether that matters. A more disreputable part of my joy, or fun, no doubt,
was witnessing the spectacle of members of the audience, from high and
low, leaving early, some shyly, as if out of regret and respect, but others
brazenly, as if insulted or mildly outraged, without realizing that they were
equally and inevitably part of the theater Cage had created of the occasion,
that their leaving was in effect predicted in Cage's preparations, which
produced a construction to be delivered independent of the audience's expectations or responses or needs (except those of audibility and physical
comfort)—that in his eyes, leaving his performance may or may not have
been as accurate and telling a response to his work as staying would have
been. Why are you there? Or in Thoreau's way of speaking, where do you
live?

I attended the next week's lecture to see what a second experience would
reveal, and, doubtless, to count the house. I would not guess who sat
through all of all six lectures, or who could distinguish one from the others.
I am reminded of Danto's recurring in various of his pieces to Warhol's
film *Sleep*, a roughly six-hour string of shots, often repeated, of a man
sleeping. Danto confesses that he did not sit through it all (or did he say
this about Warhol's *Empire*?). Was leaving the screening artistic bad faith
or faintheartedness on Danto's part? Part of the background of the joke
here is that eight hours is typically and wisely said to be the span of a good
night's sleep. Is a span of six hours good enough? What is any good about

watching a moving picture of such periods of sleep (undrugged, and not for the purpose of studying sleep)? Here I do not feel like asking whether the object is art, but whether it is a film, which Danto does not question, or, I believe, take the film to question. To say it is a bad or boring film would seem not to be in on the depth of the joke; and how would one support such a judgment? After Hitchcock experimented in his film *Rope* by using no editing, shooting each reel of film in one take, he concluded that a film, meaning a good film, had to be edited, that is, cut. Does Warhol's *Empire* challenge that judgment? Only on the condition that it is, and is accepted as, a good film.

To view, or watch, or scan, or stare at all-but-unvarying motion picture footage of the Empire State Building for just over eight hours will cause various states of consciousness. Where would the interest lie? How does the fact of unvarying motion picture footage *hold* interest as a projected still slide would not, and as the building itself does not?—anyway not in a form that would be expressed by fixing oneself at the place of Warhol's camera and staring at the building for eight hours (what would count as *watching* it?)—or at any other still artifact out of doors. As a declaration or exploration of motion and still photography, or of demanding awareness of the fact of viewing film, the concluding sequence of fixed camera shots of empty cityscapes that concludes Antonioni's roughly contemporary *Eclipse* is a thousand times more interesting and pleasant to view than (I wager) *Empire*. Perhaps that is precisely what *Empire* implies is dangerously beguiling in such a film as *Eclipse*. Here is an instance of what has caused me to speak of modernist art as, over a couple of centuries, calling increasingly, in some new way, for philosophy.

A test of artistic worth announced by Wordsworth is the desire to *return* to a work, to behold it again. This seems all but fantastic to consider in the case of experiencing the Cage lectures or the Warhol films. Yet what if I go on to suggest that we take *Sleep* as a comment on an old motif of sculpture and painting, even forming a test (whether by confirming or mocking it may be left open) specifically of a thesis of Michael Fried's about the development of modern painting in discovering that overcoming an unwanted theatricality requires denying the presence of the beholder, by depicting an otherwise absorbed, oblivious subject? Has Warhol's film shown that this is true or untrue of film more generally?

What do these recent comments of mine, or readings, at best amount to? They do not count as what Kant defines as aesthetic judgment, because they do not claim to speak with necessity and universality, an essential mark of which for Kant is that I am willing to impose them as demands that others share my pleasure in the objects, see that what I see in them is as if there to see. I find that I am not vividly interested in whether others agree with me about Warhol's films, or perhaps no more interested than I would be in whether they understand and like a joke I like, which may be no small matter. But this is not the role I have counted on from the great arts, which is rather to prepare my experience for judgment by making experience mine, and to show the world, I might say show the justice of the world, to deserve judgment. Yet I remain grateful to the artwork or art world objects, as it were, for their still strange interest to me, and particularly, I think, for making me voluble, making me loosen my tongue and express myself. This is also no small matter. On my reading of Wittgenstein's *Investigations*, it is concerned with the human terror of inexpressiveness, of suffocation, alternating with an equal terror of exposure, as if speech threatens to become unable perfectly to refer to objects of my interest or to give expression to my states of being, or else to refer and give expression so fully as to give myself away. It is the version, or threat, of skepticism that I claim Wittgenstein's *Investigations* stakes itself on identifying and dispersing, ceaselessly.

But here I seem to be proposing a way to distinguish the objects Danto calls postmodern from ones most would call modernist—among which I count Wittgenstein's *Investigations* itself—not by whether one contains a set of properties (sensuous or conceptually derived) that the other lacks, but by the role they play in our lives, by how we treat them, by whether, for example, I have, in order to allow myself and the object to be revealed to each other, to do the thing Wittgenstein calls "turning my investigation around," which I understand as having to turn myself around, reorient my life with the object. I do not have a list of criteria that distinguish these addresses to objects from what Danto means by speaking of our "participating" in performance and installations and being "transformed" by them. So I conclude with a further example.

Godard's film *Two or Three Things I Know About Her*, from 1971, takes place in a cityscape of demonic juxtaposition, with equal parts of decay, junk, and construction amid a growing forest of babbling one- or two-word signs, done with big letters in primary colors, as if made for giant children who will learn nothing beyond them. It is the sort of scene Danto has declared himself struck by as wonderful (an experience not foreign to me), and which Godard seems to despise and to admire America for bringing into the world. The film contains Godard's early figure of the housewife/prostitute, symbolizing late capitalism, surrounded in her modern kitchen by every familiarly garish product purchasable from a supermarket, underscored by a sound track sometimes unyielding with its sounds of cans being opened and of pots carelessly slammed on a stovetop and, outside the windows, of trucks and cars and trains spelling out our dependence upon them. But suddenly, from nowhere, the opening phrase, or quasi-fragment, of Beethoven's last string quartet is heard, lasting some three seconds. The modified repetition and the responding phrase do not follow. This happens again in the film. The ache for the responding phrase is so strong for a moment as to convince us that we are apt for prayer. Grant that the Godard film is a masterpiece of postmodernist filmmaking, at any rate one that positions itself against a tradition of complacent, derivative modernism and humanism and liberalism and the rest, as strongly as any postmodern object. How do we understand the gesture of its quoting the Beethoven, this Beethoven? Is it to emphasize the lastness of the quartet? Is it to say that its opening fragment is to be regarded as complete, in other words, that there is no established way of going on from it, to an answering fragment? Does this mean that there is hope for us in learning how to go on, or that there is not? T. J. Clark, in *Farewell to an Idea*, speaks of Beethoven as Jacques-Louis David's brother, both of them sources of a long period of modernism that is over. Is Godard's quotation of Beethoven taunting us with the memory of an experience we can no longer have, or trust? Or is he proposing that we learn from it, if such an experience is any longer open to us, that we shall have to find it in unheard-of forms, within landscapes of ideals that seem merely blasted? It is in opting for the unheard of that I have from my first credible encounter with Wittgenstein's *Investigations* undertaken to inherit that work as an achievement of modernism, from which it follows that I have come to understand some future of philosophy—however else, and without supposing that any separate field of philosophy will continue to be known as aesthetics—to be itself irreducibly aesthetic.

〴〳 〴〳 〴〳 〴〳 〴〳

Response

I was deeply moved by the fact that Stanley Cavell should have seen the two of us as having followed parallel paths in what one must call our philosophical lives, which has meant that we have more in common with each other than with any other philosopher of our generation. That makes it all the more interesting that we should have turned out so differently. I think the history that we shared is rather richer than his sparse narrative of actual crossed paths, but even so it remains more a history of perceived philosophical otherness than of actual encounters. It underwrites William James's wry observation that philosophers must travel in herds of one, like the rhinoceros. The otherness tinges even the episodes we shared.

I cherish the memory of that bright afternoon near Walden Pond when, for an improbable moment, Stanley, Sidney Morgenbesser, and I played ourselves in a scene for what proved to be the only feature-length film in the tragically brief career of the filmmaker, David Brooks, who was regarded, I have been told by Larry Kardash—curator of films for the Museum of Modern Art—as the rising star of the underground film movement of the 1960s. Though he was my student, David took it upon himself to tutor me on the films of his peers, and we frequently attended screenings in one or another grimy venue in downtown Manhattan. It was at Anthology Film Archives that I first saw *And the Wind Bore Him Down to the Sea*—the film in which Stanley, Sidney, and I played our roles in a scene for what was to be a film of quest. Three philosophers, arguing about the external world, stop to pick up a hitchhiker, whose quest the film narrates, but they pay him as little attention as they pay the real world itself: they exist in a world of their own.

The philosophers are next seen carrying on with their interminable argument while playing a somewhat strenuous game in the meadow that David had found beautiful enough to gather the equipment he needed, borrow an expensive vehicle, and photograph the philosophers at play in. As it happened, he had misloaded his camera, and the footage came out red when developed. He was at first devastated—someone had lent him professional apparatus, someone else had lent the Land Rover, the philosophers had given him themselves, and he had ruined an opportunity little likely to happen again. When I called him a while later, he was his characteristic cheerful self: he had decided just to use the footage the way it was, and it came out almost as Stanley described it—"ten or fifteen seconds of blurred red footage capturing three almost recognizable grown men inexplicably playing kick-the-can in a large meadow." It is here that the difference in our responses to art shows up. Stanley doubtless saw the film through the perspective of Hollywood movies, for which he has an understandable passion. My perspective was more sympathetic. It is important that the "three men" were philosophers, and that, while playing kick-the-can, they are continuing the argument they had been engaged in when they picked up the hitchhiker. And it is important that the world of the philosophers is in monochrome. Hegel had spoken of philosophy "painting its gray in gray," but "red in red" was even better for the artistic purposes of David Brooks's film. The rest of the film is in full color—the colors, one might say, of the external world: the meadow was green under bright blue skies, the philosophers' faces were red from the unaccustomed exertion of the childhood game they were caught up in. The philosophical episode, by contrast, is monochrome. David's father had wanted him to be a philosopher rather than a filmmaker—and in rescuing the "ruined" film, he was declaring for life in the real world and making a point about the life he rejected for himself. It was a magnificent example of artistic improvisation, and taught me something about philosophy and art at once. I adore Stanley's brilliant discussions of the comedies of remarriage of the 1930s. It is philosophy as we both want it to be but as it rarely is. Mostly it is red-in-red discussions of the external world, unwinnable like the game of kick-the-can, which stops without coming to an end. You can stop playing the game, but you cannot come out a victor. But I think his artistic passion inflects the way he viewed a film that was definitely not Hollywood.

The great merit of Stanley's paper for me is its raising the issue of "the end of philosophy," and in underscoring the way that we differ, I would say profoundly, in what he regards as "what seems right, and irreversibly innovative, in Wittgenstein's later work and in the work of [his] teacher, J. L. Austin." He certainly did not cite with approval my obiter dictum regarding Wittgenstein's later philosophy—that "It is beautifully written and thought, but philosophically of no significance whatsoever." This may be overstated—let's say it is overstated and even in bad taste—but for better or worse, I believe it true, and what truth there is in it will explain the further differences that divide Stanley and me in the philosophy of art and probably everything else that interests us enough to philosophize about it.

Let's consider one of the most famous passages in *Philosophical Investigations,* where he provides an almost paralyzing example of why Wittgenstein believed we do not need the kinds of definitions that almost define the practice of philosophy in the West—of justice, of knowledge, of love, of the soul, for example—in the great Platonic works to which the rest of philosophy is said to be a footnote. Wittgenstein uses the humble example of games, and concludes that we all more or else know which are the games, are able to define the common properties in virtue of which, say, chess and kick-the-can are games—despite not having a definition. Would we be any the wiser if we had one? If we followed his injunction to "look and see," we would indeed find it hard to see what kick-the-can has in common with pinochle or blind man's bluff. Wittgenstein's disciples in the philosophy of art said works of art are like games—we can all pick them out without having a definition of art, so we do not need one. What got me interested in the philosophy of art was that two things, looking more or less identical, were such that one could be a work of art and the other not. Duchamp's *Readymades*, much of Warhol's work of the mid-'6os, including his *Brillo Box*, certain paradigmatic works of minimalism—a single lit florescent bulb by Dan Flavin, a row of bricks by Carl Andre, a pile of hemp by Robert Morris—the hateful idea of "picking out" was of no help in explaining why one of a pair of indiscernibles was art and the other not. In my view, we needed a definition, and it would make us a great deal wiser. My effort, almost from the beginning, was to provide one.

Cavell is somewhat leery of the use of the term "artwork"—there is the fastidious Austinian speaking, for whom the *OED* lists accepted usages that may at best include "work of art" as "American" and "rare"—though I imagine that by this time it has become accepted English usage. He allows me the usage specifically for the admittedly somewhat barren kinds of examples from the '6os that meant so much to me philosophically, which he calls "artwork art," listing a few examples that even he might tolerate, without quite asking what makes "artwork art" art, when the real question is what makes art art, whether we are speaking of Rembrandts or Warhols. That was my concern. One had to find out why such aesthetically unrewarding objects were art along with all the aesthetically rewarding ones. My friend Ti-Grace Atkinson, when she was hammering out a philosophy of feminism, paid considerable attention to the case of lesbianism—not because she believed all women should be lesbians, but that somehow the principle of feminism had to include it as more than a deviation from the norm. The '6os demanded definitions where the '5os thought we could get along without them. Wittgenstein was philosophically worthless in this context. And so I found him everywhere that I felt definitions were needed—in the theory of knowledge, the theory of action, the philosophy of history, the philosophy of mind, the philosophy of philosophy.

In two different books, *What Philosophy Is* and *Connections to the World*, I undertook to put philosophy in a nutshell and explain what makes it different from other kinds of inquiries. Since it plays so little role in the ordinary circumstances of everyday life, it is easy to say, since one cannot find it there, that philosophy must be on holiday—and, in saying that, to believe that one has gotten rid of it. Twentieth-century philosophy found the philosophy it had inherited baffling, and tried to turn it into something else—into science, into the study of consciousness, into linguistics, into "the problems of men" (Dewey), into nonsense (Wittgenstein). Nietzsche taught that it had all been disguised autobiography, and Derrida that it was all a form of literature, by which, I think, he meant that questions of truth and falsity were irrelevant to it. All this is evasive action, in my view, since the effort was to assimilate it to something more tractable and discard whatever was left over. But it left unaddressed the question of what philosophy had actually been. I obviously can do little more here than refer to the books just cited, but my overall sense is that the great philosophical clashes are between total visions of reality—whether, for example, reality is mental, material, or both—and that there is no nonquestion-begging way in which these can be arbitrated.

I don't think this is entirely true about the philosophical clashes between Stanley and myself. I think those differences can in principle be resolved. But probably not by us. What makes us different is in the end what makes us *us*. The difference between our philosophies is in part the difference between the lives we have lived, which are pretty similar, but mainly is the different people who led those lives. In Stanley's case, the result has been some wonderful writings that I do not have to accept his philosophy to admire. His writings on screwball comedies are enriched as much by the literature he has read and the love affairs he has had as by the philosophers he has studied and been convinced by. I *know* something comparable can be said about me. I think that is what connects and separates us. Toward the end of an essay I mention in my response to Lydia Goehr— "Beautiful Science and the Future of Criticism"—I addressed Hume's problem of finding anything that was his self when he looked within and found only a mosaic of impressions and ideas.

> What bonds the self into a unity is of a piece with what brings histories and essays into unities—and Hume as psychologist and man of letters would similarly have found a unity that parallels what he found lacking between Hume as skeptic and Hume as man of the world. . . . The principles, whatever they are, that enable us to tell and follow stories, to construct and read poetry, are the principles that bind lives into unities, that give us the sense of chapters ending and new ones beginning. The future of criticism consists in making these principles explicit.

That is also the future of psychology. We, as individuals, write our lives by living them: we are such stuff as texts are made of. It is very hard, I believe, to think outside what makes us what we are and find ways to agree and disagree on what counts as philosophical truth. At least it is for Stanley and me, the texts of whose lives may not be so outwardly different but, let's face it, whose philosophical personalities are as strong as they are. The philosophers we admire did not make us into the people we are. It is the other way around. The differences between selves, however parallel their lives, is indelible and intractable. But that does not prevent me from embracing Stanley with a kind of love for his difference, for his depth and brilliance as a thinker, and for the beauty of his soul.

4

For the Birds/Against the Birds

The Modernist Narratives of Danto and Adorno (and Cage)

Lydia Goehr

The First Deception

> Thou wast not born for death, immortal Bird!
> No hungry generations tread thee down;
> The voice I hear this passing night was heard
> In ancient days by emperor and clown.[1]

These lines from John Keats's "Ode to a Nightingale" of 1819 sustain the rhetorical question Kant posed in 1790: "What is more highly extolled by poets than the bewitchingly beautiful song of the nightingale [sung] in a lonely stand of bushes on a still summer evening, under the gentle light of the moon?" Kant speaks of the beauty of birdsong, as of nature more generally. He finds beauty too in art. Yet the conditions of beauty are not, for either nature or art, what one would expect. For, from an aesthetic perspective, we find a natural object beautiful if we regard it as purposeful, as if its meaning were derived from something like human intention, but an artwork beautiful if we regard it as purposeless, as though, through the creative act of genius, nature was its source. However, Kant continues, from a moral perspective and given the very same objects, we want to see them for what they really are and don't want to be deceived. So if someone tricks us into thinking we are hearing a song of nature, when really it is artificially produced, a basic condition of our appreciation is disturbed. Kant accordingly tells of an innkeeper who determines to trick his guests into thinking they are listening to a bird when behind the bushes a young boy sings in imitation.[2]

Kant is well known for having overturned the traditional demand on art that it should stand to a natural or to an ordinary, everyday object in a relation of mere copying. Hegel extends the argument when he refers to the many examples of fully deceptive imitation in the history of art. He writes of the grapes of Zeuxis that were long regarded as art's triumph: so like the real thing, as the legend has it, living doves tried to peck at them. Like Kant, Hegel is unimpressed by these "tricks" of imitation: deception, at least of man, should not be the aim of an art in service to absolute *Geist*/spirit.[3]

Keats further complicates the relation between art and nature, and now also between man and nature, because his ode in praise of the nightingale's natural song is sung under the condition of human suffering. "My heart aches," it begins, "and a drowsy numbness pains / My sense, as though of hemlock I had drunk." The last line offers no further clarity: "was it a vision, or a waking dream? Fled is that music:—do I wake or sleep?" Like Kant and Hegel, Keats draws on the possibility of deception to suggest that the nightingale's song is not always or purely a happy one, even when sung on a summer evening.

This is also Oscar Wilde's theme in the short story about a nightingale who tries in vain to help a young philosopher find a rose to please a girl. "What is the heart of a bird compared to the heart of a man?" asks the unhappy nightingale, and then immediately answers her own question: "Bitter, bitter was the pain, and wilder and wilder grew her song, for she sang of the Love that is perfected by Death, of the Love that dies not in the tomb." The young philosopher fails to get the point and instead of singing a *Liebestod* chooses to return to his books. What does logic give him that love does not? A guarantee, he believes, against his ever again being deceived.[4]

The Second Deception

The interest that motivates the present essay originates in a piece I wrote for a conference in Berlin on "conceptualisms" in music and the other arts. I called it "Against the Birds."[5] I read the philosopher and music critic Theodor W. Adorno as arguing against conceptualism in general, which is to say, against the regressive tendency of concepts entirely to subsume particulars, say works of art, as a totalitarian society subsumes its individuals, thereby denying to both the works and the individuals their freedom of movement. I focused on Adorno's critique of the composers he met in Darmstadt (Stockhausen, Boulez, and most especially John Cage), because at the same time that Adorno was arguing against subsuming particulars entirely under a concept he was also arguing against subsuming art entirely under the concept of nature and nature entirely under the concept of art. Adorno worried about the contradictions implicit to the naturalist claims about art he heard in Darmstadt, for it was a misleading naturalism used to justify highly technological or unnatural forms of production. Adorno sometimes objected more to the deceptive character threatened by the claims than to the actual music produced. Darmstadt, he might have described it, was "mass deception."

My title "Against the Birds" played against a title John Cage once used for a book, "For the Birds."[6] Cage didn't do much with the title; nor at first did I. So I began to think further about Cage, and then more broadly about the pervasive use of birds, birdsong, and birdcages in the history of music, until I arrived at the thought that knowing this history might help further elucidate Adorno's critique. Such a history would match what Adorno, with Horkheimer, described as the dialectic of enlightenment, because contained within that description was a story of the dialectic between nature and art, i.e., about how nature comes, in the civilized name of reason and art, to be dominated by humanity but incorporated simultaneously into a most uncivilizing discourse of myth. Enlightenment, as they did say, was "mass deception."[7]

In their account, the end of the enlightenment dialectic occurred earlier than the 1960s with the catastrophic culmination of the Fascist movement in Germany. Still, they argued, the tendencies they saw in Germany before the war were present afterward, in Germany as well as in postwar capitalist countries like America. Moving my attention from Europe to America (or from Darmstadt to New York), I noticed that the Manhattan philosopher and art critic Arthur Danto also was calling upon the dialectic between art and nature ("nature" albeit now under the guise of the commonplace), to comment on the conceptualist, Fluxus, and minimalist movements of the postwar years. At this moment it occurred to me that Danto's and Adorno's postwar, American and European accounts might each very well be illuminated by their comparison.

In general, Adorno writes more about music, Danto more about the visual arts. Both write about John Cage. Both, moreover, link thoughts about art's relation to nature to those about art's relation to the commonplace. Hegel originally provides the link when he speaks in the same sentence of "the hard rind of nature" (*die harte Rinde der Natur*) and of "the common world" (*gewöhnlichen Welt*) as equally giving the mind more trouble than the products of art "in breaking through to the idea" (*zur Idee durchzudringen*).[8] However, the connection goes further than this. For the dialectic that starts out between art and nature becomes over time one between art and the commonplace, where "the commonplace" becomes the concept precisely to demonstrate the loss of what the concept of "nature" once implied, namely, beauty and freedom. If this is right, then it also plausibly follows that the artists of the '60s who seek a meaning for art in the commonplace are those who become too content to accept the loss of a certain sort of meaning in art. Or, contrarily, those who continue to see beauty either in nature or in art are those who no longer find beauty in the commonplace world. Whatever the attitude adopted toward art or nature, it is historically inseparable from the attitude adopted toward the commonplace.

Shared by Adorno and Danto, so I want to show, is a deep philosophical commitment to preserving a difference between art and nature or between art and the commonplace, simultaneously to reveal the deceptive character of what they both interpret to be contrary assertions of identity. In these assertions both find the terms to articulate the idea that art has come to an end conceptualized as either a triumph over or a defeat by deception. This essay ultimately focuses on how both philosophers assume theses about identity and difference to interpret the culmination of their particular historical narratives of modernist deception. I nevertheless argue that just as their arguments are *about* identity but *for* nonidentity, so similarly, however preoccupied they are with ends, their arguments are in fact for continuation.

In what follows I do not describe either of their historical narratives in full, only the terms of their endings. I do, however, offer a brief narrative of my own. It focuses on music in the last two hundred years, and mostly on opera, at least until the final stage, where I turn specifically to John Cage and his *Bird Cage*. Despite its brevity, one may see the various ways birds have entered music's domain, first by symbolizing all manner of freedom, escape, return, love, knowledge, and identity, then by the more conscious formal uses whereby correspondences are established between artistic creation and the inspirations of nature. Gradually, the Kantian trauma of being deceived by a boy imitating a nightingale becomes a trauma about a reality sustained by mechanical artifice. Finally, there is a dialectical last stage where appeals to birds and their songs are made (almost philosophically) to challenge the very distinction between art and nature. The narrative is written deliberately to reach a fork in the road, to pursue either the path of Danto or that of Adorno.

The Operatic Birdcage

In the beginning was the name, but a promise also of financial reward. Mozart marks this beginning in 1798 when Madame Vogelsang aspires to sing like a nightingale so that she may earn 2,000 ducats a year. Papageno has a different aspiration when he names himself the "bird catcher known throughout the land," since what he wants to catch "in his net" are women. Yet the women are rarely waiting to be so entrapped, as we hear in the birdlike songs of Nedda, Manon, Mélisande, and, of course, la Rondine. Usually their songs show them rather to be fighting against the odds. Rossini thus narrates a patriarchal story of a town that condemns a young girl to death even though the crime is small, only to discover at the last moment the guilt of *la gazza ladra*. Which seems, temporarily at least, to be the fortune denied to Agathe in *Der Freischütz* when, innocently believing that in the song of the nightingale she hears the arrival of the man she loves, she finds herself the target of a shooting contest: "Don't shoot," she sings, "I am the pigeon!"

Madame Vogelsang later becomes the more reflective Meister Vogel-gesang, when the woman who desires to sing like a bird is transfigured by Wagner into the man who desires only to understand the rules of her song. Meister Vogelgesang accompanies Meister Nachtigall to the opening round of a song contest, only to discover that the appreciation of Walther von Stolzing's first song belongs not yet to him at all, but only to Hans Sachs, who apparently knows something no one else yet knows. Indeed, he generates for the other masters, for Walther, and for the opera itself a dialectical drama about nature and art to demonstrate the conditions of Walther's special genius: his song sounds "so old" and yet is "so new" as "a bird sings in the sweetness of May." Sachs argues that though a song should concur with the rules of art, it shouldn't concur, to use Kant's term, too "punctiliously" (*Pünktlichkeit*), for otherwise the song will show more its academic form (*Schulform*) than its (natural) beauty. Those who follow rules too literally are pedants; they suffer from *Beckmesserei*. Those, contrarily, who show genius produce songs as exemplary models to encourage the always-needed reinvigoration of the rules. Only with the recognition of the genius's respect for rules and of the masters' respect for genius is the

conflict between nature and art resolved. At this moment, the genius happily joins the mastersingers' community.

This happy ending is, however, put to a Nietzschean test by Bizet, when
Carmen proclaims in her *"Habanera"* that it's not so easy for a community
to cage a rebellious bird—be it a gypsy, a woman, or a genius. Her claimed
freedom challenges the Wagnerian illusion of contentment at the *Meister-
singer*'s end, since the question remains what Walther will sing the next
day after his acceptance into the community, or, indeed, whether he will
ever sing again.

Walther sings like the bird of spring in part because he is in love. So
does Olympia, and no less than like a nightingale when she is made by Of-
fenbach to sing to her ardent Hoffmann. Yet there is a difference between
him and her, for whereas he's a man, she's only a mechanical doll. Hoffmann's obsession with his doll transforms the Kantian fear of human artifice into one of mechanical artifice. Olympia sings as an imitating parrot,
singing "Ah-ah-ah" as if she were experiencing sublime pleasure. But this
is only an "as if." What she really is doing, because this is all she can mechanically do with her ice cold lips, is affirming the words of her besotted
man. Her pleasure is false, but it deceives the man who loves her. However, the deception is entirely his—the desire and its product.

The same pattern occurs in Hans Christian Andersen's story "The
Nightingale," later made into an opera by Stravinsky, but motivated by Andersen's deep passion for the singer Jenny Lind. In the story, on hearing
the mechanical nightingale's song, the townsfolk proclaim it to be the very
best bird they can imagine, whereupon the narrator remarks that they
make the bird sing again and again—even though it is the thirty-fourth
time. Unable to learn its tune, they, like Hoffmann, prefer this bird to the
real thing. "With a real nightingale you can never know what is going to
come next, but with the artificial bird it's all set. That's the way it is and
that's the way that it's always going to be. You can explain it, you can open
it up and see the human ingenuity—how the pieces are put together, how
they work, and how one thing follows from another."[9] Apparently the
people don't see the Beckmesserish tension. They understand the song according to the rules or the mechanism, but they can't internalize it, which
is why the real nightingale has to return, as Walther von Stolzing has to return, to demonstrate how the song should properly be sung.

Kant worries about the boredom experienced when hearing the same
song repeatedly. He worries that once we've grasped the point or rule of a
song's pattern, there's nothing left to stimulate the imagination. It turns
out that his worry cuts across the distinction between the real and the arti-

ficial nightingale, because, in his view, it doesn't matter whether the bird is real or artificial; it's the repetition alone that annoys him, the boredom and the tastelessness, as he describes it, of an ever-repeating song. Kant actually questions whether we ever really enjoy song of any kind. Even in the case of a genuine birdsong, might we not really be appreciating only the little bird that produces it?[10]

It's often claimed of repetition that discontent taints what seems initially to feel like satisfaction. When no challenge is given to listeners by a mechanically repeating toy or when what it sings is entirely predictable, the song assumes a quality of what Hoffmann earlier and Freud later calls the uncanny, marked by the ability of a mechanical object to deceive us into thinking it is real, but also by our knowing in our boredom that something is amiss. Freud writes about the infantile repetition compulsion, arguably played out by the contemporary Glass cages of minimalist music, from which the question arises whether this essentially repetitive music symbolizes some sort of mystical transformation, a difference triggered in and for consciousness, or merely the dulling of a mind that has become overly enamored with artifice.

Mimi and Rudolfo make love to the coming of spring, but Puccini denies this duet to his Butterfly. Pinkerton fails to return as he said he would with the robin redbreasts in the happy season. Since he doesn't appear, it occurs to Butterfly that maybe the happy season comes less often in America. Sharpless holds from her the truth and declares himself "ignorant about . . . ornithology." "Orni?" she asks; "thology," he repeats. With Danto, we shall later have to ask of what use ornithology can ever be, if all one wants to know is what it's like to be a butterfly in love.

Before this, however, a nice connection emerges between Butterfly's question and Andersen's tale, for, in the latter, we hear that the "whole city talked about the remarkable bird," and "whenever two people met, the first one needed only to say 'Night—!' before the other said 'Gale!' and then they sighed and understood each other."[11] The verbal rupture in the term suggests a society fractured by heartless or mechanized design—a "tin ear or a tin heart," which, of course, is also what one might accuse Pinkerton of having. Such a society of men is portrayed in Walter Braunfels's opera *Die Vögel* of 1920, based on Aristophanes' much older play. This opera tells of a society (Germany after World War I) being built anew, trying to escape the problems of the old society, only to end up in a condition much worse, where the birds even assume control of the air. The freedom promised by the naturalized society of birds becomes totalitarian control, according to which, following Aristophanes, humanity is severed not only from nature but also from the gods. In a proud moment the birds sing of their power and control, but the words they sing forecast their inevitable fall. So too, and not least in his most decadent opera *Salome*, Richard Strauss draws upon Wilde's play to make Herod sing in his sickness of hearing a terrible "beating of wings," to signify the "chill wind" that is blowing throughout his land.

In German, to say that *"man hat einen Vogel"* is to recognize the madness of the man. Thus Herod might well have appeared again in 1969 in Peter Maxwell Davies's *Eight Songs for a Mad King*, although now the king is English and is called George. Maxwell Davies makes explicit use of bird voice techniques to convey both the madness and the broader sense of our becoming caged or imprisoned by the patterns of our thinking. This work introduces the final theme of the present narrative, the formal transfiguration of bird sound into musical sound or, better perhaps, into fully composed music. When Bartók earlier in the century, but Messiaen later on, notated folksongs and birdsongs, they didn't intend to trick listeners into thinking that they were hearing the "real thing"; they were interested in the possibilities and difficulties of notation, of techniques of recording, and of composing in an advanced musical language, despite their sometimes naturalist and, in Bartók's case, nationalist claims. When Messiaen composed *Saint François d'Assise* in 1983, he created an extraordinary "dawn chorus" to demonstrate the most modernist tension between advanced compositional technique on the one hand and the call of nature and of the gods on the other. An intentionally religious work, *Saint François* links the voices of the birds to those of the angels, as "God's messengers," to prevent the birds (read "humans") from assuming a total authority of their own.

In 1985, Messiaen's student, Michaël Lévinas, composed *La conférence des oiseaux*. In this work, following the description of one critic, the singer-actors perform human and birdlike movements while a tape produces sonorities derived from actual birdsongs.[12] It is comparable to Jonathan Harvey's *Bird Concerto with Piano Song* of 2003, which projects digitized samplings of Californian birdsong around the auditorium. Apparently, this work isn't anything like David Tudor's older *Rain Forest*, but it does similarly beg that the question of art's relation to nature be posed. Another critic recently declared that in all these sorts of works, the birdsong at last assumes the ontological status of a found object.[13] Yet, on closer inspection, there is very little that is actually "found." Just as the young boy with all the intention in the world imitates the nightingale from behind the bush, so now, with all the machinery one can imagine, the birds are heard in the concert hall. Still, the thought of an art's being found, or of a music's being natural, carries its dialectical weight through the ongoing commitment to aesthetic appearance, which is exactly what Kant saw so clearly, even if the naturalized character of the appearance is anything but natural. In writing of something like "found art," Kant describes cases where one stumbles across natural objects and attributes to them a purposiveness as if they were products of human design.[14] In the modern cases, the coin falls on the other side, when we attribute to products of high artifice the character of their being without human design to find in them some quality of nature's intentionless immediacy. Whatever the complexity involved, the critic who sees in contemporary works the character of their being found draws a conclusion most relevant to our concerns, namely, that with these works an end has finally been reached. No more mere twitterings of birds, he says almost against the entire history of women's song (they were hardly ever "mere twitterings"!), and no more mere copies of nature, he says against the history of pedantry, but nature itself finally entering and thereby perhaps liberating the auditorium of contemporary musical sound.

Cage's Parrot

In 1972 John Cage produced an event in downtown New York entitled *Bird Cage*. It was named after a beer coaster belonging to a working-class bar in Philadelphia. It took place over two evenings and consisted (following the CD) of twelve tapes of birdsong (recorded in New York State) spliced by the voice of a speaking man, Cage himself. At a significant moment, Cage and his parrot engaged (a little like Hoffmann and his doll Olympia) in a repetitive play of imitating voices. As the advertising for the CD says, Cage wanted the tapes to be heard by people "who were free to move" and where birds were "free to fly"—and that, apparently, could happen still in downtown New York.[15]

Generally in his works Cage articulates the trajectory of music's bourgeois historical passage. He raises the question of music's relation to birdsong to make explicit what is involved in our concept of music. In reference less to the works than to the proclamations he makes on their behalf, his thought is that, contra Messiaen, birdsong need no longer be composed into musical form because it's already music. One needn't transfigure natural or ordinary sound into music because it's already what the compositional act shows it to be. The traditional psychological, if not also ontological gap that has long maintained a difference between music and birdsong is now closed. Music finds its origin by being returned to that from which it sought under the condition of enlightenment to separate itself, namely natural sound. Through the reincorporation of natural or everyday sound into the concept of music, the concept is brought to self-understanding by being shown no longer to need its artificial or deadening (Western) aesthetic history. In this passage, music meets its natural maker, finds its concept and identity, and, as paradoxical as it here sounds, is liberated from its cage.

To present Cage's argument in this particular way is to use it, as one may use many of the proclamations of the Fluxus artists, to sustain an account of the end, if not of music's *production*, then at least of music's traditional (enlightenment or bourgeois) *conception*. For it is the tension between production and conception (or product and concept) that lies deep within any thesis on the end of music or art.

Adorno and Danto

More or less explicitly, Adorno and Danto both interpret the history of the arts in terms of the Kantian (or Western) dialectic between art and nature or in terms of the arts' (bourgeois) separation from the world of the everyday. Influenced by Hegel and Nietzsche, they also dialectically trace their accounts back to ancient Greece, to Plato's fear of the arts, generating what Danto calls the disenfranchisement thesis of art by philosophy, and back also to Greek myth, motivating Adorno's concentration (with Horkheimer) on Odysseus and the Sirens. Nietzsche provides one specific link when, in his discourse on good and evil, he describes the dangers of attempting to "translate man back into nature" or to use the "eternal basic text of *homo natura*" as a way to confront man with man and then man with "the *rest* of nature," especially when this confrontation is "hardened in the discipline of science." For what this discipline does is disenfranchise not only art but also humanity, closing its ears as Oedipus's ears are closed. Actually it is the ears of the sailors that are closed. Nietzsche's point, however, remains when he asks: can anyone, whether Oedipus or a regular sailor, any longer hear the siren songs of the "old metaphysical bird catchers"?[16]

Both Adorno and Danto read the movements of conceptualism, Fluxus, and minimalism as challenging or at least polemicizing the basic distinction between art and life, to deny the difference in favor of proclaimed assertions of identity. "Art is Life and Life is Art" proclaim the Fluxus artists,[17] or Cage, with much more of an edge: "Art has erased the dividing line between life and art. Now it is up to life to erase the dividing line between life and art."[18] Does Cage not in fact give quite new meaning to Nietzsche's early proclamation that only as an aesthetic phenomenon is life justified?

Both Adorno and Danto acknowledge that the identity claims aren't straightforward, yet they read them at the extreme, as strong assertions of identity. Cage's birdsong doesn't really deceive the listener into thinking it is the "real thing." Warhol's *Brillo Boxes* (Danto's favorite example) don't really look like their supermarket counterparts. And yet the strongest claim to identity and of perceptual deception, that we could somehow mistake one for the other, is necessary for both their arguments to work.

Consider Cage's best-known work, *4'33"*, where, even though there's nothing to hear except the real, ordinary, or natural thing, the noises that happen to be heard are nonetheless framed by institutional time and space, and are deliberately so framed to bring attention at least to the traditional strictures of performative time and space in the artificial concert hall. Contrast this work with, for example, Max Neuhaus's installation in Times Square called *Times Square*. Unlike others who apparently encountered the work without anyone's help, when I visited the site, I heard nothing until I was told (in fact by Danto) what to listen for. It was an almost monotone sound, a murmur or tremor, almost like the large chord of a cathedral organ and thus almost a pillar of sound separated from the ordinary sounds of the square, intended to be separated and experienced as separated, such that when one walked across the square, it would be as if one were passing from one sound space into another, then out again on the other side. Neuhaus's work is site- and sound-specific, a sound sculpture upon which, as Danto more recently informally remarked, one can spray no graffiti.

Cage's work is more traditionally constrained than Neuhaus's by factors of time and space. And yet Neuhaus claims his work to be a work, whereas Cage claims with his work to challenge the very concept. Cage uses his "work" to make the constraints of the work concept explicit; still, Neuhaus's use might be the more subversive. My question here is whether it is more effective to challenge the work concept from the outside or the inside, by an explicit idea or by changing conditions so as to compel a change in our understanding. Adorno definitely thinks the latter: a new aesthetics, he says, can be inferred neither from a philosophical idea nor from empirical investigation; it can only be developed by reflecting from inside the musical experience itself.[19] I think Danto would concur. Neither he nor Adorno bases their account on works that proclaim themselves philosophical works or, better, works of philosophy (if indeed any really do). Neither is so interested in an account of an art *become* idea or philosophy. They are both rather more interested in a history of art production that compels at a particular historical juncture—through experience—a certain sort of philosophical interpretation and, with that, liberation from a certain sort of deception.

Both sidestep the actual, metaphysically styled statements made by artists themselves about their works. They do this more or less deliberately to show, following Adorno first, that philosophical criticism articulates a significance for the works, which the works can't do themselves in the languages in which they're created, and a significance of which the artists aren't necessarily aware. Danto makes a different point. For a long time the production of the arts fell under the same historicist master narrative as the philosophical thinking about the arts. As philosophical critic his aim is to make explicit the terms of this master narrative, to release or rescue art from its authority, and thereby to bring the narrative to some sort of end. Danto thus describes how the concept of art is realized in or by the works themselves, though it is his own act of philosophical interpretation of these works that makes the art act explicit.[20] Like Adorno's view, Danto's really does depend on the relation he assumes between himself as philosophical critic and the works themselves. In Kantian terms, though one speaks "as if" the conceptual development occurred entirely in the works themselves, it couldn't have done so had there been no additional act of philosophical reflection.

For Danto, the concept of art is brought to its modernist fulfillment when art passes over (via philosophical reflection) into its posthistorical (or better, posthistoricist) condition. Adorno too gives an account of such a moment, though his tone is quite different. Rather than seeing the concept as realizing itself in any sort of positive gesture of self-knowing (even by the philosopher), he worries much more about an art production that has fully compromised itself to its concept. For here art might meet its maker, but the maker is now merely one of concepts. He thinks much about the contemporary impossibility of producing a noncompromised or literally "nonconceptualized" art. When he writes that there can be no poetry after Auschwitz (a statement he later modifies), one of the things he says he means is that society has so declined that there is (almost) no space left anymore for a noncompromised art to be produced. (Almost) all art has become conceptual in the very worst sense. To have a (almost) gapless society is to have society totally administered, where even, as in Braunfels's *The Birds*, the air is controlled and nothing slips out of the net. Such a society prevents what at least great art was formerly able to achieve, namely, a refusal to conform to society's demand for a conceptually fitting art. The "almost" is stressed here to maintain in Adorno's thought about art the possibility of its refusal, the refusal of what too much conceptual reflection sometimes brings when it rids itself entirely of any Schillerian trace of the naïve.

Danto reads art's history, with art's preoccupation with distinguishing itself from natural or ordinary objects, in terms of its ability to be the world's conscience, to take a stand at a distance, to interpret the world. Adorno reads art's commitment to aesthetic appearance as being how art sustains its separation from a society he regards under the condition of late modernity to be false. Through truthful forms of aesthetic appearance, art destabilizes society's deceptive appearances. Adorno uses philosophical critique to expose the dialectical relation between aesthetic and social appearance. Danto prefers to pit art less against society or social appearance than against philosophy, given philosophy's positivist need specifically to stabilize its concepts with definitions. Adorno does this too, but sees in this positivist philosophical need a corresponding (and regressive) social need. Danto isolates this philosophical need to explain how it long dominated the practice of art, only ceasing when, in the moment of the '60s, art went as far as it could in making the question, what is art? explicit to the philosophical critic. Overall, Adorno makes the social theory embedded in his view explicit in a way Danto has generally been far less tempted to do.

Danto

Danto is a philosopher and critic of the '60s. He places the starting point of his philosophical work in Manhattan at a moment when he almost accidentally witnessed the production of art and music by artists such as Warhol, Rauschenberg, and Cage. In that moment, artists challenged the "Artworld" to explain the difference between works of art and their perceptually indiscernible counterparts. By attempting (intentionally or not) to erase the essential difference, the artists made transparent to the artworld and to its philosophical critic what it is. Danto went on to describe the difference in terms of what he calls the "is of interpretation"—as opposed to the "is of identity"—according to which it's possible to attribute to an artwork all sorts of world-constructing (expressive, symbolic, and metaphorical) properties and all sorts of art-historical (expressionistic or representational) properties that are denied to the indiscernible counterpart, especially when, as with everyday Brillo boxes, the observer is more interested in cleaning than in beautifying the world. The interpretative context of the

artworld, with its history of styles, is what allows an object or image regarded as ordinary in the supermarket to be "transfigured" into an extraordinary work of art, where the transfiguration marks less the act of making
one thing into another thing (as in "found art") and more the acknowledg-
ment that how we encounter and interpret a work of art is categorically
different from how we treat an (albeit perceptually identical) ordinary
counterpart. Danto's use of the term "transfiguration," with its sacred history, plays perfectly into his modernist version of what was earlier called in
Germany (following Hegel) *Kunstreligion*. By the 1960s, one might say, the
religion of art was secularized once and for all—or desublimated to mark
the loss, as Danto puts it, of "the sublime"—by a theory about the artworld
that turns on just that moment when artists challenged that world to accept into the domain of art an object that looks no different from a supermarket commodity. What, in Danto's account, marked this deep gesture of
secularization on the part of contemporary art marked, in Adorno's account, also the calamitous triumph of commodification.

In 1964, in his "Artworld" article, Danto was most concerned to argue
for an ontological victory won by modern artists (beginning with Fauvists
and Impressionists) when deception became no longer an issue for those
artists in the production of their art. And yet, precisely when deception
was no longer the issue, something new became possible in art, namely,
that an artist could now produce something that not only looked like the
real thing but was just the real thing itself. To sleep in this bed or not to
sleep in this bed became first the correct question and then the incorrect
question for anyone looking at Rauschenberg's overlooking Platonic bed.

In other words, critical to Danto's argument was that the attempt to
erase the gap between artworks and ordinary objects only succeeds insofar
as it made transparent to the philosopher (as spectator) what the correct
philosophical task regarding art now is, namely, to explain to what the *gap
or difference* amounts. The argument turned out at this moment to be thoroughly dialectical. For the philosopher to explain the difference to counter
an identity being asserted is not to render art philosophical but, instead, to
grant art its liberation from philosophy. In the attempt to effect what Danto
calls a "logical symbiosis" between art and the ordinary, art is brought to
some sort of end, though not to the end of its production. It is rather only
released from a progressivist master narrative dominated by its need to
live up to philosophy's demand for art's self-definition.

Burdened by this need, art was long disenfranchised from itself. This
ended when art entered its posthistorical stage, when, apparently under
much more democratic (American) conditions, it was no longer burdened

by a developmental (European) history of styles or materials. At this moment art was allowed truly or for the first time to be *for its own sake,* which is to say, paradoxically, 150 years after philosophy first declared art's freedom in these terms—a historical turn that only suggests that philosophy's declaration in 1800 suited philosophy far more than it did art. Whatever the story in 1800, for Danto it was only in the 1960s (in America) that art was liberated from its history of productively repetitive art historical attempts to say what art is, and could now fly free as a bird claiming its independence— at least from philosophy. Here, not incidentally, is a little piece of social theory present but rarely made explicit in Danto's theoretical account.

No problem it seems now for art: art is liberated. But why not then speak less of art's end and more of its new and continued life in freedom? And why not speak rather of philosophy's end, or at least of the end of its domination of art? Is it not the real consequence of Danto's view that in liberating art from its philosophical burden, a dominating philosophy of art is brought to an end, because, by so interpreting art's liberation, philosophy can finally ask and answer its own essential ontological question: what is art? After it has asked and answered the question, what is there left for the old dominating philosophy to do?

Danto recognizes the possibility that philosophy might have become gray, grown old, or left itself (impotent) with no more of a task than that of passive understanding. In freeing art from its dominion, philosophy plausibly loses not only its perpetual antagonist (they have always been at war) but therewith its own developmental form of ongoing thought. In a comparable gesture of release from the very idea of historical development, Philip Glass once declared of music that it is best "experienced as one event, without start or end."[21] Without beginnings and endings, music just happens. His idea was for the spectators to lose their sense of time and to release themselves from the burden of historical time perhaps most of all. For Danto, such a release marks the moment of the happening of the posthistorical Happenings. But is this now how one ought also to understand philosophy, as having become the kind of activity that "just happens"?

In some sense, yes. In attempting to overcome its age, metaphysical philosophy, in its posthistorical condition, does allow art to happen as it wants, but it also gives itself over to a most productive form of criticism. Danto argues that the philosophical answer to the question, what is art? is that a work of art embodies and is about its (artistic) meaning. Criticism amounts to showing how works *embody* and are *about* their meaning. The criticism must be rich enough to compensate for the age or even impotence that the traditional metaphysical philosopher now feels, yet it must not assume a developmental direction or internal logic of its own. It must embrace what Danto describes as art's new pluralism, the fact that art is no longer constrained by having to move in a certain way or to be of a certain style. Thus, art production and criticism now do the work of the artworld, freed of the obligation to be historically developmental. And the traditional philosopher must sit back and accept the change without irony or cynicism.

Of course, for Danto, philosophy does not give way to criticism *überhaupt*. To the extent that it continues, it does so under the nondominating guise of what he calls "analytical philosophy," which assumes no historicist course and makes no historicist assumption. Danto explicitly links the liberation of art to that felt or asserted by the so-called common-sense philosophers or logical positivists earlier in the twentieth century, when, in celebrating their access to the ordinary world through either common sense or logic, they severed their theories from the highfalutin' metaphysics of German historicism and idealism. These philosophers claimed, as the artists later claimed, that access to the world, even if not immediate, was far less muddy than the (German) idealist metaphysicians had led us to believe. For the positivists, the birds flew forward in the pure flight of scientific progress unobstructed, so they believed, by any historical gaze. Many have said in either celebration or despair that this move too marked another sort of end of philosophy. To be sure, Danto has not always been entirely convinced by the positivist flight himself but, with this doubt, he has not then been led back to the disenfranchising historicism of idealist metaphysics. He seeks rather a place somewhere and more modestly in between.

In a recent book, *The Abuse of Beauty* (though he's used the example many times before), Danto employs for an epigraph a saying from an imagined character aptly named Testadura, the hardheaded one: "Art is for aesthetics what the birds are for ornithology."[22] In 1967 Barnett Newman reversed the saying to turn it into a deep criticism of aesthetic theory: "Aesthetics is for art what ornithology is for the birds." Apparently, Newman had the philosopher (of music) Susanne Langer in mind when he said this. If Pinkerton falsely promises Butterfly he'll return with the red robin, so aesthetics, Newman is telling Langer, is "for the birds": worthless, useless, "impotent," and thus even "sharpless." The phrase "for the birds" found its common currency during World War II, when enlisted men in the U.S. Army had to do menial tasks regarded as no better than picking up the shit of the officers, an idea that itself picked up on the original meaning whereby birds eat the droppings of horses and cattle. Recall, Cage used the phrase for a book title but didn't do much with it; Danto does, and asks accordingly whether aesthetic theory can tell us what it's like for art to be art, if ornithology can't tell us what it's like for a bird to be a bird. His nicely paradoxical answer is, as we already know, that as soon as aesthetic theory can tell us what art is, it sets the bird that is art free from its cage.

The phrase "for the birds" has a longer association with the shittier side of life than perhaps Danto knows. If Butterfly once suffered from the false promise of Pinkerton and then the false pity of Sharpless, so the nightingale once suffered equally from the words of a Viennese music critic, who attempted already in 1854 (and then later influenced Langer) to fix the terms for a philosophically respectable aesthetics of music. His name was Eduard Hanslick, and he was ridiculed as the pedant Beckmesser in large part for attempting this very task. Hanslick denied exactly what Cage claimed. Humanity, Hanslick argued, doesn't learn from nature how to make music. "Nature does not give us the artistic materials for a finished, pre- or ready-made tone-system only the raw stuff which we then make serviceable for the music." So far so good, but then his derision of nature came in the next remark. It is not, he wrote, the "voices of animals" but only their "entrails" that are important to us in our music, for with the latter we make the strings for our instruments. The promise of the nightingale's song, he was telling us, as Kant was before him, is best left for the birds, or even better for "the sheep," that the violin, in other words, is better played by humanity with guts.[23]

In the 1950s Danto attended the lessons on Buddhism by Dr. Suzuki at Columbia University. So did John Cage. To record his experience and his memories of Cage, Danto recently wrote an essay surely ironically called "Upper West Side Buddhism," given Cage's so-called "downtown" musical aesthetic. "It is widely known," he writes,

> that [Cage's] 4'33" was inspired by Robert Rauschenberg's white paintings, done when he was at Black Mountain College in 1951. Cage said that he saw them as "airports for shadows and dust"—or as "mirrors for air." The deep point was that they were no more empty than his own 1952 composition was silent. The panels themselves collaborated, one might say, with the environment, so that the ambient lights and shadows became part of the art, instead of being aesthetically erased in order to allow a response to the pure, unsullied blank. If a wayward pigeon dropped shat on the white, that would be part of the work, at least in Cage's view. (Rauschenberg, on the other hand, stipulated that the panels be repainted, to keep them fresh.)

Those who took Cage's course in experimental composition at the New School in the 1950s enlisted the surrounding world to create compositions. A case in point was Dick Higgins's 1959 *Winter Carol*. The carolers decide on the length of time within which they go out to listen to the sound of falling snow. Snow, of course, is naturally poetic, because of the hushed beauty it creates when it falls. But when Cage talked about the environment becoming art, he was not thinking about an agenda of beautification. It was, one might say, like applying phenomenology's "brackets" to experience, letting things be, just as they are, without imposing any interpretations.[24]

In focusing on how a natural environment "becomes" art, Danto highlights a crucial aspect of Cage's composition, namely, that naturalness resides less in the material per se than in the emergent experience of the work, the process or performance. Cage's works are not static or fixed objects but "open works," processes of becoming that show the natural world in its dynamic state. For Cage, performance art, which music can be as soon as it gives up its attempt to be an object art, stresses more the *becoming* of nature than it does any static notion of *Being*. Music is the paradigm (perhaps alongside dance) of the would-be objectless art. "You say: the real, the world as it is," Cage writes. "But it is not, it becomes! It moves, it changes! . . . You are getting closer to this reality when you say as it 'presents itself'; that means that it is not there, existing as an object."[25] Cage calls for "an art which imitates nature in its manner of operation,"[26] where it is the manner of operation, not the demand for copying, that governs the thought. This conclusion is profound: the point is not after all that musical sound should sound identical to natural sound, but that art should reproduce the world by actualizing what is already going on in the world.

By stressing the manner of operation and not the copying, Cage claims to close the gap between art and world (or nature) by returning us to a world from which our human experience has long been severed. The purpose of Cage's argument is to expand the concept of experience and thereby to make a transition in philosophical understanding possible. It looks as if his view approaches one of Danto's most central points, that what the eye sees had become by the '60s entirely insufficient to tell one whether what is seen is art. We used (wrongly) to think the eye was sufficient and art production sustained the belief, but now, given the new production, we know that it never really was. More is involved in one's experience than "merely" looking and listening if one wants to know what something is.

Whereas, however, for Cage, the expansion of experience involves moving *outside* the traditional or historical parameters of the music world, for Danto, the expansion of experience involves the interpreter's becoming conscious of how much knowledge provided by the artworld sustains the interpretative act of the mind's eye. And yet, these contrary moves, outside and inside the worlds of music and art, are both introduced to promote a similar philosophical conclusion whereby one comes to *know the concept* either of music or of art.

Danto acknowledges the impact of musical innovation on the postwar avant-garde movements when he writes that "overcoming the gap between art and life became a kind of mantra for the avant-garde artists of the early sixties. It was certainly a point of principle with Fluxus artists, so many of whom came to art through music as conceived of by Cage. Yoko Ono trained as a musician, had studied Zen before joining Fluxus." But still, and correctly, Danto sees many of the significant steps to have already been taken by Duchamp, in the permission he gave to "make art out of anything," from which Danto concludes that "the combined force of Cage, Duchamp, and Zen constituted an artistic revolution of an unprecedented kind."[27]

Closing the gap was certainly part of Cage's own self-conceived project. However, as we've already seen, this project was tempered by his belief that in closing the gap one does not thereby identify a fixed object called a work with any static object from nature or the commonplace world. Instead, the idea was to show through musical performance the emergent quality of the natural world around us. I would like to call this view "emergent naturalism." Its fundamental question demands reformulation. The question no longer asks (in an ontological vein) what makes musical and natural sound different or the same; instead it asks how one comes to experience the natural world through music in the right "naturalistic" way. To this question Cage offers his most famous answer: one comes to experience both nature and music aright if one opens one's ears—to another sort of thinking and listening—by putting one's Western institutional mind to rest. Sound, like experience, must be freed from "all psychic intentionality." It must "be itself" and not be used merely as a vehicle of (Western) human theory and feeling. We are "part of nature" and "must learn to exist like nature, simply existing without purpose."[28] As is well known, Cage was inspired by Eastern religious doctrines of chance and indeterminacy.

Although Danto has always been firmly committed to the internal claims and history of the Western artworld, he still says that he has found something inspiring in Cage's claimed relinquishing of intentionality, in how

Cage "represented the world" without either "mind or hand." I think "represented" is no longer the right word; one would do better now to speak of how the artists allowed the world nonintentionally to *emerge* in their art. Regardless, Danto writes of how the artists that came out of the Suzuki class committed themselves to producing art without effort, intention, or design, and in this commitment found the "secret promise of politics, of art, of writing—a knowing effortlessness in which the object and the agent collaborate to achieve a mutual fulfillment."[29] I'd like to believe that Danto less concurs with the view than finds in it that unprecedented revolutionary moment from which he draws his conclusion about the end of art. Were Danto fully to concur, he'd have to separate himself more radically from the Kantian–Hegelian legacy regarding art's relation to nature than I believe he really would want to do. For, in this legacy, it was never the aim to deny to the artist or to the aesthetic contemplator of the arts the effort of human labor, discipline, and knowledge. On the contrary: the appearance of effortlessness in a work of art was always considered a hallmark of genius. That no effort is made or demanded at all, well, that's quite another thing and probably better left (more appropriately) to the birds.

Another way to show the potential contradiction here is to refer to Cage's book *For the Birds*, and to suggest that it is best read as dedicated to the birds, but thereby also to humans to listen as birds listen, which is to say, to listen not *to* but nonpurposively *from*, as if one were already within nature. And yet to state the very fact that birds listen to sounds as music is to attribute to them the character of being human or the ability to listen with a thoroughly naturalized or idealized intention. From which the question arises whether the intentionality of our listening is ever really relinquished or, rather and more plausibly, Cage is asking only that a certain Western conception of intentionality or purposiveness be put aside.

For Danto, the continuation of art making as effort and labor doesn't have to imply art's continued allegiance to a dominating philosophy. All he needs to say is that what sustained the paradigm change in the '60s, or what artists historically had to claim and to do in order for him as philosophical critic to do what he had to do, was quite different from what art *is* and what it continued to do after the philosophical claim had been made. Indeed, Danto speaks of how the Warhol *gesture* with the Brillo box installation was meaningful only so long as it was not yet understood; when it was understood, it was no longer necessary. In other terms, it is the contradiction between what was said or gestured and what happened thereafter that allowed art to assume a new form, more conscious of itself, yet paradoxically freed from the philosophical demand for self-consciousness that formerly so burdened it.

Equally for Cage, a relinquishing of Western intentionality, or a freeing of music from the burden of the (Western or European) museum aesthetic, does not have to mean that artists give up on discipline altogether. It just has to mean that the discipline of a Zen master suggests something entirely different and far less alienating for how art relates to nature than the idea of discipline encouraged by the restrictive conditions of Western labor. For only the latter has sustained the purportedly deadening routine (if one sees it as such) of the concert hall.

And yet, I think that an important difference has also emerged here regarding Cage and Danto's respective attitudes toward discipline. Most of what seems to count for Danto when he fills out his "is" of interpretation is what artists and critics have mastered by way of artistic theory and the history, as he put it in 1964, of the last fifty years of New York painting. For Cage, however, what counts is also the history of craft or of what has been done by way of technique in the actual making of art. Danto argues in the case of Warhol, for example, that an artwork's being made "entirely . . . by hand" seems to fall out of the vocabulary in an artworld devoted to producing copies that are also not copies as the objects of art. But, for Cage, the element of making is retained even if he willingly hands over much of the compositional activity to the increasingly less intentional performers, computers, and birds. Whereas Danto focuses on the move toward "ideas" or "theories" of art, concluding, thereby, that nothing would be an artwork "without the theories and histories of the Artworld," Cage focuses more on an alternative, naturalized, or Eastern view of discipline. The difference here might ultimately be one of emphasis, emanating from the different foci of critics and producers, but it does potentially reveal a profound difference of attitude regarding what matters for each in the production of art.

What more is at stake in confusing the two claims, that relinquishing intentionality is the same as relinquishing discipline? The answer takes us now to Adorno's view and to the question again of the conditions of continuation for both philosophy and art given the thesis that an end has been reached. Not always fair to Cage, Adorno reads his claims deliberately at the extreme, intent to expose in them the larger potential for deception, or music's place in the broader dialectic of enlightenment. Thus when, for example, Cage insists that one put one's Western mind to rest in the production of art, Adorno reads the claim as if Cage is thereby advocating a future governed by a mindless philosophy—and this Adorno fears perhaps more than anything else.

Adorno

Adorno argues in a most Kantian vein that to relinquish control or to deny labor is to give up too easily the tension that for so long has governed the relation between art and nature. Having been made into stark opposites more or less around 1800, art and nature began to call upon each other (electing their affinities) without, however, trying to become each other. Nature called upon art for its construction and form as art called upon nature for its spontaneity and immediacy. With this argument, Adorno wants to refuse an identity between art and nature precisely to preserve a dynamic difference between them, for only in the yearning to have what the other has does each side continue to gain something thereby. To assert an identity between art and nature or art and life, or even to maintain that one has finally been achieved as a matter of historical progress, is to break from an aesthetic past that was formerly sustained on the basis of a dialectical interaction of differences. To so assert the identity has, for Adorno, profound consequences for art and society.[30]

One argument he offers against a false naturalizing aesthetic is given in Freudian terms. It shows how, in the '60s, artists, like individuals, came to feel socially emasculated (as a Freudian extension of alienation). To compensate, they felt compelled to produce the sort of art that was formerly produced in the heroic or revolutionary age. And yet they could not actually produce heroic art. So, to compensate again, they declared their desire to renounce control of their art as if they were also renouncing control of their weakened egos. Recognizing their impotence, they preferred "to drift and to refrain from intervening, in the hope that, as in Cage's *bon mot*, it [would] not be [the composer] speaking, but the music itself"[31]—as in fact music spoke for itself as an humanist ideal in 1800. But rather than producing a heroic art for humanity, they apparently now sought to produce an art for the birds, as if giving up on humanity altogether. How, Adorno asked rhetorically, could an intentionless art contribute to transforming the weakness of the contemporary ego into what they still seemed to desire, namely, an aesthetic or heroic strength? Finding no convincing answer, he proclaimed their products as impotent or paradoxical as their aim. One may at least ask whether this argument does not similarly suit the pop artists of the '60s, who intrigued Danto and who so willingly relinquished beauty in favor of the sort of graphic excitement that always secured sale of the image. But one may also ask whether in fact such artists were, as Adorno says, either really feeling so emasculated or feeling compelled to seek some sort of compensatory aesthetic or heroic strength in the first place.

To liberate art from intention is to liberate art from effort, from thought, from philosophy, from humanity's development. Adorno thus describes the relinquishment of "development" in terms of art's having fallen into a stasis or into a social or positivistic congealment. Art might now "just happen," but it has nowhere to go, and if it does try to go somewhere, it tends not to go where we want it to, and where it thinks it is going is often precisely where it doesn't and can't go—namely, back to nature. Adorno doesn't want philosophy to go the way of art: philosophy should not end even or especially when it deceives itself into thinking self-reflectively that it has come to some sort of self-understanding (pace Hegel) either of itself or of art.

Adorno argues that claims of immediacy end up at the same dangerous extreme as claims of total control, whether it masters the work of art or the society within which the work is produced. He writes repeatedly of how concepts and categories become naturalized, self-evident, or commonplace so that their historicity or social meaning and construction is sublimated in the name of being, product, or essence. Here Adorno meets Danto with their mutual argument against the worst trajectory of German historicism. Adorno's *Aesthetic Theory* distinctively begins with a strike against everything in art, but also in modernity more generally, that has come to assume the appearance of self-evidence, only to ask whether art (and everything else) has not thereby come to an end. To assume a naturalized appearance is tantamount to following enlightenment's drive into unfreedom. The naturalism is false insofar as it conceals the total control of labor and construction that is actually required for the naturalized appearance to sustain itself as such.

Adorno compares this sort of false naturalism with the necessity or naturalness that attends a beautifully constructed work of art, when it strikes a viewer as if it could not have been created otherwise. An artwork from the moment of its creation has "elements that appear natural and self-evident." However, these moments are natural only as "second nature,"[32] and second nature, being the product of art, is quite different from a first nature that's claimed to be work's model, matter, or inspiration. Only as second nature is an artwork recognized to have its basis or mediation in human labor and effort. Only as such is the artwork recognized to be both beautiful appearance and ordered construction. In this argument, Adorno moves between two meanings of "nature," between a work of art's appearing natural, as if spontaneous, and its being naturalized through the imposition of order. To confuse second with first nature, order with spontaneity, is to establish an identity or a reduction (what he otherwise calls a "phantasmagoria") where the dialectical tension ought rather to be maintained. Adorno notes that Kant recognized the crucial difference when he described the work of art as a product of genius, *as if* no labor is involved in the production—the purposiveness without explicit purpose. But Kant then forgot his own insight when he reduced his judgment of the birdsong to a concern only with the little creature that produces it.[33]

Another way to make this point is to note Adorno's double use of the idea of second nature. On the one hand, one may acknowledge the labor that goes into making the artwork even as it appears "natural" (this idea invokes Kant's "as if"); on the other hand, something appears as second nature when its labor is concealed in such a way that we proclaim the artwork produced "naturally" or without "force," as when we declare that some activity "has become second nature" to us or that we "did it without thinking." When Adorno comments on Kant's failure to distinguish the song of the bird from the little creature that produces it, he shows how easy it is for the first idea of second nature to be confused with the second. For what birds do, they do without thinking at all, whereas what geniuses do, they do by transcending the enormous body of thinking and know-how that contributes to making them the artists they are.

Adorno reads much of the proclaimed radicalism of the postwar artists as regressive, as taking a further step toward social conformity. In the threatened collapse of the gap between art and nature, he sees a fall into a totalitarian pattern of identity thinking. Instead of maintaining their difference from nature, artworks now assert an identity, because nature is now thought to stand for everything society is not. Artworks would rather be like nature than like social products, but the nature with which art now seeks its identity has been destroyed, as much as art has been destroyed, by society, which means that nature is no longer alive nor anything like that which artists are now constructing in their imagination.

In a world given over to the praise of commodity, Adorno argues, natural beauty has been "transformed into a caricature of itself," and cannot therefore be the nature that is claimed to reveal itself to the new artists in its immediacy. To try then to appeal to an immediate nature to differentiate one's new art (as Cage does) from the world of artificial products is perversely to accept the social alienation one is trying to overcome when trying to restore nature or naturalness to the world. In other terms, Adorno argues that given the total expansion of the exchange principle, nature is increasingly being invoked to fulfill "a contrasting function," to mark the difference from that from which people want to distance themselves. However, by being so utilized, the idea of nature is thereby integrated back into the reified world to serve what the social world wants of it. This is a typical argument in Adorno's philosophy (as also in Nietzsche's), that certain kinds of appeals, say, to nature, beauty, freedom, individuality, and truth, are used to oppose the existing social order, but are actually reabsorbed by this use back into the order, thereby keeping it in place and rendering the appeal to "something different" futile.[34]

Adorno sees little difference in his critique—in music, philosophy, or society—between a mystical union with "immediate nature" or, at the other end of the spectrum, the pedantic following of rigid rules. He regards both as symptomatic of totalitarian thinking, of the sort of positivistic thinking that demands certainty to overcome ambiguity, immediacy to overcome mediation, directness indirection, sameness difference, and order chaos. With Cage in mind, he thus describes the cruelty with which contemporary composers throw culture "into people's faces," even if this is a fate both culture and people deserve. That it is deserved means that when composers act this way they do so less to be barbaric than to show what people have done to culture and culture to people. The cruelty of the composers' acts only backfires, however, when, by appealing to an "exotic, arty-crafty metaphysics" (*exotisch-kunstgewerbliche Metaphysik*) they find themselves back in the exact same place from which they are trying to escape. Adorno sometimes remarks that what he most admires in Cage is his protest against "the dogmatic complicity of music with the domination of nature," as well as his refusal to yield to the terror of the technological age. However, what he cannot accept is Cage's rationalizing tendency to retreat into claims of (phenomenological) immediacy, which, linked to the "enclaves of sensitive souls," remind Adorno of Rudolph Steiner's eurhythmics and healthy-living sects.[35]

A different way for us to think about the dialectical interaction between art and nature is to recall the pioneering work of Pierre Schaeffer and his *musique concrète*, out of which a principle emerges for contemporary music, that music should be heard, as one hears it in urban and natural space, without attention paid to its mechanical source. Still, I want to stress, it's not so easy to distinguish the purported radical nature of this claim from Wagner's own rationale for concealing the orchestra at Bayreuth in the name of creating a pure space of sound, a pure aesthetic illusion. By contrast, in David Tudor's *Rain Forest*, the principle seems to reverse itself insofar as all one sees in this work are the instruments of sound production, even if what one hears is something approximating a rain forest. The point of this work, as I understand it, is that you have to be there to understand it; it is *not* a work made for recording, even if, on some level, it is all about the technology of sound production. The listener has to see the mechanical sources and participate actively with the mechanical means while yet experiencing something that tells about the audible world of natural or everyday sounds. The issue, again, is whether a work that wears its artifice on its sleeve tells us more about the workings of nature than a work that hides behind the veil of immediacy or naturalness.

Adorno is always seeking a dynamic place between extremes, between, say, pure chance and total control, or, in the case of Cage, between his works of "chance" and those of total "preparation." In so doing, he increasingly distinguishes the concept of art from that of a work of art, to show how the former moves toward its demise the more it gives itself over to what the concept of a work wants most, namely to preserve as *fixed* the labor, preparation, and articulation that individuates it. The more fixed or articulated the work, the more art loses what it wants to preserve, namely, the resistant aesthetic dimension of what is not prepared or articulated, or what Adorno describes variously also as its "mimetic," "spontaneous," "silent," or "speechless" comportment or expression. Recall that Danto reads the challenge of the supermarket commodity as helping to bring the concept of art to its self-knowing (via philosophical interpretation); he vicariously celebrates the Warholian excitement about the commodity for the philosophical knowledge it makes possible. Adorno contrarily emphasizes the pyrrhic victory of an art that concedes entirely to its commodification, to being a work or product of art. For to reach the extreme of work- or objecthood is to concede what the culture industry has come to demand of it, that it *look* and then *be* no different from any other product of exchange.

And yet, at the other extreme, if, as Adorno reads Cage as sometimes doing, the work retreats into pure art or music, into a condition of total speechlessness or nonintentional immediacy, and thereby denies its status as a work, then, with its claimed isolation from the social (Western) production of art, it renders itself utterly impotent to do what it wants to do, namely, to show the possibility that the Western world that has lost its music might still be different from how it presently is. In this argument, total isolation or retreat has the same ideological character as total compliance. In all these arguments Adorno assumes that an artwork is true to itself when it maintains the tension between its inherent but contradictory impulses, to appear as both made and unmade, fixed and spontaneous, product and process. After that, the matter is to decide whether and when contemporary society admits such works to exist and upon what terms.

For Adorno, what survives at this moment of transition or triumphant commodification are works that in a deep sense have betrayed the aesthetic concept of art. However, that they have betrayed this concept doesn't mean that they have also betrayed history; on the contrary, history, as society, demands what art has become in the form of its works and deserves what it itself has brought about (though, having said this, Adorno often remarks on the banality of the thought that allows one to rest too comfortably with the belief that because the world is now ugly, art should be ugly too). Given the tension between history and the aesthetic, the philosopher's critical task is then to distinguish between contemporary works that now too happily comply with the times and those that still somehow refuse to do so.

To comply with the times is, for Adorno, to comply with the horror of the times but in denial of the horror (as he sees the situation after World War II). Thus he expresses utter skepticism toward the sorts of claim he hears Cage making about his music when, for example, Cage writes that it does not "attempt to bring order out of chaos nor to suggest improvements in creation" but serves "simply" to wake us up "to the very life we're living, which is so excellent once one gets one's mind and one's desire out of the way and lets [the music] act of its own accord."[36] An excellent world? Maybe, though perhaps not so excellent a youth. Apparently Cage's emergent naturalism was motivated partly by the insult he felt in younger days when one of his works, *The Perilous Night* (1943–44), was dismissed for sounding like "a woodpecker in a church belfry." Erik Satie, who much inspired Cage, once specified that one of his own works (humorously, his *Sonatine bureaucratique*) should be played "like a nightingale with a toothache."[37] Cage worried at this time that his work, like Satie's, would not be taken seriously; for Satie, at least, this was the point. But Cage, so it is said, could not forget the moments when his mother told him that his music was "for the birds"![38] Recall now Danto's remark that Cage is not "thinking about an agenda of beautification." Perhaps this is right, but certainly Cage isn't seeking his naturalism in a world of horrid sounds. Adorno is also looking for beauty, though, like for Cage, this has nothing to do with "an agenda" as such "of beautification." However, unlike Cage, Adorno finds he just can't put his (Western) mind to rest enough no longer to see the horrid world around him: horrid sounds and horrid acts. For Adorno, there is something deeply false in even trying.

"Excellence" is a term often used in reference to human labor. Cage rather speaks of the excellence of the world around him. Adorno argues against the latter way of speaking, not the former. But if excellence in human labor is still sought, he argues, it should be sought in the shadows and ruins of human labor, that is, in what the world, in its arrogance and overconfidence, has discarded through other, much worse and destructive acts of labor. "Consciousness," he writes, "does justice to the experience of nature only when, like impressionist art, it incorporates nature's wounds."[39] If nature is wounded, this is because of what humanity had done both to nature and to itself. The composer Terry Riley once wrote that "the music has to be the expression of spiritual categories like philosophy, knowledge and truth, the highest human qualities. To realize this, my music necessarily radiates balance and rest."[40] Why "balance and rest," Adorno asks again of his contemporaries, in a world that no longer admits of either in truthful form? If art is to mirror life, why think of the life that exists or appears under the spell of society's untruth? Why not focus rather on concealed life, on the life that has been lost or historically brought to death? If beauty or truth is still to be found, why not look in the places veiled from what appears now as horror to the eye?

An interesting difference has emerged. Whereas Danto is brought to distrust what appears to the eye for the perceptual illusion it might promote of a false identity between an artwork and an ordinary object (by those who cannot "see" the difference), Adorno is brought to distrust the eye as an extension of a greater distrust of the illusions that modern society promotes in the name of the true, the good, and the beautiful—the forerunners of the more contemporary term "excellence."

With Cage, Adorno argues against a static relation of art and nature in favor of a dynamic one. Yet he vehemently rejects the idea that nature shows its beauty (now) directly. "Natural beauty is the trace of the nonidentical in things under the spell of universal identity. As long as this spell prevails, the nonidentical has no positive existence."[41] However (and here is the final dialectical turn), even in administered society, there remains the possibility of beauty in both art and nature only so long as it is acknowledged that the beauty shows itself indirectly in intimations or splintered glances. Why this extreme "negative capability," to quote Keats, the originator of the thought? Because at the same time that beauty is seen momentarily in intimations of art, those intimations will most likely arise in *works* of dead or liquidated form, works, that is, that truthfully show art and nature in their contemporary degraded condition. Thus, in these works, if something beautiful appears, it does so only as a remainder or reminder of what was once possible in art and of what nature once stood for. Adorno is always asking how artworks that point to something lost or dead can point also to something still hopeful, and how they can do this without regressing into empty forms of conformity.

"The song of birds," Adorno wrote at the end of his life, "is found beautiful by everyone; no feeling person in whom something of the European tradition survives fails to be moved by the sound of a robin after a rain shower." However, "something frightening lurks in the song," though not so much in the song itself, but in the spell within which the song has historically become "enmeshed."[42] With this remark Adorno points to one outcome of the passage of enlightenment, namely, how nature fell into myth when it was subjected to the demands of fate or when the song of the bird assumed a false mythical status in an artificial world that forbad exactly the expression of that song. During the Enlightenment, natural beauty was increasingly repressed, transfigured into a idea solely for art or a myth for contemporary (in)humanity.

On this basis of this argument Adorno draws a most important conclusion, that only an artwork that frees itself from the myth of nature has any chance of helping nature or natural beauty to recover. Such a work will be autonomous or true to itself—an artwork that seeks its justification precisely *not in nature but in art*. This is the "determinate negation" of art under the modern condition of autonomy, i.e., the idea that art will not give itself up to a false (heteronomous or unfree) claim of naturalism. An artwork committed to art, responding to art's own or internal material needs or developmental logic (the latter, at least, to which, Danto says, art needs no longer to respond), has the potential to release or rescue both nature and art from their mutual spells of mastery of each other, and thereby to show between them the continuing possibility of a fragile dialectical interaction. This will be an artwork that has not complied with the times and has taken the side of destroyed nature. The idea, here, that one shouldn't give up on art forms part of Adorno's argument for preserving in the artworld a resistant stand against a society that has (almost entirely) submitted to an "anything goes principle," which, for some Europeans apparently more than for some Americans, connoted an unbridled power and optimism associated with a totalitarian society in which the leaders did "anything" as an everyday, "banal" commonplace, even the most extremely evil things, just because "everything" was "now possible."[43]

Adorno once concluded a critique of Darmstadt with a negative utopian gesture that he took from Kant's promise of "perpetual peace" (*ewige Frieden*). Whereas Kant apparently saw in that promise a concrete possibility, Adorno rather sees a negative expression more appropriate, he believed, for modern times. Thus, his last line asserts, "The form of every artistic utopia today is: to make things of which we do not know what they are."[44] However, by "not knowing," Adorno was not advocating a mindless philosophy or art. Instead he was asking us to give up our trust in social domination (a trust he said we have actually come to desire) in order to open up a space for good or geniune art to be produced. In other words, he was arguing vehemently for the continuation of (unforced) social labor and individual thought: art and philosophy in dialectical tension. In large part, he argued this way to avoid the suggestion that to him alone the bird now sings, since he desired to be no Siegfried. But then he reminded us: the bird does not directly sing to anyone else either. Nor are there any metaphysical bird catchers left in town, so that even when a song is heard, we won't know whether it is truthful. One can no more blindly trust claims of truthfulness than claims of naturalness, even if it does seem to be a little bird that sings in the tree.

The Song of the Pipes

Danto sees in "the end of art," in that moment of the '60s, a positive moment of liberation, when art was released from the philosophical burden to come to know itself, even if as it did so, philosophy came to know art. Art production didn't cease, but the philosophy of art came to know and answer its essential question. Dialectically, I suggested, this was far less art's end than the end of a dominating philosophy of art. Danto's posthistoricist pluralism for art presents a strong challenge to what, in Adorno's work, is a continuation of a master narrative, albeit now premised entirely on the tension of a continuing dialectic. Another essay on this theme would focus its attention here, and rightly so, on the pluralist versus the monological implications of the thesis of the end of art.

On Adorno's part, he sees an end of art when art's production compromises itself to identity thinking. He understands this end to have come to dominate both philosophy and society. He rejects the terms of any absolute or positive ending of a Hegelian-styled dialectic that precludes the possibility of continuation, for to so announce such an end is tantamount to agreeing to its terms. Unlike Danto, he does not stress the severing or liberation of art from philosophy, but seeks only to distinguish autonomous from compromised art, and then autonomous from compliant philosophy. Not only does he stress the continuation of art and philosophy in their fragile and necessarily antagonistic relationship to each other; he also describes that continuation in terms of the specific challenge it potentially presents to an administered society under the extreme condition of modernity. Whereas Danto more or less celebrates the advent of *pluralism* for a philosophically liberated art, Adorno focuses on an art and nature wounded by society's extreme *polarization*. If this essay were to be written yet differently again, it would be written in terms of the challenge Adorno poses this time to Danto to tie the end-of-art thesis to something more explicitly social and political.

And yet, each somehow challenges the other regarding their optimism and pessimism, their hope and their resignation. I put this point in this distanced way, however, to leave it open as to which theorist represents one side or the other. As both Danto and Adorno have shown us, appearances, in art or in philosophical theory, can deceive.

Most of all, it has been my point to show how well Adorno and Danto are read as having offered, for art and philosophy, the terms for their continuations over and above their endings, and, between art and nature, the differences over and above the identity. Endings and identities are points reached on the way. They might be devastating or catastrophic, but they are not thereby the last points in the discourse of either philosophy or art. The continuation of art, whether it reflects a positive conception of liberation for Danto or a negative conception of autonomy for Adorno, follows from specific acts of criticism performed in the shadow of philosophical critique. For the birds/against the birds—this is a false choice if, as I have argued, in assuming a critical position in relation to the song of the birds, Adorno and Danto seek not messages but, instead, a philosophical (and social) significance. A critical part of this significance consists for both in a continued search for beauty and, attendant upon this, for a truthful release from the deceptions of eye, ear, and mind.

Thus, I return to my beginning, to Keats to join his song of the nightingale finally to his human song of the pipes. For, if the argument has gone through, it is only when the two songs are brought dialectically together (as they were composed the same year) that beauty remains connected to truth, as truth to beauty, where in the end, so the song says, this "is all ye know on earth, and all ye need to know."[45]

〽 〽 〽 〽 〽

Response

Lydia Goehr's paper is a tour de force. If her account of Adorno's philosophy of art is as faithful as her account of mine, then the paper is authoritative on three counts: on the two philosophies of art and then on their comparative analysis. That she has been able to interweave all this with her own historical account of the theme of birdsong in opera is a miracle of ingenuity. Birds, to be sure, figure in my philosophical mises-en-scène mainly as dupes via the often-quoted anecdotes in Pliny, and obliquely in the legendary putdown of aesthetics by Barnett Newman as "for the birds." I think Cage is wrong in saying that birdsong already is music, when what he ought to have said that it can be, and that it is music as he understood it when, for example, the nightingale emits its warble within earshot of any performance of *4'33"*. It would be as if Duchamp were to have claimed that all urinals are sculpture, in contrast with saying that any of them can be. Or had said that everything in the world is a ready-made, when in truth he had somewhat exacting criteria for ready-mades, chief among which is absence of aesthetic distinction. Someone can approach the ontological question of art in a kind of Mahayana spirit, by saying that everything is art, that each and every thing passes into the realm of art together, much as we all enter nirvana at once. But my approach is that of the "Lesser Vehicle": objects have to earn the status of art, one by one, the question always being how. A colleague might have asked Duchamp, "Marcel, why not a sink? Why not a bathtub?" and he, with his characteristic *gentillesse*, would doubtless have responded, "Why not indeed?" leaving it to others to make the necessary move, my question always having been what that consists in. And so with birdsong. "Why not barking and meowing?" I have the most affecting memory of walking past the bandshell in Kaliopani Park in Honolulu, which is next to the Honolulu Zoo, just after a concert. All the animals were singing—tigers, elephants, monkeys—and went on with their postperformance chorus as the musicians packed their instruments.

Cage's declaration was radical enfranchisement, abolishing really the boundary between music and sound by making sound music, and then making music something that required neither rehearsals nor conductors nor concert halls. Against that leveling agenda, my philosophy of art falls away. As Goehr knows and shows, my question has from the beginning been what makes the difference between outwardly indiscernible things, only one of which is an artwork. Thus I find it charming that Björk sang to the accompaniment of a popcorn machine, as I would have had she sung in the bird shop, to the accompaniment of caged larks. It would not automatically have been "for the birds," in Newman's sullen use of the GI epithet. I have retained, I think, a sense of quality in the face of the radical openness of avant-garde art in the '6os. I'd like to keep open the possibility of birdsong being art. But Cage's openness has the consequence of putting philosophers out of work, since nothing would be left for them to do. I would not have been charmed, in contrast with Stanley Cavell, by Cage's "lectures" at Harvard, when he spoke, as it were, in tongues, giving a performance of sorts rather than what he was paid to do, namely deliver a set of talks. I am really quite old-fashioned in such matters.

I did not draw, then, quite the radical teaching from Suzuki that Cage did, and Cage's Fluxus followers. They really did believe that the line between art and life could be erased, and I thought that it could not be, but one could not tell in any given instance whether it had been or not. So my task was more or less as follows: given that an object might be an artwork, what would be true of it that would not be if it were a mere real thing? Imagine walking into a space in which there are ladders, buckets of paint, drop cloths, bottles of thinner, boxes of spackle, rollers, and brushes. Just such a work was created by the Swiss artists Peter Fischli and David Weiss. To all outward appearances, the work looks just like a room in which those objects are found merely because it is being decorated. But in view of Fischli and Weiss's art—or even merely its possibility—one can no longer be sure, in entering such a space, whether it is a work of art or not. Given that it *is* a work of art, what *must* be true of it? That is the problem my philosophy of art attempts to deal with.

I never met Adorno, but for what it's worth, I did get to know his fellow critical theorist, Herbert Marcuse, who was my colleague for two quarters in La Jolla in 1973. Based on my discussion of contemporary art with Herbert, I believe I have a fair idea of what Adorno would have said about the art that interested me. That year, Martha Rosler, who has since become quite famous as an artist, exhibited in the university art gallery a work of installation art called *Garage Sale*. It was her M.F.A. thesis. *Garage Sale* really was a garage sale, and all the items were for sale. Herbert, who was, as a radical, predictably conservative about art, despised it, believing that it celebrated rather than criticized bourgeois values. He did not quite deign to write about it, but one of his disciples, Sandy Dykstra, published a critique in the local paper, to which Martha sharply responded, and for a while the frontier of art ran through La Jolla. I—naturally—admired the work, and since Herbert and I had become pals of a kind, the head of the graduate program in visual art—the poet David Antin—invited the two of us to debate the issue one evening, just for the faculty and students. There was no grandstanding, and I think I got across to Herbert that the work was both a garage sale and about the meaning garage sales have in our culture. In fact it was a kind of self-portrait. One worked through concentric rings of the artist's soul. The innermost ring was pretty intimate. One could buy pieces of her underwear, and even—I think—photographs of her lovers. I know Herbert saw that there was more to it than he had appreciated, but he was as stubborn as I imagine Adorno would have been, whose book, as Lydia points out, "begins with a strike against everything in art, but also in modernity more generally . . . only to ask whether art (and everything else) had not thereby come to an end." Actually, as I have indicated, Rosler's work "showed the traces of human labor and effort"—it was not dumped but arranged. "All the worse," I am sure he would have said.

Marcuse was also a pessimistic man, but one who had been surprised by the adoration of young people who regarded him as a prophet. There he was, suddenly in the midst of young admirers, and for a moment it must have seemed to him that utopia was almost actual. He had lapsed back into his pessimistic mode when we were thrown together at the edge of the continent that year, and he no longer had great faith in young people to enact his vision. But I don't think, from what I have heard, that Adorno had the soft side Herbert now and again displayed. His was a deep pessimism, with settled dispositions, and he was something of a scold. Mine, by contrast, is a deep optimism. Wittgenstein said that the worlds of the happy and the unhappy differ, but Adorno's world and mine differed actually, and I don't know that my optimism would have survived, living through what he did. When his world changed, his guilt in having survived it suffused his entire outlook, but I was at a different point in history and geography, and the world more or less underwrote my optimism. I survived three years of military service in Africa and Italy, but simply counted it as luck—and no one can feel guilty for being lucky. But I think there is more to it than that, and it has to do with the sheer *Geworfenheit* of Adorno being European and me being American.

Lydia told me that what Adorno worried about was that art was always in danger of being enlisted as an arm of political power, and it was certainly true in mid-twentieth-century Europe that aesthetic rectitude was defined in terms of political rectitude. Marxism and Fascism both believed that art must express political reality—and then set about to guarantee that this was true by hounding artists into conformity. Max Beckman's art was exhibited as clinically degenerate, Malevich's was suppressed as bourgeois and hence unsuited to a proletarian society. Fascism had Italian and, to some degree, Spanish variants. In America, there were socialist realists in the '40s, as well as regionalists, both of whom condemned modernism as respectively bourgeois and reactionary, or un-American and irrelevant. Artistic dictatorship is flagrant in the criticism of Greenberg, and after the war, the use of the figure was politically impugned in Germany, where artists were pressured into abstraction—the presumed artistic style of the victors. The blessing of being an artist in America is that the government never gave a damn, and with some exceptions, artists were protected by the First Amendment. In his memoir of the late Leon Golub—a harsh critic of American foreign policy in his paintings—David Levi Strauss recalls him saying, "You know, in many countries in the world today, you and I would have been thrown in prison or shot a long time ago. But here we're more or less left alone to keep working, even celebrated once in a while." Political dictatorship of the arts was never a felt danger in America, so one was never exposed to the chronic anxiety that evidently drove Adorno. He lived through the '60s, when everything was all at once possible as art, but he didn't believe in it, or didn't feel the liberation—indeed the exaltation—that I felt. His previous experience ruined the '60s for him.

What I loved was the way that ordinary life was being moved into art— that you could make art out of soup cans or soup pots (as in what German artists like Sigmar Polke and Gerhard Richter called "capitalist realism"). Pop art was felt as liberationist everywhere in the world. One might have thought Adorno would have imagined that the art of common reality would have indemnified pop art against political takeover. My sense is that he felt that art had gone to hell and that it could even so be taken over in the name of some new repressive order. He was in the unenviable position of someone who could neither eat his cake nor have it. My attitude was always the exact opposite, which seemed to me the only reasonable way to think and live. I'll admit that that may be one of the unacknowledged benefits of being an American.

Having your cake and eating it too defines the essential politics of art in America, and lately I have been working at making it philosophically viable. Politicians, with rare exceptions, have supported artistic freedom in America. Their question has been whether it is justified to use taxes to actively support art that goes against the taxpayers' presumed moral attitudes. Because of our pluralistic society, there will always be some taxpayers in America whose moral values will be offended by some art—even the *Mona Lisa* violates the Second Commandment. My feeling is that if the First Amendment overrides the Second Commandment, it overrides most of them. The usual liberal defense of the First Amendment is that the right to free expression of ideas contributes to the common welfare, and that this right then entails a duty to support such freedom, even if it means supporting ideas that go against our grain. That means we might find ourselves defending the rights of those whose attitudes are hard to swallow, but we are bound to defend them on the condition that ours remain defensible as well.

The end of art, as I understand it, did not occur to me as a philosophical idea until Adorno had been dead for some years. I have just suggested a way of meeting Lydia Goehr's challenge to make my end-of-art thesis "something much more political and social." If everything is possible as art, then everything is underwritten by the First Amendment: artists have a right to make anything any way they like, barring the commandments that trump the First Amendment, like prohibiting murder, so the art world is the very model of the pluralistic society in which I believe. It immediately entails the end of a certain form of art criticism, namely, that form which insists that there is only one right way for something to be art. As an art critic, I have found a philosophical position that accords with my natural bent, though I admit it took me some time before I was able to accept the pluralism forced upon me by the recognition that art had come to an end. Lydia says, cleverly, this was not art's end so much as philosophy's end—for once the essential philosophical question was found, there was not a lot left to do philosophically except to find the solution and then pack up. My view is that it really means the end of politics, or in any case the end of art criticism as ideology. Lydia proposes that the end of art came to mean in my case "a new and productive kind of criticism." I'd like to end my response by commenting on that.

In 1984, I published my essay on the end of art in the spring and became an art critic in the fall. I did not, however, become an art critic on philosophical grounds, but through a sort of fluke. True, the publication of *The Transfiguration of the Commonplace* helped bring it about, since it was read and discussed in the art world, and that led to my being asked to write critical pieces for *The Nation*. But like everything important in life—or in my life, at least—it happened by chance. And it did, I think, lead me to write a lot more philosophy of art than I would have written, had it not taken over and in certain ways transformed my life. I delivered the Mellon Lectures in 1995, and published *After the End of Art* in 1997. I delivered the Carus Lectures in 2001, and published *The Abuse of Beauty* in 2003. Four collections of critical pieces were published as well, as well as two volumes of philosophical pieces. There was and is a lot to do in the philosophy of art beyond the philosophical definition of art.

I have certainly no regrets that my philosophical life took this turn, but I have now and again, and especially recently, wondered what I would have done had it not occurred. There were two growth buds in my philosophical

writing that I would almost certainly have nursed into branches: the concluding chapter of *Connections to the World,* which advances a basis for re-
habilitating the idea of the so-called *Geisteswissenschaften;* and the concluding paragraphs of my essay "Beautiful Science and the Future of
Criticism," in which I sketch a thesis in philosophical psychology, based
on the thought that the mind has the structure of a text. Both of these
would be robust pieces of analytical philosophy, and would, I think, be as
interesting as anything I have ever written. Neither, so far as I can see,
would lead me in the directions Lydia Goehr proposes for me—but I am
deeply grateful to her for the insights that her effort at seeing my thought
together with Adorno's have yielded.

Notes

1. John Keats, *The Poems,* ed. Jack Stillinger (London: Heinemann, 1978), 369.
2. Kant, *Critique of the Power of Judgment,* Part 1, Book 2, Deduction of Pure Aesthetic Judgments, section 42, tr. Eric Matthews (Cambridge: Cambridge University Press, 2001), 182.
3. Georg Wilhelm Friedrich Hegel, *Hegel's Aesthetics,* trans. T. M. Knox (Oxford:
   Clarendon Press, 1975), 1:42–46.
4. Oscar Wilde, *The Works of Oscar Wilde* (Leicester: Blitz Editions, 1990), 292–96.
5. Lydia Goehr, "Gegen die Vogel. Theodor W. Adorno über Musik, Konzept und
   dialektische Bewegung," in Christoph Metzger, ed., *Conceptualisms in Musik,
   Kunst, und Film* (Berlin: Akademie der Künste, 2004), 97–114.
6. John Cage, *For the Birds: John Cage in Conversation with Daniel Charles* (London:
   Marion Boyars Publishers, 1981).
7. Theodor W. Adorno with Max Horkheimer, *The Dialectic of Enlightenment,* ed.
   Gunzelin Schmid Noerr, tr. Edmund Jephcott (Stanford: Stanford University
   Press, 2002); phrase taken from the title for the chapter on the culture industry:
   "Aufklärung als Massenbetrug."
8. Hegel, *Aesthetics,* 1:9 (retranslated).
9. Hans Christian Andersen, "The Nightingale," in *The Stories of Hans Christian
   Andersen,* tr. Diana Crone Frank (New York: Houghton Mifflin, 2003), 145.
10. Kant, *Critique of the Power of Judgment,* 126.
11. Andersen, "The Nightingale," 144.
12. Paul Griffiths, "Carried Away on the Wings of a Bird," *The New York Times,* Au-
    gust 16, 2003.
13. Andrew Clements, from a review in *The Guardian,* April 11, 2003.
14. Kant, *Critique of the Power of Judgment,* 240, within a discussion of the contrast
    that animals make of the "raw materials" [bloße rohe Materie] of nature with
    those same materials being taken to have the sort of order and purposiveness as-
    sociated with products of art.
15. John Cage, *Bird Cage* (music CD), EMF CD 013, 2000.

16. Friedrich Nietzsche, *Beyond Good and Evil: Prelude to a Philosophy of the Future*, tr. Walter Kaufmann (New York, Vintage, 1989), sec. 230, 161.

17. Wim Mertens, *American Minimal Music*, tr. J. Hautekiet (London: Kahn and Averill, 1994), 21.

18. Ibid. 109.

19. Cf. Theodor W. Adorno, "Vers une musique informelle," in *Quasi una Fantasia: Essays on Modern Music*, tr. Rodney Livingstone (London: Verso, 1992), 321.

20. Danto's view is worked out in many of his writings; in this essay I am drawing mostly on his "The Artworld," *Journal of Philosophy* 61 (1964): 571–84; *The Transfiguration of the Commonplace* (Cambridge, MA: Harvard University Press, 1981); and the essays in *The Philosophical Disenfranchisement of Art* (New York: Columbia University Press, 1986). Cf. also his art-critical collection, *Unnatural Wonders*, with its pertinent subtitle, *Essays from the Gap Between Art and Life* (New York: Farrar, Straus & Giroux, 2005).

21. Mertens, *American Minimal Music*, 71.

22. Arthur Danto, *The Abuse of Beauty: Aesthetics and the Concept of Art* (Chicago: Open Court, 2003).

23. Eduard Hanslick, *Vom Musikalisch-Schönen: Ein Beitrag zur Revision der ästhetik der Tonkunst* (Wiesbaden: Breitkopf & Härtel, 1966), 150; my translation. Even if Danto is not aware of Hanslick's argument, he is aware of the general point, as one sees when he quotes these lines from William Butler Yeats: "Once out of nature I shall never take/My bodily form from any natural thing" ("The Artworld" 582).

24. Arthur Danto, "Upper West Side Buddhism," in Jacquelynn Baas and Mary Jane Jacob, eds., *Buddha Mind in Contemporary Art* (Berkeley and Los Angeles: University of California Press, 2004), 56.

25. Quoted in Christopher Shultis, "Silencing the Sounded Self: John Cage and the Intentionality of Nonintention," *The Musical Quarterly* 79, no. 2 (1995): 319.

26. John Cage, *Silence: Lecture and Writings* (Middletown, CT: Wesleyan University Press, 1973), 3–13; Mertens, *American Minimal Music*, 104.

27. Danto, "Upper West Side Buddhism," 57.

28. Cage, *Silence*, 12.

29. Danto, "Upper West Side Buddhism," 51.

30. This is an argument Adorno presents in *Aesthetic Theory*, ed. Gretel Adorno and Rolf Tiedemann, tr. Robert Hullot-Kentor (Minneapolis: University of Minnesota Press, 1997), in the sections on nature and art, or on natural and artistic beauty. However, it is an argument also complicated later on, as we shall see, when art is made by Adorno to take nature's side in refusing what humanity has done to nature, humanity, and art.

31. Adorno, "Vers une musique informelle," 283. The composer refers in Adorno's text to Webern.

32. Adorno, "Vers une musique informelle," 275–26.

33. Cf. Adorno, *Aesthetic Theory*, 61 ff. and 178 ff.

34. This paragraph draws on Adorno, *Aesthetic Theory*, 67–68.

35. Adorno, "Vers une musique informelle," 314–15.

36. Cage, *Silence*, 12.
37. Quoted in Calvin Tomkins, *The Bride and the Bachelors: Five Masters of the Avant-Garde* (London: Penguin, 1968), 97 and 104.
38. I was told this by Daniel Herwitz.
39. Adorno, *Aesthetic Theory*, 68.
40. Terry Riley, quoted in Mertens, *American Minimal Music*, 45.
41. Adorno, *Aesthetic Theory*, 73.
42. Adorno, *Aesthetic Theory*, 66.
43. I am drawing here on Hannah Arendt's thesis on the banality of evil [*Banalität des Bösen*] as a critique of the commonplace or self-evident, as developed in her *The Origins of Totalitarianism* (New York: Harvest Books, 1973), where she epigraphs her argument with a line from David Rousset: "Normal men do not know that everything is possible." By quoting this sentence (taken from Rousset's commentary on what was done to human beings in the concentration camps) she is clearly posing the question as to what normality should be in contrast to what it has become normal to think it is. Adorno also takes up the theme of banality throughout his writings, especially as part of his critique of "self-evidence."
44. Adorno, "Vers une musique informelle," 322 (translation amended).
45. Keats, "Ode on a Grecian Urn," in *The Poems*, ed. Jack Stillinger (London: Heinemann, 1978),373.

5
Photoshop, or, Unhanding Art
Gregg Horowitz

In one crucial respect, Arthur C. Danto's impact on contemporary philosophy of art is unmatched: by force of argument[1] and example,[2] he has made it possible, and perhaps even necessary, for philosophers to engage with contemporary art. It has long been a philosophical reflex to hew to the spirit of Hegel's owl of Minerva and let the dust settle before passing judgment or, absent the patience to wait for a form of life to grow old, to pretend to think and write from a perspective distanced from the hustle and bustle of everyday life. However, under the influence of Danto's own "posthistorical" approach to questions of art, attaining a view from the future has ceased to be an unquestionable philosophical virtue. To be sure, other influential writers on art, such as Charles Baudelaire, Clive Bell, and Clement Greenberg, have shaped their aims and approaches in the teeth of the new but, until Danto, only Theodor Adorno and R. G. Collingwood argued that systematic philosophical aesthetics had to test itself specifically against the art of its own time.[3] Collingwood's influence has been sharply limited by his fusty choice of community theater as artistic exemplar, but Danto, by contrast, has chosen to think centrally about contemporary visual art, which is now, as Greenberg announced in 1941,[4] the dominant art of our time. With its tight formal and institutional connections to fashion, ephemerality, and sensuous immediacy, contemporary visual art embodies and expresses our historical moment in plastic images; to examine it philosophically is thus to tackle the contemporaneity of contemporary life, its unprecedented lack of historical mooring, as a problem in need of philosophical interpretation. For showing us a way to think about contemporary art as a way to think seriously about the lightness of our being, Danto has earned the gratitude of all current philosophers of art.[5]

This debt being acknowledged, it nonetheless needs saying that philosophical engagement with "the contemporary" requires a breathtaking leap in the dark that, on sober reflection, we might be grateful not to have to make. Philosophy characteristically aims to make phenomena intelligible by building for their rational kernels a better jewel case than the disposable shells they originally come in, and therefore is especially poorly equipped to handle ephemerality. But if "the contemporary" is not an especially promising concept with which to begin philosophizing, "the new," which is the concept by means of which Adorno orients modernist aesthetics to opacities in modernist art, is a philosophically familiar call to make sense in the future of what in the present moment is unexpected and shocking. The concept of "new art" is an anchor for reflection in the midst of violent historical experience. But "contemporary" art—art that is not just accidentally of its moment, as all human artifacts are, but essentially so—lives and dies in its moment and so is strangely timeless. It makes no special claims on the future. It may be that our art is contemporary in this sense, which no doubt would be expressive of something about our historical situation. But if reflective rationality is not itself to become another fashion, merely one among the plural and evanescent "isms" through which we experience and grasp our time in thought, then philosophers must learn, following Danto, how to think about the timeless transmutability of the contemporary.

To think about the present while simultaneously being disarmed by it—to think about it as disarming—requires an ability to bear exactly those uncertainties and ambivalences philosophers have traditionally sought to overcome. Careful readers of Danto know that he has taken this imperative one step further by recommending that we come to enjoy our immersion in the ephemeral.[6] Readers of the following essay offered in honor of Danto and in gratitude to him will see well enough, however, that the way of happiness is not mine. To my eyes, the path through the contemporary is not yet well enough marked for us to discern which fork leads to happiness and which to suffering. So much is clear, I think, in the art of Andreas Gursky, with which I engage here. Still, it is a signal achievement of Danto's to have made vivid, hence unavoidable, that we may and must find such a path nowhere else than in the midst of contemporary life.

[1]

Over the last two hundred years, through the agency of Hegel and a certain line of interpretation of him, an ancient tension in the philosophy of art has taken on new urgency. Plato, famously, struggled to open up some space between art and philosophy so that the philosopher might resist the temptation of art's magic and thereby come to see art clearly or, as we might say now in an unconscious echo of the original Greek problem, come to theorize about it. Plato opened this space, however, only in order to show that art's invitation to indiscipline, its cultivation of sensuous experience, remained active within philosophically disciplined thinking as an inexplicable spur to further philosophizing. We might put Plato's achievement in the form of a paradox: he sought to bracket, if only for one reflective moment, the power of art, in order to show that no philosophy of art could succeed finally in bracketing the power of art. It is a pungent irony that in this way Plato actually succeeded in unleashing the power of art, for only when philosophy arises as the highest discipline of thinking that is nonetheless unable to tame its enemy does that enemy take on the fearsome prospect of untamability.[7] Art's expulsion from the city follows inexorably.

The modernist version of Plato's high regard for art emerges when Hegel argues that if philosophy is born out of its unending conflict not merely with sensuous experience as such but with the authority of sensuous experience, then philosophy is intrinsically haunted by the power of art. (I suppose that if one were a Platonist, one might prefer to say that this thought reemerges in Hegel, but the distinction between emerging and reemerging must lose some of its charm for us if we are to think seriously about being haunted.) To say that philosophy is intrinsically haunted by the power of art is to say that art has an authority that philosophy recognizes as having been overcome as part of philosophy's own proper past; this recollected authority is what Hegel has in mind in saying that art is *and remains* for us a thing of the past. Hegel thus takes up Plato's thought about his intimate relation to a practice he never quite trusted, but in a way that casts a suspicious light on philosophy's need to be systematic. Systematic thinking, Hegel suggests, is our way of coming to terms with what we already know cannot be brought to bay through any particular act of comprehension. A system is measured by its power to prepare a place for the stray element that otherwise would derail thinking. If philosophy is systematic thinking, it is because it has already experienced anxiously the authoritative demand of some element that it has yet to confront openly. Art, then, *remains* a thing of the past in Hegel's formulation because in no imaginable future will its obsolete authority dissipate once and for all. Out of this certainty of the limits of its power—which is to say, out of its anxiety—historical cognition is egged on to philosophical systematicity. Art's exclusion from historical intelligibility follows inexorably. Philosophy of art is haunted, we can say, because it has a date with a power it believes itself to have trumped already.

Because systematic philosophy of art takes its bearings from a future experience it is dedicated to not having, it is apt to begin thinking philosophically about art by thinking about works that haunt us. This is what happens when philosophers try to come to grips with great works of art that, regardless of our knowledge of the contexts in which they were composed, exercise a power that exceeds our historical understanding of them. But there are also some works of art that haunt by embodying the authority of sensuous experience not directly but, instead, *despite*. That is, the sensuous authority of some works of art expresses itself not as a supercognitive claim on our attention but rather subcognitively, in the latent form of the undertow of an experience that has not yet been properly undergone. This, for me anyway, is the quality of my experience of some photographs by Andreas Gursky. One of a group of students trained in Düsseldorf by Bernd and Hilla Becher, the most significant and influential postwar German photographers, Gursky was the subject of a mid-career retrospective at the Museum of Modern Art in New York in early 2001. Others in the Becher student cohort were Thomas Struth (who has since been the subject of a similar one-artist show at the Dallas Museum of Art in mid-2002), Thomas Ruff, and Candida Höfer, and, in light of their accomplishments, it gave me pause when I heard that Gursky was to be the first in his class to garner for himself a show of such scope in a major American museum. Gursky's work is unresolved in so many crucial ways that it would, I thought, better suit the judgment of his career to defer the satisfactions of retrospection. And the show itself did nothing to convince me otherwise. The very latest images, the diptych called *Stockholders Meetings* (2001) completed after the retrospective had been scheduled and so as if on commission, were marred by a cartoonish literal-mindedness that cast a negative glow backward over the entire exhibition.

My aim in this essay is neither to develop this criticism further nor to retract it. Rather, I want to try to come to terms with why, despite the manifest irresolution of Gursky's art, I find myself haunted, in the sense described above, by several of his photographs. Some of them, such as *Prada I* (1996) and 99 *Cent* (1999), loom in my memory despite my aesthetic scruples, thereby expressing a latent authority with which, my capacious ambivalence nothwithstanding, I have not yet grappled. Having a deferred experience of the authority of these pictures is not, of course, the same as knowing what it is in them that is authoritative, and my aim in this essay is to make this strange *post hoc* experience intelligible. However, to say of Gursky that his pictures have a deferred or latent authority is strange, for if ever there were a photographer for whom everything is on the surface, he is it. His pictures are so sedulously pleasing (they have what Carter Ratcliff, echoing Hollywood lingo, calls "lavish production values"[8]) that the prospect of a reflective search for their deep and buried significance is at first glance absurd. But then this thought occurs to me: perhaps the authority I am puzzling over rests not in the noble self-possession and withholding of power characteristic of great works of art but rather in the wasting of a power that is itself so colossal that it needs enormous pictures over which to be dissipated. Perhaps, in other words, the authority of Gursky's images is not so much a function of power held in reserve but a trace of power now gone. And this thought sets us on a promising track, because Gursky's significance (which made a mid-career museum retrospective appropriate) arises from his being among the first serious art photographers to have made important use of the postphotographic computer technology for the manipulation of photographs called Photoshop.

[2]

Photoshop—for anyone still unfamiliar with it—is the end of photography as we know it. It is software with which to manipulate photographic images before the printing process: one can use it to rearrange the elements of already existing photographs, add bits of photographic and nonphotographic content to them, and even invent wholly new photographs from digital inputs. While Photoshop no doubt will not be the last such technology, it was the first with sufficient power to break the evidential link between photography and the world (which is why the brand name Photoshop is now used as a generic label, as is Kleenex for absorbent tissue paper). Philosophers characterize the evidential link broken by Photoshop in terms of *counterfactual dependence*: were the object not present in front of the lens when the shutter opened, the photograph would not show it. A photograph is counterfactually dependent on the world in a way that a painting, for example, is not. While it may be true that Kahnweiler posed so that Picasso could paint his portrait, Picasso could have painted him even had the picture dealer not been in Paris in 1910. The painted portrait could have been done from memory, for instance, but not even a Picasso could have photographed Kahnweiler from memory. A painting has no counterfactual dependence on the world at all, in the sense that nothing specific about the world needs to be true for a painting to show us the world that way. A painting of a unicorn might be a highly realistic and therefore charmingly fantastical depiction, but a photograph of a unicorn is a fraud—in fact, the more realistic, the more fraudulent. This evidential link between what we see in the picture now and what really was in the world at a moment in the past is what Photoshop has definitively broken. If one can make a photograph at one's desk, what experiential or epistemic authority can accrue to a photograph simply because its maker went out into the world with her Leica? Now, every time we look at a photograph we need to wonder whether it is testimony or fabrication. No longer an answer, every photograph is now a question.

The irony of Photoshop's impact on photography is that in attacking the basis of what was a specifically photographic practice, i.e., the use of the camera to make pictures, the new technology has flung the art of photography into the modernist whirlpool just as photography, when it was a new technology, seemed to do to the art of painting. Photoshop transforms photography from a technology with a uniquely powerful capacity to show us our world compellingly into a set of antiquated techniques, which, to all appearances, was precisely the fate that photography imposed on painting. Photography may continue to exist as a hobby or a specialty taste, as does painting, but its privilege in capturing the visual world is passing away. Indeed, more and more photographers and filmmakers have stopped using the phrase "shooting pictures" and—sticking with hunting metaphors—have begun to refer to the record made by the digital camera as "first capture." That sinister "first" is where photography loses its privilege.

We can use this moment of photography's modernist crisis to make a general observation about the relation between art and technique. Photography thrived as a practice for as long as its techniques, specifically camera and darkroom techniques, were constitutive of an artistic skill. This conjunction of technique and art has been expressed beautifully when the art of photography was defined as "the challenge of finding the one place to stand from which the world, compressed into two dimensions within the picture frame, makes sense of itself."[9] The Photoshop capacity to make photographs with no counterfactual dependency on the world means, however, that the proper place to stand now can be invented rather than discovered, virtual rather than real, and this is tantamount to denying that the camera, which occupies a real optical perspective, is a proper tool through which the photographer can assist the world in making sense of itself. The technique, the skill in using the camera, and the art, the intelligible picturing of the world, thereby break apart on the shoals of Photoshop.

Put otherwise: Photoshop brings it to pass that a particular authority to depict the world from someplace within the depicted world melts away. Because we cannot tell by looking whether a photograph is entirely invented, we are now rightly suspicious that every photograph reveals to us nothing but how its creator wants the world to look rather than how the world is. Photography's special perceptual authority is thus undermined. And this soldering of the meaning of the image to its maker is what photography did in the nineteenth century to the techniques that used to be necessary to achieve visual intelligibility in painting. In the face of photography, the techniques of illusionistic painting—perspective, modeling, tonal relations, and so on—became so many "mere techniques." The phrase "mere technician" is a caustic slur on an artist because it suggests that the artist has confused exercising her powers, which is of course a precondition for making art, with making art. In falling between the world and the image, a "mere technique" is simply *too* subjective. It is an aspect of a practice that has no artistic justification because it expresses nothing about the world.

The danger that an artist might end up being nothing but a technician tends to haunt the early stages in the development of an art when the promise of a technique looms larger than the problems it can reasonably address. In his *Lives of the Artists*, Giorgio Vasari delivered the following world-class screed:

> The most imaginative and captivating painter to have lived since Giotto would certainly have been Paolo Uccello, if only he had spent as much time on human figures and animals as he spent, and wasted, on the finer points of perspective. Such details may be attractive and ingenious, but anyone who studies them excessively is squandering time and energy, choking his mind with difficult problems, and, often enough, turning a fertile and spontaneous talent into something sterile and laboured. Artists who devote more attention to perspective than to figures develop a dry and

angular style because of their anxiety to examine things too minutely; and, moreover, they usually end up solitary, eccentric, melancholy, and poor, as indeed did Paolo Uccello himself. He was endowed by nature with a discriminating and subtle mind, but he found pleasure only in exploring certain difficult, or rather impossible, problems of perspective, which, although fanciful and attractive, hindered him so much when he came to paint figures that the older he grew the worse he did them.[10]

Uccello's mistake was to confuse a condition that was necessary for his art with one that was sufficient for it. Now, where we hear a distinction between necessary conditions and sufficient ones, we must sense a definition being proferred. In Vasari's criticism of Uccello we can make out the bare bones of a definition of a living art as a practice in which technical mastery of the means of art making is a way of rendering the world intelligible. From the perspective of this definition, we can understand why the wrecked careers of techno-geeks like Uccello commonly litter the early history of a significant artistic technique; it takes a whole history of experimentation to work out the expressive possibilities of a technique, and Uccello was a martyr in the court of trial and error. But the definition also puts us on the trail of understanding why a similar fate so often awaits those who work late in the history of a technique, for it is possible for an *entire* art to be reduced to mere technique when, in the wake of decisive technological changes, there is no longer any artistic significance to its inherited means. Easel painting made fresco obsolete and the pianoforte made the harpsichord an emblem of the old-fashioned. The coming of synchronized sound to movies destroyed silent comedy, although in that case the replacement of slapstick by screwball might strike us as a net gain. The coming of color to movies, on the other hand, has reduced black-and-white pretty much to two expressive possibilities: it can signify "yesteryear" or "independence from the studio aesthetic." (Come to think of it, these are perhaps not two different possibilities after all.) Color is now the technological air that filmmakers breathe. And as our being oxygen breathers establishes a range of possible life forms for us and rules out others, so too does color rule out certain artistic possibilities. We could multiply examples, but the point is by now clear. Technological development wipes from the face of the earth wave after wave of expressive possibility. But in that brief moment in time before the expressive force of its basic techniques vanishes beneath the waves, a disappearing art enters the age of the virtuoso in which the techniques, rather than bringing the world to us, arrogantly interpose themselves between us and the world. This is the photographic air Gursky breathes.

[3]

Despite having just argued that the art of photography is being undermined by digital technologies, I am not sure that I have pursued the irony inherent in this argument far enough. It is hard to shake the thought that if photography, by gutting the significance of manual techniques, really was responsible for turning painting away from its traditional projects of portraiture, landscape, and so on, thereby setting painting on its modernist path, then photography had it coming. This formulation may sound unpleasantly vengeful, but its point is to bring out how something in photography, some ambivalence about its relation to the lost authority of the painter's hand, has portended digital manipulation all along. If my hunch is correct, then Photoshop, which should be understood, I will argue, as the uncanny return of the *deskilled* hand, is as much a fulfillment of photographic art as an overturning of it. Let us return to the question of the relation of photography to painting to explore this issue.

The thought that Photoshop heralds instead the return of the *skilled* hand holds an immediate attraction because one of the characteristic features of the new technology is that it permits photographers powers of invention that have until now remained largely the property of painting. It seemed, after the birth of photography, that one still had to have the touch of Van Gogh to turn the night sky into *Starry Night*, whereas when a proud parent shows off a snapshot of the new baby, no one stares intently at the picture and asks, "How did you do that?" As photography took on itself the authority of the immediately recognizable image, painting sank down into the residual authority of the hand or, as it is frequently put, the artist's touch. However, it is a historical oversimplification to say that photographers all along quietly accepted the segregation of their medium's authority from that of painting. As early as 1857, the Swedish photographer Oscar Gustav Rejlander produced a "combination print" called *The Two Ways of Life* that is an allegory of the wages of sin. In order to show the same young man both resisting temptation and giving in to it, Rejlander shot several photographs and then printed them as one. He needed this process to achieve in a photograph the articulated narrative that was properly at home in history and allegory painting. To our eyes his picture is comic, and in 1890 even Rejlander's most loyal defender, Henry Peach Robinson, saw its shortcomings.

Here this astonishing group, consisting of about thirty figures and attempting the highest poetry in art with so much success as to gain respect, if not approval, from all, was put together. Any one but an enthusiast would have seen the impossibility of success with such a subject in such materials, but amid difficulties that would have scared most men, Rejlander saw only the end, and if he did not succeed in reaching it, his failure was almost as honorable as complete success. . . . Apart from the subject, which is allegorical, and partly carried out by the use of the nude—now ruled, and rightly, to be outside the natural limitations of the art—the picture is a marvel of skill and excellence.[11]

A veritable Uccello of the camera was Rejlander, with his supreme technical mastery in the service of inartistic ends.

It is worth observing, however, that Peach Robinson brings not one but two charges against Rejlander: first, allegory is impossible in photography; second, the nude is outside the limits of the art. Although we might be inclined to hear the second complaint as mere Victorian prudishness on Peach Robinson's part and so as gratuitously added to the first, the two criticisms are really of a piece. Allegory requires that an image be capable of standing for itself and at the same time signaling an altogether different meaning. Allegorical meaning arises on the site of an evacuation of some primary significance about which we may say, for instance, that "the story is not really about hares and tortoises." But because the authority of photographs rests on their counterfactual dependence on the world, they are too much in the grip of their subject to sustain the drift required for the alighting of allegorical meaning. The subject of the photograph is too concretely there, too much with us in the space in which we encounter the image, to be transported without remainder into the space of another meaning. Nowhere is the limitation of the concrete more palpable than in the nude photograph, where the naked person is too close, too stimulating, to be seamlessly integrated into the space of another meaning by the "art" of photography. That Peach Robinson's insight into the danger of nakedness is not merely an expression of specifically Victorian attitudes can be seen from the fact that the naked body only entered art photography when it was distanced by means of techniques such as radical cropping, soft focus, low lighting, and so on. (Today, similar ends are commonly achieved through implicit or pseudo-surrealist narrative.) Thumbing through amateur photography magazines and Web sites reveals that the nude is, of course, all over photography, but, in a back-door confirmation of Peach Robinson's charge, only as that subject the anxious dissimulation of which is the price of art. The denial of its undeniable concreteness leads photography not toward allegory but toward anxious noodling at best and outright mendacity at worst.

While the arrogance of the naked body is the most powerful example of how the authority of the photograph rests on the absence of the distantiating work of the mediating skilled hand, it is by no means the only one. So much would be attested by, for instance, anyone with a scientific interest in the motion of racing horses or, less disinterestedly, in the order of their finish. The unavoidability of photographic significance that arises from its counterfactual dependency on its subject is not, however, an unmixed blessing, for, as Rejlander and Robinson both saw, something is also lost in its wake. Photography's authority pitches its tent in the mansion of the real, but the loss of the mediating hand causes a collapse of the distance between the image and the real. The thing comes too close. Or, perhaps more precisely, in bypassing the hand's power to bring the real toward us in the form of an image, photography at the same time negates the hand's power to hold the real off. Photographs fulfill the hunger for images, but they fulfill it too proximately—too immeasurably, as I will soon start to describe it—and so also have a threatening edge.

The foremost symptom of this threat of proximity is the persistence in the history of photography of the tendency toward pictorialism that Rejlander exemplifies. In the images of photographers as diverse as Julia Margaret Cameron, Ansel Adams, and Edward Weston, we can see different forms of "painting envy" at work in the tension between the regressive authority of the image to compel recognition and the technical effort to put the immediately recognized subject at a measured distance. Now, despite how this may sound, pictorialist envy is not a merely negative project, for in the absence of the measure of distance afforded by the hand, the history of photography is driven forward in pursuit of properly photographic methods with which to blunt its own overwhelming recognitive authority.[12] This is not to deny that there have also been nonphotographic expressions of the effort to blunt photographic immediacy. In his *Florence* series, for instance, Gerhard Richter painted over photographs of that intensively photographed tourist mecca. This is clearly an extreme tactic, however, which in the end amounts to more an effacing of the photograph than a dimming of its authority. What such extreme tactics paradoxically reveal is not the authority of the hand—the very idea that Richter might paint Florence rather than photographing it is risible—but rather its sheer idiocy. In the face of the photograph, the hand becomes a blunt tool, a club, even, rather than that delicate instrument refined in the crucible of the history of painting. In consequence, the authority of the working hand essentially falls just outside the dialectic of photographic history, which is kept in motion by the tension between the overwhelming fidelity of vision and the *irrevocably displaced* fidelity of touch.

In light of this perpetual ambivalence at the heart of photography about its own authority, it would not be unreasonable to see Photoshop as the latest weapon in the pictorialist arsenal. And there are certainly grounds for seeing it as merely a recent contribution to the retoucher's arts of cropping, airbrushing, and so on, with which Gursky began his career as an image manipulator.[13] However, such a judgment misses something crucial about the radical power of the new technology. To see why, we must first take a pass through the received story, to which I referred earlier, of photography's responsibility for the onset of painting's modernist crisis. According to that story, photography was a technologically progressive step that, because of its unmediated and automatic access to the visual world, turned the accumulated techniques of the history of painting into so many unnecessary troubles. This miracle led nineteenth-century critics to call photography the death of painting because centuries of practical knowledge that had developed with the purpose of rendering the world visually intelligible became obsolete in a flash.

There are several respects in which this familiar story of the advent of photography is too crude, but let us focus for now only on one. The idea that photography was the source of the rupture in the history of art between the premodern and the modern treats its invention as a bolt from the blue or, at least, from outside the history of visual art. But such an assumption does not hold water. We know that the optical, mechanical, and chemical know-how required for photography was in place for at least a century before the actual invention. That nobody in the eighteenth century, that great age of tinkerers, put all the pieces together could be explained, I imagine, by the absence of the one special genius. However, when the invention finally happened, it happened more or less simultaneously in several industrial nations. The copyright disputes in the early photographic industry can be explained much more straightforwardly if we forget about genius and grant that what had been lacking was not the way but the will. There had to be a *need* for a device that would let the world produce its own image without relying on the skill of an artist before photography could come into existence. That means that the crisis that, on the standard view, the invention of photography purportedly caused was, in fact, itself the cause of the invention of photography. The invention arose on the site of an already compelling deauthorization of the hand.

That the received story is performing a *mythical disavowal* of the crisis of the hand can help us to understand why it typically narrates its events from the point of view of the progressive ideologues of photography. It always seems to be a part of the legend of early photography that second-rate painters like Paul Delaroche declared painting dead when they felt the world-historical impact of the first image made without the human hand. I realize that the point of such myths is to convey being swept up by overwhelming historical force and that it is no criticism of an exclamation like "it took my breath away" to point out that breathing is a precondition of exclaiming. Still, one cannot help but sense the historical stagecraft in these tales. The mediocre painter is fighting some sort of losing battle and photography presents itself as the way out, so he announces himself to have had an eye-opening insight and, with the nonperceptual authority of historical necessity, declares painting dead, i.e., declares the crisis resolved in his favor. The claim that painting was dead must be heard, I am suggesting, as a moment of imaginary liberation for artists living through a historical malaise.

All mythical tales of disavowal respond to a narrative crisis that is betrayed by a telltale repetition of the moment of origin. In the case of these legends about the birth of photographic authority, that moment is the de-authorizing of the hand, which, despite being narrated as having happened and been surpassed *back then*, continues to generate a pictorialist tropism in the history of photography. Even within this artistic practice that arises just where the hand loses its power—or perhaps especially there—the tension between recognitive immediacy and measured distance remains a structuring tension. Critical interpretation of the history of photography must explore, therefore, how photographic image making drove a wedge between the work of the human hand and the work of rendering the world intelligible, but at the same time it must also acknowledge that this deskilling was not and is not easy to swallow. A world that cannot be measured by the human hand is not a human world. Unease in the face of the immeasurable world explains why photography remains perpetually haunted by pictorialism and also why Photoshop, despite seeming to be a powerful tool in the pictorialist arsenal, in fact threatens to wreck photography by removing the tension within it between fidelity and invention, between immediate recognition and the memory of distance. Photography practiced straight may have let the world take care of itself, but it did so by leaving the hand out of the picture. Photoshop enables the return of the hand, but the hand it brings back is an idiot hand. With Photoshop we finally see that the idea of meaningful handwork is a motivating illusion of the modern imagination, a point Gursky seems to be making in his detail of a Constable painting such as *Untitled X* (1999), which strips Constable's brushwork of its mysterious power of illusion. One wonders in the face of this disillusionment, however, what measure might still be available—whether the world can still be made intelligible from a human perspective at all. Perhaps what Photoshop has begun to reveal is that a world in which invention and intelligibility are entirely riven is in crucial ways an impossible world. In any case, this is the world taken up by Gursky's pictures.

[4]

How to take the measure of the world has long been the problem at the heart of Gursky's photographs. It is one of the central problems that ties his work to the history of painting, understood specifically as the labor of rendering the world visually intelligible. Gursky takes up from that history the task that I will call "crafting a face," by which I mean making a form that enables us to recognize the world by visually expressing the world's concealed structure. Solving this problem is more complicated than it may sound at first. For an image to have the form of a face, it must look like a face. That is not enough, however, for a mask also looks like a face. To be a face, an image must also reveal what lies behind, even though, unlike a mask, a face cannot be removed without damaging what lies behind (or perhaps it can be removed, in which case it turns out that it was only a mask after all—this is the point ghoulishly lived out by Leatherface, the pointedly named protagonist of the horror film *The Texas Chainsaw Massacre*). What we want of an image that makes the world intelligible, then, is that it be a *semblance of a face, or an expressive mask*. This is the task that Photoshop complicates immeasurably.

Let me begin to make this point with reference to a slightly juvenile, pre-Photoshop image of Gursky's called *Breitscheid Intersection* (1990). In this photograph, workers are laying a grid over a road embankment in order to give it shape, perhaps to prevent it from eroding. Grid laying is also the preparatory structural work of the illusionistic painter, who uses it to organize the spatial relations of a painting in an optically convincing way. Gursky "props this task up," so to speak, using the embankment so that the grid being laid by the workers is brought parallel to the picture plane as it would be in a demonstration of perspective. At the same time, the grid remains entirely below the image's horizon line, thus identifying grid laying with ground laying and further reinforcing the reference to painting. Gursky is, in short, showing us the substructure that keeps the ground orderly. This structure will be masked, however, when the last posts are deleted and the rest of the landscaping details added. Adding and deleting detail is, of course, the ability that Photoshop puts in the hands of the photographer.

That Gursky identifies hiding structure with pictorial illusion is also shown in another pre-Photoshop image, *Cable Car, Dolomites* (1987). In this picture, unlike in *Breitscheid Intersection*, the element that does the hiding, the cloud bank, is plainly visible. Because the hiding is incomplete, the trick is ultimately revealed and we can see, with a little effort, the cable from which the car is suspended, but the use of clouds to do the work of dynamic concealing and revealing brings out another relation to the history of painting that informs Gursky's work. In several pictures, Gursky toys with the history of the romantic sublime in German painting, specifically in Caspar David Friedrich. Friedrich's paintings, such as *Monk by the Sea* (1809) and *Cross on the Mountain* (1812), are technically brilliant but slightly queasy combinations of pagan nature worship and pious Protestantism, the culminating example of which is *Large Enclosure* (1832), a heretically audacious masterpiece in which we see the earth from both the proximal point of view from which the space of human life is visible, and the god's-eye point of view from which the earth's curvature is visible.[14] Because Friedrich's pictures so often show nature as the place where humans are dwarfed by the immensity of the divine, to see the structure of nature is to see ourselves being unable to find a position from which to encompass it visually. The complete absence of the human figure in *Large Enclosure* is a precondition for its being an allegory of the human position between the natural and the divine because, after all, a visible figure placed at the station point would expose the contradictory perspectives combined in the painting.

Compare *Large Enclosure* with Gursky's *Rhine* (1999). This is a Photoshop picture of an icon of the German romantic imagination in which Gursky has removed all human figures from the eerily regularized banks of the river, leaving only the stairway on the far embankment as a reminder of the comings and goings of people. Yet what a difference even one figure would make in softening this almost industrial landscape. In the history of painting, the human figure is almost identical to verticality, as if standing upright were the very mark of being human.[15] A single figure thus would interrupt and humanize the formal horizontality of the photograph. But Gursky must be making an ironic observation about our wish for a vision of something human because, after all, the straightening out of the river is the *unmistakable* mark of the human. We are looking at the naked structure of the human world, and the presence of a recognizable human figure would serve only to conceal that structure. The human form, in short, is not the face of this world even as this is manifestly a world of human making. Gursky's Photoshop depopulation allows him to complete the work of constructing the human world by removing the final impediment to seeing it: us. The human world is thereby exposed as antihuman.

The complement to the Photoshop elimination of the overfullness of the world is the use of the technology to overpopulate the world, as seen, for example, in *99 Cent* (1999). In this image, Gursky intensifies the color of the eye-catching offerings, all identical in price and endlessly proliferated throughout the discount store. In *Chicago Board of Trade* (1999), he reproduces the traders, literally reiterates their figures, to fill out the image with overwhelming detail. It is as if the structure of the world he wishes to depict needs more detail, more stuff, if it is to show itself, but at the same time the increase in visual information overwhelms the eye. At this point we might also note that the sheer size of Gursky's images contributes to the mismatch he is displaying between quantity of information and visual intelligibility. The stuff through which we try to see the world gets in the way of the world we are trying to see.[16]

Another way to make this same point would be to say that the world we are trying to grasp keeps disappearing behind the techniques we use to grasp it. This reference to the disappearing world, the world hovering at the edge of vision, brings to mind another moment in the history of art that is at work in Gursky's vision: impressionism. It is one of the great mysteries of contemporary taste that impressionism has become the official "beautiful art" of our day because, insofar as they are of a world that keeps disappearing behind the fleeting impressions out of which we try to make sense of it, really great impressionist paintings are morbid. If impressionism is beautiful, it is the beauty of the subjective afterlife of the stable world, the beauty of a memory both fading and fixed. This tension between the fleeting and the stable, the impression and the world, is part of the attraction that the new world of leisure and lassitude had for many French painters in the second half of the nineteenth century—think of Seurat's *A Sunday Afternoon on the Island of La Grand Jatte* and Renoir's *Luncheon of the Boating Party*—and Gursky pays direct homage to this subject matter in, for example, *Ratingen Swimming Pool* (1987). But what Gursky most crucially takes from impressionist painting is not its subject matter but rather a formal property, its progressive detachment of surface from subject, in which he sees at work the decomposition of the visual intelligibility, the face, of the paintings. Monet's *Water Lilies*, for instance, in which lateral spread opens up an encompassing world that is nonetheless only for the eye, can be seen standing behind *Schiphol* (1994), a picture in which Gursky uses the windows of an airport terminal to rethink the role of the visual envelope as presenting the world but simultaneously keeping it at a distance. In this case, Gursky is thinking not just of the reiteration of the elements *within* the picture but also of the serialist reiteration of entire pictures. If every picture gives us not the world but a fleeting impression of it, then to envision our relation to a stable world, we need to multiply the images and vary them ever so little each time. It is as if, rather than seeing the world by means of our impressions of it, we see the impressions themselves, and we get to the stable world only by judging the differences between them. The stable world thereby becomes an invisible something that is inferred to subsist "beneath" all the impressions. Serialism is the negative faith that the world, despite being visually unintelligible, remains *the one unrepresentable thing*.

That photography is inherently a serial art to begin with, Gursky must have learned from his teachers, the Bechers, who are devoted photographers of disappearing worlds. Their method is to choose instances of one type of structure, usually relics of an earlier age of industrial technology such as mine heads or industrial façades, and photograph them for what they call "typological exhibition." The Bechers are, in a sense, inheritors of the famous documentary project *The Face of Our Time*, in which the photographer August Sander systematically, hence sublimely, aimed to catalogue all the social types in interwar Germany. Such works perfectly exemplify the photographic ideal of letting the world make sense of itself by finding the right place to stand, which is, by definition, face on. But what the Bechers' typologies demonstrate is that no single image is up to the task. The structure of the specific world of, say, mining reveals itself only when we compare several images and come to see the underlying structure that gives rise to a characteristic "face." But such faces are only characteristic because, as façades of industrial structures, their appearance is a matter of aesthetic indifference. It is only by accident, so to speak, that they are expressive of their structure, only because no one cared enough about how they look to cover them up cosmetically. And that is also why they are allowed to fall into terminal disrepair. The intelligibility of the world the Bechers show is essentially connected to its ephemerality. It is an intelligibility that arises only at the moment of ruination.

Gursky's images cannot look more different than the Bechers', and one cannot help but wonder what the teachers think of the direction their stu-

Hong Kong and Shanghai Bank (1994)

dent has taken. But, in the end, I do not think Gursky has fallen that far from the tree. He sees in the unease about handwork's inability to render the world intelligible the motive for the Bechers' compulsive attraction to industrial ephemera, but he also sees that photography, in its faith in the self-evident, is itself a relic of the industrial age.[17] Photography gives us every insignificant detail of the surface of the world, but our world, the structure of which is hostile to the human hand, is in fact utterly incomprehensible when seen photographically. In its color-coding, which is supposed to help us navigate inhuman spaces, and its ordered repetitions, which are supposed to manage visual overload, *Siemens, Karlsruhe* (1991) already mimics the world that has gotten away from us, but in *Klitschko* (1999), the self-representing world of the photograph is a nightmare. The structure of this world is both utterly vivid and completely beyond our grasp. We made this world, yet in no meaningful sense is it ours. Gursky shows us the structure of what has no expressive face. Or, if you prefer, he shows us the expressive face of the unintelligible world. From the point of view of the question of whether we can comprehend the world, it comes to the same thing.

Gursky's procedure is something like this: he first makes photographs that are counterfactually dependent on the world. But because those images are immediately recognizable, they lie.[18] Gursky then transforms the image so that it becomes, as Freud says of the nodal point of dreams, ultraclear, and thus incomprehensible. *Hong Kong and Shanghai Bank, Hong Kong* (1994), for instance, is a hyper-real image because the detail visible in each window is sharp, as if we were standing right in front of it, even though we are far enough away to see the whole tower. The image is hard to bring into focus, but not because it is smudged. Quite the contrary: the image is illegible because Gursky has overprinted the latent content of the structure, the organization of work, onto an image of the structure itself, in order to show that latent and manifest content cannot be made to fit together visually. In just this respect, however, it is reminiscent of Rejlander's *Two Ways of Life* and the incoherence of the very idea of photographic allegory the earlier photograph displayed. In the same vein, Gursky's images of contemporary systems of production show us that there is no image that can mediate the relation between the human scale of work and the economic scale of the pound and the dollar that measure it.

Atlanta (1996) brings this theme out most powerfully by showing how a structure built for habitation maintains its visual integrity by means of a hard-to-detect cleaning staff. They are the people who work to erase the counterfactual dependency of states of the world on the human presence in it. They are the Photoshop workers of the hospitality industry, who keep the world orderly and fresh and incomprehensible—"faceless" is the word I am looking for. Their hands work to hide the earlier presence of guests, but because they also work to hide that their hands were needed to do that work in the first place, the erasure they perform is actually a double era-

Atlanta (1996)

sure. That is why they must leave little notices in our hotel rooms to tell us
that they were there. The first task of the cleaners, then, is to erase history,
but their work is not done until they erase the signs of the labor that went
into the erasure of history, leaving behind a fresh-scrubbed world. This
makes the cleaners Gursky's ambivalent proxies within the picture, for
just as a battalion of maids is a sign that the order of the world is un-
friendly to the traces of the human body, so too is Photoshop a technology
with which we erase both the presence of the world and the presence of
ourselves as erasers. We do not do this by destroying images, of course, for
we are far from iconoclasts. We make our images and then disappear inside of them. Gursky's images struggle to show this, which is to say they
try to show the face, which is now only a mask, of the world that has gotten
away from us.

  Let me conclude with a photograph, *EM, Arena, Amsterdam* (2000), that
is one of Gursky's scariest. To say so is not to deny that *Amsterdam* is in
many respects a typical Gursky image. A grassy field is overlaid with a manifestly human design. The colors are pumped up to bring out the contrast
of green and white, and the figures are too detailed for the distant overhead

EM, Arena, Amsterdam I (2000)

perspective. Everyone is in motion yet at the same time photographically frozen. This photographic stopping of time reveals the *order* of the motion, which is, in this case, everyone turning away from the injured player. No one looks at him, no one pays attention to the face of pain. But that's not exactly right. The other players are actively turning their backs on the injury because the referee uses his hand to wave them off. And being waved away by someone's hand is, in a sense, a response to immeasurable pain. In the way *Amsterdam* points toward what we do not see while never quite allowing us to see it, it is practically a summary of Gursky's work, so much of which, we can now say, is seen from the referee's point of view. Our technology grants us just enough distance to remain unmoved by the player's face, even though it is the same technology that brings the grimace of pain insufferably close. But the world that cannot move us despite maximal visual proximity is, in principle, the world without a face; it is the world in which our eyes are no longer of any use in the task of recognition. Working with Photoshop, this is the dilemma Gursky confronts over and over, and this is why some of his images haunt. Working at the roadblock, which is also an intersection, of the shocking clarity and immediacy made possible by Photoshop, Gursky discovers there an encounter that is always just out of reach. The undeniable beauty of his photographs, which this paper has largely evaded, is thus a hysterical masking that compels attention to something we cannot yet witness.[19] Whether this sort of masking eventually becomes expressive will have significant bearing on the visual arts in the age of their unhandedness and is therefore a question of pressing concern for aesthetes. Whether we can craft a face that is fit to measure a world that has unhanded us is a much more general problem for the future of the human world. Its significance, therefore, remains immeasurable.

◀▮ ◀▮ ◀▮ ◀▮ ◀▮

Response

Although Gregg Horowitz is right in saying that the focus—I would say the occasion—of my work on the philosophy of art has been contemporary visual art, this is not because I consider the latter to be, as Clement Greenberg claimed, the dominant art of our time. I have no idea which, if any, of the arts today is the dominant one, but I would suppose it must be one of the popular or mass arts, like rock or film, since it is through these that the myths people need to help define their lives are accessible and compelling.

It is, rather, because the problems that engaged me as a philosopher emerged through the avant-garde art of the early '60s, where the question was vividly raised of what made one of a pair of largely indiscernible objects a work of art and the other not. This happened in music in the '50s through John Cage, and in dance in the '60s with Merce Cunningham and the Judson group. Noel Carroll has composed for contemporary dance a narrative that parallels the one (or ones) I have composed for the visual arts, leading to the same situation in which there is no outward difference between dance and ordinary bodily movement. And Borges, as I noted in my response to Daniel Herwitz, showed that the same possibility was thinkable if not entirely actual in literature. It was something that emerged across a broad spectrum of the arts, and, in the visual arts, through a number of movements—Fluxus, pop, minimalism, and conceptual art in the '60s—without this meaning that the visual arts were dominant. It is quite contingent, a matter of my own interests and knowledge, that they seemed to me, in the '60s, to be calling for a philosophical definition of themselves from within, which I then tried to supply as a philosopher.

I have, since childhood, had a keen interest in painting and in affiliated arts like drawing and prints, but my interest in the problem raised by indiscernible counterparts was initially almost entirely philosophical. The problems that interested me in the '60s were differentiating actions from bodily movements that outwardly resembled them, and distinguishing illusory from veridical perceptions when there were no internal grounds for doing so. The differences in both cases lay outside the indiscernabilia, and the philosophical question was to explain them. The result would have been a theory of action in the one case and a theory of knowledge in the other. It had never occurred to me that there were questions of the same sort for art, though of course there was the problem, which Nelson Goodman had made much of, in distinguishing originals from fakes. Goodman's strategy was to deny the problem, in effect, claiming that sooner or later differences could emerge under close looking. That, I thought, did not answer the question, which for me required finding which differences explain the difference between art and nonart. Had it not been for *Brillo Box* and like works, I would never, I think, have written philosophically about art. Had I been asked, for example, to talk about art in 1963, I'm not sure I would have had anything much to say. But *Brillo Box* turned out to be a kind of Rosetta Stone for the philosophy of art, and I have found, after forty years, that I have not exhausted its conceptual richness. It opened up dimensions in the concept of art that were scarcely recognized before it came on the scene.

To the degree that photography has played a role in my philosophy, it has mainly been through the way the simple snapshot has served as an example of how representations relate to the world: the snapshot is "true" when its shapes, colors, and values are caused by what they resemble—and in this the snapshot is a useful model for thinking about certain basic kinds of knowledge, so far as the latter is analyzed as justified true belief. A belief, and hence knowledge, is justified when its causes and truth conditions are of a piece. Skepticism enters when it occurs to us that nothing internal to our representations justifies us in believing them true or is caused by what would make them true if they were true: when nothing internal to our representations justifies a belief that either of the two main connections to the world—truth and causation—hold.

Gregg Horowitz is entirely right in finding a basis for photographic skepticism in the revolutionary software program called Photoshop:

> The Photoshop capacity to make photographs with no counterfactual dependency on the world . . . Put otherwise: Photoshop brings it to pass that a particular authority to depict the world from someplace within the depicted world melts away. Because we cannot tell by looking whether a photograph is entirely invented, we are now rightly suspicious that every photograph reveals to us nothing but how its creator wants the world to look rather than how the world is. Photography's special perceptual authority is thus undermined.

In brief, Photoshop does for the perceptual authority of photography what Descartes's *malin genie* did for the cognitive authority of perception. I might observe that photography did not quite do to painting what Horowitz claims it did in the nineteenth century—"soldering . . . the meaning of the image to . . . the techniques of painting that used to be necessary to achieve visual intelligibility." Descartes explicitly speaks of the mind as a picture gallery—by which he would have had to mean a gallery of paintings or drawings—from the examination of which we have no way of knowing whether they correspond to anything in the world, or even whether there is a world for them to misrepresent. All the techniques of painterly verisimilitude were known to Descartes, who was a student of optics and had—or is believed to have had—his portrait painted by Hals. The virus of the *malin genie* antedates Photoshop in inducing radical doubt in the seeker after certainty. And one would have expected this, at least to the degree that the snapshot is a fair model of the basic cognitive episode in which our basic representations are taken to accurately capture the world.

Horowitz's paper is brilliant and pioneering, quite apart from the co-
gency of his criticism of the work of Andre Gursky, which has, so far at
least, only used digitalization as an enhancement. He has not taken it "all
the way." I have no quarrel with the criticism, which I find compelling, and
I applaud his effort to deal with the Bechers' work and the influence of
their photographic philosophy. But I would like to bring forward a few observations from the history of art that seem to me to bear on Horowitz's
main claim about Photoshop, and somewhat blunt its radical edge. Photoshop just makes it easier to do what has always been an option.

First, according to Hans Belting's masterpiece, *Likeness and Presence,*
the mediation of the hand would have been enough to discredit claims of
pictorial authenticity in the period in which the devotional image was ascendant in Christian art—roughly from the end of the Roman Empire to
the beginning of the Renaissance, when aesthetic considerations began to
take over. A picture was deemed authentic precisely when it was
acheiropoiēton— "not made by hand"—hence not made by an artist's hand.
The paradigm was the image of himself that Christ caused to appear on
Veronica's veil. The image was Christ himself, as much so as any relic that
might have been part of his body, like blood or foreskin (but perhaps no
integral body part, in view of bodily resurrection). Saint Luke is often pictured as a painter, but the image of the Madonna credited to him was believed to have materialized on his panel by miraculous transfer: the Virgin
realized that Saint Luke was not up to the task of "capturing" her. A third
example would be the image of Jesus on the Shroud of Turin. Even today,
pictures are miraculous to the minds of the faithful only when their power
cannot be explained through painterly intervention. Their main purpose
was their power to intervene on behalf of their owners. Technologically
speaking, the authentic picture was nearer kin to photograms than to photographs, but the actual presence of the saint in the icon far outweighed
the degree of resemblance between the two.

From this it follows, I think, that the painter was no more than a *pis aller*
so far as the production of pictures was concerned, as is tacitly conceded
in a wonderful painting of Saint Luke I have more than once commented
upon, in which Guercino shows him sitting before a panel on which an
image of the Madonna appears. The style of that image is archaic relative
to the high skill of Guercino as a Baroque master. Guercino knew enough
art history to realize that painting at the time of Saint Luke would hardly
have been as capable of presenting visually credible images as was Guercino himself. That indeed required the discoveries of the Renaissance that
were accessible to seventeenth-century masters. But Saint Luke did not

paint the image he sits before: it was a miraculous image, due to the grace of the Virgin. The angel standing beside Luke is astonished by it, not because of its likeness to the Virgin, but because it is the Virgin herself, as much so as Christ's face on Veronica's veil. No painter was capable of that! The ability to paint likenesses was small compensation for the defining incapacity of artists to create the real thing. Better a crude but miraculous picture than a mere semblance, however exact.

But Horowitz is entirely correct in saying that it was with reference to images of the kind that Guercino and Paul Delaroche were capable that Delaroche declared, upon learning of Daguerre's invention, that painting was dead. Images that looked just like reality could now be made without learning to copy nature by drawing or painting it. All such skills were now built into an apparatus that could do the work for you. The camera would have meant nothing in the period Belting discusses in *Likeness and Presence*. Nor would it have meant much in the history of Chinese painting, which probably explains why the Chinese never invented it. We all know how little it meant to the Chinese when the principles of perspective were explained and demonstrated for their benefit. The achievement of verisimilitude, on which Victorian anthropologists based their claims of European superiority—and that generated the concept of primitivity—was laughably irrelevant to the societies stigmatized by it.

This history of the relationship between painting and photography was, for decades, a history of what in the Renaissance were called *paragone*—arguments in which the arts were compared, usually invidiously, as their practitioners competed for social advantage. The sculptor worked in noisy, dirty circumstances, while the painter's studio was neat, clean, and silent: he could paint to the accompaniment of lutes or participate in learned dialogue with his subjects as he portrayed them. In terms of a *paragone* on photography and painting, photography defined visual truth, which Ruskin, in defense of the Pre-Raphaelites, accused painters, from Raphael onward, of having sacrificed in favor of pretty tales. The American "Pre-Rafs," as they called themselves, praised one another's work by saying that one would think it had been produced by a camera, and dismissed the tableaux of the Academy on grounds of visual prevarication. These painters aspired to the effect of handlessness. Or, to take the opposite position: photography was stupidly literal, whereas painting was like poetry—not limited by the real world, the artist could paint his visions. Whereupon photographers modified reality to conform to their visions, and photographed the results. Lady Julia put her models in medieval garments, or dressed them in wings like fairies. Henry Peach Robinson created sentimental mises-en-scène for Victorian sensibilities. It took no time at all for photographers to disguise the visual world to exploit the assumptions of what Horowitz identifies as "counterfactual dependence" to instill false beliefs in viewers. Matthew Brady put Confederate uniforms on dead Union soldiers and arranged them on the battlefield to convey illusions of victory. I believe Timothy Sullivan did the same.

It is possible to argue that modernism was the product of these rivalries. Manet, according to Clement Greenberg, effected the thin shadows of the photograph in his portraits to enhance the sense of reality, inadvertently became the first painter to achieve the flatness Greenberg seized upon as the essence of painting. Or painters strove for effects unavailable to photographers, who in turn invented pictorialism. In his essay for the present volume, Hans Belting describes Picasso's efforts to erase the boundaries between photography and painting in an act of precocious postmodernism. Not long ago I invented the term "photographist" to designate artists who use photographic means to nonphotographic ends. Today everything goes. The *paragone* of painting and photography is a dead genre.

What, in view of the history just reviewed, does the advent of Photoshop change? It changes things only insofar as it matters whether we believe a given photograph is intended to represent a given reality or not. I don't think Cindy Sherman has had recourse to Photoshop, but it would not greatly matter if she did, since there has never been an intention in her case to use photography for anything but fiction. The great *Untitled Film Stills* of the late 1970s appropriated the genre of the still for fictive films, though since they were never taken from real films at all, her photographs are fictive twice over. Photoshop would at best have helped her achieve the effects she sought. Her work was counterfactually *independent*, if that means anything. The photographs are not about what was in front of the camera, but about whatever they are about—not about Cindy Sherman in a nurse's costume, but about the role she was playing, namely, of a nurse; not about Cindy Sherman made up to look like a jaded housewife, but about a jaded housewife in a film never made. What difference would it make if there were things in the photograph that were not there on the "set"?

This would not quite be true of Nan Goldin's photographs in her *Ballad of Sexual Dependency*, since her project was to show the people in "Nan's World" just being themselves, including Nan herself. I don't think Nan Goldin digitalizes, but if she did, so what?—so long as her viewers are not misled about what they see in the photographs. If we learned that she had used Photoshoppery to make the black eye her lover Brian gave her look worse than it did, it would be artistic misrepresentation—making Brian look even worse than he was and herself more deserving of our sympathy. But if she showed herself with a black eye she never had—well, that would be a visual lie, given her intentions. On the other hand, because of her feeling for her friends, it would be quite consistent for Nan to make them look more beautiful than they really were—out of friendship or even love.

I think we could accept the news that Atget got shopkeepers to add some manikins to the crowded store windows he photographed in Paris— so why would we object if there were a technology that enabled him to get the same crowded effect by exploiting it? Replace Atget with Gursky and ask what difference it would make if he were to have added some merchandise to make the store interior in *99 Cents* even more crowded, or used digitalization instead to achieve the same effect? From this perspective, it seems to me, Photoshop has roughly the function that retouching has had in achieving an image satisfactory to the photographer.

In general, then, my view of Photoshop is that so far as art is concerned, it is but a tool. It is, on the other hand, more than that with photographs whose function is to achieve visual truth, to convey information, to reproduce the look of the world. It would have been extremely useful to those bent on diminishing the impact of the Abu Ghraib photographs to say that it was all Photoshop, with no truth in it. By demonstrating that the photographs of abuse by British soldiers were fabricated, the Blair administration escaped censure. But so far as I can see, Photoshop has merely (!) contributed to the rising mendacity that has overtaken the way information is transmitted to the public, making it easier to control the minds and spirits of the population and more and more important to protect the freedom of the press independently to investigate the truth that photographs pretend to offer. But that has been true of press photography since at least the American Civil War.

I wish I were better able to grasp Horowitz's concluding interpretation of Gursky's *EM*—"The world that cannot move us despite maximal visual proximity is, in principle, the world without a face; it is the world in which our eyes are no longer of any use in the task of moral recognition." The grinning mugs of the tormentors in the Abu Ghraib photographs are certainly an element in our moral recognition of violated dignity and aborted rights. The uninhibited pleasure in the evidence of erotic cruelty immediately evoked in viewers moral repugnance and shame, even without—or especially without—the intervention of Photoshop. It was just homemade photography with the aid of cheap digital cameras, the images sent flying from laptop to laptop, from Baghdad to Baltimore and beyond, with the implicit message "having a wonderful time; wish you were here." It is just because photography is taken to consist of *acheiropoiēton* images—images made without hands—that Horowitz speaks of a world that has "unhanded us." Would hands—I means hands used in the act of drawing or painting— really have made a moral difference? I feel that it is in pursuit of the insight in the final paragraph that Horowitz composed his paper—so I wish I could respond to it with something better than my present unclarity in respect to his meaning.

Notes

1. Arthur C. Danto, *After the End of Art: Contemporary Art and the Pale of History* (Princeton, NJ: Princeton University Press, 1998).
2. Danto's art criticism published in *The Nation* has been collected in five volumes so far, starting with *The State of the Art* (New York: Prentice Hall, 1987).
3. R. G. Collingwood, *The Principles of Art* (Oxford: Oxford University Press, 1958), and Theodor W. Adorno, *Aesthetic Theory*, tr. Robert Hullot-Kentor (Minneapolis: University of Minnesota Press, 1998).
4. Clement Greenberg, "Towards a Newer Laocoon," in Greenberg, *The Collected Essays and Criticism*, ed. John O'Brian (Chicago: University of Chicago Press, 1988), 1:23–38.
5. Speaking of gratitude, I owe a personal debt to Kathleen M. Eamon, a graduate student in philosophy at Vanderbilt University, who assisted me in assembling and tracking down the references for this essay.
6. Arthur Danto, "Symbolic Expressions and the Self," in Gregg M. Horowitz and Tom Huhn, eds., *The Wake of Art: Criticism, Philosophy, and the Ends of Taste* (London: Routledge, 1998), 97–114.
7. Danto treats Plato's arguments in "The Philosophical Disenfranchisement of Art," in Gregg M. Horowitz and Tom Huhn, eds., *The Wake of Art: Criticism, Philosophy, and the Ends of Taste* (London: Routledge, 1998), 63–80.
8. Carter Ratcliff, "The Seeing Game," *Art in America* 86, no. 7 (July 1998): 89.
9. A note of scholarly embarrassment here. My drafts of this essay attribute this quote to the curator Peter Galassi. However, somewhere between first draft and final polish, the source of the citation disappeared, and now I cannot track it down. If the idea is Galassi's, I apologize to him for my carelessness; if it is not, I apologize to him all the more, and also, of course, to whomever I have stolen it from.
10. Giorgio Vasari, *Lives of the Artists* (London: Penguin, 1998), 1:95.
11. Henry Peach Robinson, "Oscar Gustav Rejlander," in Beaumont Newhall, ed., *Photography: Essays and Images* (New York: Museum of Modern Art, 1980), 105.
12. Peter Galassi makes a similar point about how the history of photography must be comprehended dialectically because it has been driven both by artistic concerns and by commercial, scientific, and idiosyncratically personal forces operat-

ing under the radar of the canonizing concepts of art photography. *Andreas Gursky* (New York: Museum of Modern Art, 2002), 10.

13. Galassi's catalogue essay cited in the previous note recounts the development of Gursky's techniques of manipulation beginning as early as 1991. I owe thanks to Jay Bernstein for pressing on me the danger of overstating the difference between Photoshop and other sorts of image retouching.

14. My discussion of *Large Enclosure* relies on ideas more fully developed by Richard Wollheim in *Painting as an Art* (Princeton, NJ: Princeton University Press, 1990).

15. The significance of the upright posture to visual form is explored by Rosalind Krauss in *The Optical Unconscious* (Cambridge, MA: MIT Press, 1994).

16. Norman Bryson makes a closely related point, although he draws a happier cognitive conclusion than I do, when he writes that "Gursky constantly links the macro- and micro-levels of social knowledge, so that we are able at one and the same time to take in the overall picture—every floor of the Shanghai Bank, for example—and to inspect minuscule details (individual work stations, tiny cells of corporate activity)." Bryson, "The Family Firm: Andreas Gursky and German Photography," *ArtText* 67 (November 1999/January 2000): 76.

17. At this point I am disagreeing with Alex Alberro, who charges Gursky with "a highly superficial, aestheticized approach to the site of labor." This disagreement will grow deeper when, very shortly, I turn to analyze *Atlanta*. Let me say here, then, that Alberro's criticism of Gursky's aestheticism is very compelling and that I do not take myself to have responded to it at all fully. Alberro, "Blind Ambition," *Artforum* 39, no. 5 (January 2001): 113.

18. In an interview, Gursky tells of having visited industrial sites and being surprised by what he calls the "socio-romantic air" of their appearance. In other words, their appearance did not disclose the true nature of their functioning, and so they—sites of globalized capitalist production—could not be truthfully photographically documented. "After this experience," Gursky continues, "I realized that photography is no longer credible, and therefore found it much easier to legitimize digital picture processing." Cited in Alex Ohlin, "Andreas Gursky and the Contemporary Sublime," *Art Journal* 61, no. 4 (Winter 2002): 29.

19. I owe thanks to Fred Rush for pointing out to me the closeness between Gursky's concerns and the tradition of reflection on the technological sublime.

6

At the Doom of Modernism

Art and Art Theory in Competition

Hans Belting

[1]

On December 28, 1964, the Eastern Division of the American Philosophical Association held its sixty-first annual meeting. One session was devoted to the topic of "the work of art." In retrospect, there could not have been a more noteworthy historical coincidence. For at that moment, the art scene had abandoned any safe definition of the artwork as it had dominated the exhibition walls in the glorious days of modernism. Artists themselves had started to deconstruct the visual profile of the artwork as a beautiful stereotype in gallery production. Anything was welcome—in particular the strategies of the Happenings, Fluxus, and conceptual art—that would undermine the former authority of the work of art. So a new discourse was needed to treat the status of the work once it had ceased to embody the traditional expectations of art. As would be recognized much later, modernism accelerated its own dissolution at that moment.

Young Arthur C. Danto seems to have been the only one among the APA speakers who sensed the importance of what was happening in 1964. When he entered the ranks of art criticism with his memorable talk entitled "The Artworld," he developed a theory that would identify artworks that no longer looked as such. But "telling artworks from other things is not so simple a matter." When an actual bed made its entry in the art scene, the artist urged the audience to identify it not as a bed but as representing something else. This is, Danto continues, "equivalent to asking what makes it art." To see something as art, he argues, "requires some-thing the eye cannot decry—an atmosphere of artistic theory, a knowledge of the history of art: an artworld." The author, as we know, spoke of his re-cent Damascus experience when Andy Warhol's *Brillo Boxes* were exhib-ited in the Stable Gallery on East 74th Street that same year: "What in the end makes the difference between a Brillo box and a work of art consisting of a Brillo box is a certain theory of art."

Several questions arise immediately. What did it mean to speak of a "certain theory of art"? And did such a theory apply to any art, or only to that of the given moment, which, much later, became identified as the end of modernism? Had the transformation of an object into an artwork—or, for that matter, into representation—not been a problem for other times as well, even in the high days of confident figuration? But the real issue was whether there was still a momentum for a general art theory (the theory of what distinguishes any art from nonart) or art theory itself had become a victim of history and change. One wonders whether there was ever a valid art theory valid enough to survive its own days. There certainly is a secret link between art production and art theory of a given moment, although theories always claim to be general and timeless. The difference, at that moment in 1964, seemed to be the artists' resistance to, or lack of interest in, creating works that would attract an aesthetic response.

"Mr. Andy Warhol, the Pop artist," as Danto felt obliged to introduce a still unfamiliar figure, "displays facsimiles of Brillo cartons . . . as in the stockroom of the supermarket." And the speaker asked himself "why the Brillo people cannot manufacture art and why Warhol cannot *but* make artworks." A similar discussion had already taken place in front of Duch-amp's old *Readymades*, which became popular at the same moment. In Warhol's case, Danto was reluctant to provide an easy answer. He even asked whether a world of latent artworks, like the bread and wine of reality, waited "to be transfigured, through some dark mystery, into the indiscern-ible flesh and blood of the sacrament." Bread and wine indeed still looked the same after consecration, at least to the incredulous eye. Was the "con-secration" of the artwork by the artist-priest the result of a similar "dark mystery"? The mystery of turning something into the representation of something else? An object into an artwork?

For a long time, the history of art had provided a framework in which every work was assigned its proper place and thus qualified as art in a se-ries of similar art events. But this history, as Danto insisted, had recently ceased to explain any work's position in the "progressive historical narra-tive" called the history of art. The eye of the beholder had been trained to recognize art by its historical form. But the eye "was philosophically of no use" when the artwork no longer revealed its visual qualities. Danto, on a later occasion, repeated that "you cannot tell when something is a work of art by looking at it." There certainly continued to be a difference between artworks and ordinary things. "But there is no way of telling the difference merely by looking." The difference by now has become "philosophical." When art "gives rise to the question of its true identity . . . it has become the occasion of philosophy. . . . Until the form of the zquestion came from within art, philosophy was powerless to raise it. Once it was raised, art was powerless to resolve it."

Danto, who in his own way treated the old question of the identity of in-discernibles, developed a new philosophy of art that differed from most of the art theories in its independent aims while sharing some concerns of the art of his time. The relation between art as form and as concept, or the liberation of art from its own history, had haunted modern artists for a long time. The artwork itself had represented the core of the matter, as it made artists define and redefine art's "true identity," which had become a matter of doubt once it was addressed. Even the Brillo box effect, seen in retrospect, was a strategy to entertain the same question and to resist any of the received answers—a strategy that raised the question "from within art." The act of merely exhibiting objects or commodities implied the presence of art not as creation but as concept. But it is doubtful whether modern art ever functioned "merely by looking," even when it offered enough to look at.

[2]

In Balzac's novel, *The Unknown Masterpiece,* to whose metaphor and impact on modern art I dedicated a recent book, Frenhofer's friends already are exposed to another (or reversed) Brillo box effect, as they expect to see a beautiful woman on the canvas and instead only discover "a wall of painting," which in their eyes reveals the absence of representation or the tautology of art's representational tools. Frenhofer aspired to art in the absolute rather than practicing art as the visual expression of a given subject. However, his friends reject the thought of identifying art as self-reference rather than as reference to something else. Since then, the question has shifted to other areas but the problem has remained unsolved. For the problem is inherent in the hybrid that a modern artwork is by definition: it exists as an object yet represents an idea, the idea of art.

In Warhol's intention, the concept wins over the object. The Brillo boxes were the never seen, as they did not resemble any other artwork and nevertheless lived from their nonidentity with a commercial product. His boxes thus appear both as a break from art production and as a continuation of conceptual avant-garde practices. In fact, Warhol shared tendencies in the 1960s that aimed at the deconstruction of any familiar item of art. See, for example, his thirty *Mona Lisas*, which "are better than one." Gustav Metzger, a former émigré from Europe, wrote a manifesto entitled "Auto-Destructive Art" as early as 1959. His target was the artwork, since art as such cannot be destructed. In his view, only the self-destructive act would continue to rescue "a total unity of idea, site, method and timing." These terms allude to the making of art, which in the meanwhile had lost its former authority based on creation. Autodestructive art was meant to release art production from creating the artwork that was regarded as an anachronistic fetish. The new aim was to liberate the idea of art from becoming an artwork and thus from serving as a commodity on the art market.

Any such activity could only be a gesture, but the gesture came "from within art" and symbolized the artists' reflexivity within their own domain. Just one year later, the Swiss artist Jean Tinguely caused a sensation in the art world by actually performing autodestructive art in the courtyard of the Museum of Modern Art. The autodestruction of the *Hommage to New York* lasted from 6:30 to 7:30 p.m. on March 17, 1960, and left the elaborate machine in pieces. The artwork, if the machine could be considered as such, disappeared step by step in front of the audience. Tinguely indeed devised an allegory of the creative process by inverting it in mirrorlike fashion. We are here reminded of Yves Klein's saying that his pictures were the ashes of his art. Tinguely exchanged exhibition for performance, physical existence for an event in time. Art, as an idea, was not destroyed together with the artwork. On the contrary, self-effacing art revealed art's nonidentity with its visual properties.

A different strategy was pursued by Robert Rauschenberg when in 1961 he created a combine painting with the title *Reservoir*, meaning reservoir of time in a very particular way. Indeed, the picture may have been the first one in art history to contain two real clocks. The first was set when Rauschenberg started painting, and the second at the very moment he finished the picture. By recording the exact time of his working process, the artist implied a reference in the following sense: what you see here is a so-called artwork, and I have produced it in a measurable time whose short duration contradicts the nonmeasurable time of its existence as a finished piece. The working process always had been eliminated, as it were, by the seemingly timeless appearance of an artwork. Now, the work recorded its own production as a lost past whose memory is exhibited by the two clocks. Their time difference marked the time gap separating exhibition from creation, being from being made. Rauschenberg, frustrated by the mute face of the usual gallery art, even participated at live performances where he appeared together with other artists in front of the public. At such occasions, he staged the making of a picture by controlling the time with a stopwatch. In the end, he would even refuse to show the finished picture, since the allegorical act of making it was more important than its visual properties.

Symbolic gestures of this kind were evidence enough that the painters revolted against their inherited roles, especially against being confined to their usual self-expression via the artwork. A kind of nominalism distinguishes their new doubt from their continuing practice. Sigmar Pole shared this nominalism when he painted an abstract picture in 1968, but extended its painted surface by a white strip carrying the inscription "Modern Art." As a generic label, this nontitle becomes an integral part of the work or dissolves the coherence of the usual work via a commentary. Abstraction had been the very incarnation of modernism, at least of American postwar modernism. Pole's picture, via the label, makes a reference to "so-called abstraction." The nonidentity of the picture with an abstract painting invites a gesture of reflexivity that separates looking and reading as two cognitive acts. Visual evidence has become the mask for a transvisual discourse.

At the time, a happy competition between art and philosophy brought the two domains into close relations. Joseph Kosuth, the champion of conceptual art, suddenly brought this competition into the open when he coined the slogan "Art after philosophy" in 1969. Art now laid claim to that part in official culture that "traditional philosophy," as he wrote, had increasingly lost. Danto likewise spoke of "traditional art" when he wanted to justify philosophy's new claims to the domain of art. He might have easily spoken of "philosophy after art." It was surely no accident that Kosuth, as a former student of Ad Reinhardt, would embrace language and thus invade philosophy's territory. Since Reinhardt had touched the last frontiers of painting, Kosuth laid claim to language as his new medium of representation. He even accused any artist who would continue to believe in visual representation of being stubbornly "formalist." To resist any temptation of formalism, he preferred to speak of a "proposition" rather than an artwork. Artists were to "propose" ideas of art and had to abandon the "making" of art.

This is not the place to discuss conceptual art, especially because it has been subjected to substantial revisions since the 1990s, which sometimes obscure the initial intentions. But it cannot be denied that the identity of art was a common concern of both conceptual art and the new philosophy of art. The title of an exhibition held in 1967 indicated the artists' dilemma. "Language to be looked at" was a compromise between looking at an artwork and reading about art's idea. Also, Sol LeWitt's "Paragraphs on Conceptual Art," published in a 1967 issue of *Artforum*, shifted the emphasis from the artwork to its idea: "The idea becomes a machine that makes the art." Kosuth, who in Peter Osborne's view differed from Sol LeWitt as a "strong conceptualist," summarized his creed in the famous statement "Art is the definition of art," which may be said about modern art in general, however, as we will see below.

Marcel Broodthaers, the Belgian poet-artist, practiced in the same years what Danto would call an "institutional theory of art." He defined art by its institutional setting rather than by its visual expression. His installation for the 5th Documenta in 1972 turned the real museum space into the metaphorical space of modern art by using inscriptions on the four walls. In the center you saw an invisible work, or rather the exhibition site for such a work, marked by a precinct with fence. The floor inscription within the fence read "Private Property," and thus ironically identified the site as a protected zone. Its message distinguished the exhibition site as a part of museum property one had to keep out of. The distinction between art and nonart, in this case, did not rely on theory but on the institution, and thus was the museum's privilege.

Broodthaers thus "exhibited" an idea of art that one might call institutional and that was indifferent to mere visuality. You were required to control what you saw with the site where you saw it. The history of art looked suddenly like a mere memory in Broodthaers's posthistorical mirror. Art making and art theory did not represent different projects any longer. One might speak of meta-art that permanently questioned its own status. Art itself had taken leave from any "progressive historical narrative," to recall Danto's definition, and became either a retrospective project or else a departure for areas and aims never explored before. The German group Zero emphasized by its very name a zero hour in art when everything was new and a mythical beginning was promised. The "end of art" of which Danto spoke was the approaching end of modernism.

[3]

The general art public in the 1960s, however, would mistake the common target of such activities as the deconstruction of the artwork, whatever the single movements otherwise had in mind. The opposition to the traditional items of exhibition, even to exhibition in the first place, seemed to be shared by artists otherwise very distinct in their behavior and concepts. Since the artwork had been so solemnly reconsecrated by recent modernism, the new art scene looked like deliberate iconoclasm, like a bunch of movements "against" rather than movements in their own right. It seemed to announce the end of art, whereas modernism, by contrast, looked like the last stronghold of lofty ideals. This forced opposition, with its dualistic note, needs to be thoroughly revised, however, as it tends to purify modernism in retrospect and to dismiss its inherent conflicts.

This brings me to my second topic. The old debates over "art and life" reveal the desperate attempts to escape from the usual framework of exhibition art. In fact, modernism entertained an endogene and permanent crisis that, however, is not to be confused with failure. The crisis fueled creative potentials and served a project oriented toward the future that never was satisfied with even the most audacious experiments. As a result, modernism's total contrast with the 1960s does not stand up to closer inspection. On the contrary, the new art scene entertained problems with a long incubation period. The tension between idea and form, between art and the artwork, which had lingered for so long, now demanded radical solutions.

Modernist artists for so long had intended artworks to represent *art* in its own right rather than to represent something *with art*. But to represent art was tantamount to representing representation or else to representing the unrepresentable. Ideas by definition defy any simple equation with formal and visual qualities. The modern artwork thus emerged as a hybrid. As an object, it both attracted and resisted the desire to convert it into an idea. But the narratives of modern art usually isolated artistic form (style, innovation) as the purpose and target of change and progress. As a result, they dismissed important reasons underlying this continuing unrest. We cannot address these large issues here, as our aim is more modest. It may be sufficient to select a small number of modernist strategies that reveal the same urge to escape the artwork as had materialized in traditional genres like painting and sculpture.

Marcel Duchamp is the obvious choice in this respect, but he is all too often treated as the one exception from the mainstream, which he was not. Among the comments in the *White Box* is the question whether "works can be made which are not *of art*." In the 1960s, such a remark would have been turned the other way around: can art be made that does not consist of works? Duchamp was one of the first to discuss the crucial link between art as an idea and the artwork as an object. In a later commentary, *The*

Large Glass was reduced to a mere "delay" before the penetrating gaze would look through it. The work, as a brief rest for the searching eye, turned into an allegory of itself. Physical creation was preceded and partly replaced by conceptual invention. The borderline between interpretation and its object tended to dissolve. The artist's written explications even preceded the work instead of following its completion. Incidentally, the project coincided with the famous theft of the *Mona Lisa* from the Louvre, which caused such relief among artists. The thief had not stolen the idea of the picture. He only carried the object with him and left behind the empty glass, which may have inspired Duchamp's imagination to concentrate on the glass alone.

In the same years, Kasimir Malevich crossed out a *Mona Lisa* print in a postcubistic picture. He had welcomed its theft and therefore complained about its return to the Louvre as an anachronism that led him to erase the emblem of an obsolete ideal. When he devised a new type of exhibition in the 0.10 show, which opened in 1915 in St. Petersburg, the *Black Square* dominated his own room as the true icon of nonfigurative suprematism or as the icon of an idea. From then on, he did not care to exhibit his pictures upside down or mirror reversed. They came in serial production and, as specimens of a cosmic idea, were meant to float freely through an imaginary space. One had to look at them with spiritual eyes. In a telling gesture, Malevich declared the *Black Square*, despite its late origin, to be the very archetype of his whole production up to that date. In a letter written in 1927, the painter insisted that he had finally "extirpated" the old picture and extracted pure emotion from it. "The world as sensation, the ideas are the purpose of art. A square is not a picture, much as the switch or the plug are not the current. Whoever saw a picture in my icon, committed an error, since he mistook the plug for an image of the current," or, in other words, mistook the artwork for art.

Vassilij Kandinsky, again a few years earlier, had definitely other ideals and even would become the victim in a clash with the progresssivists in Moscow. But he was also driven by the obsession to liberate "the spiritual" or the spirit of art from any materiality. In his view, the very idea of art had finally become visible in "abstraction," where it was detached from any other representational purpose. He relied on a most influential, but arbitrary identification of pure form as conceptual, in that it was thought to represent art as an idea. His text, "My Career," announced the arrival of an art "that had never been personified [he uses this telling term] before." In its "essential abstraction, it still awaits to be embodied." Form, as a result, was to function as the agent of the idea. In his desire to compete with musical composition and even to transfer the theories of harmony to visual art, he began to number his works and classify them as "compositions" rather than mere "improvisations," which he regarded as exercises. However, he remained under the spell of an artwork that was to prove his own art.

[4]

Did Picasso also join this scenario where the familiar art production time and again looked uncertain and unwelcome? He seems at first to have been the most unlikely person ever to be affected by concerns of theory, and yet it is tempting to include him in the company of all those who looked for alternatives to the usual gallery production and felt under pressure to make art outside mainstream practices. Even in his cubist period, when he was acclaimed the victor in the modernist game, he sometimes felt most uncertain about painting or, for that matter, sculpture as a continuing exercise. In the summer of 1913, he made premature attempts to exchange easel painting for what would become space installation. Four years later, he chose the theater stage for what would become performance in the future. In the ballet *Parade*, he decided on the *première*, the inauguration in a theater, to present his new art and turned against the monopoly of the *vernissage*, the gallery opening.

Let us first consider the cubist period. In the installation attempt, a painted guitar player pretended to play on a real guitar: the player is part of the canvas, while his arms reach out from the canvas and seem to hold the physical instrument. The still life on the small table, with its wine bottle, newspaper, and pipe, conjures the real presence of a living artist against his metaphorical counterpart in the picture. The disorder in the living room represents the rhythm of real life, while the stylized order of the painting keeps the distance of art. The exit from the flat canvas, which half a century later would have qualified easily for an exhibition, survives in the memory of photographs. And yet the photographs are not restricted to a mere recording but inaugurate a new type of art which, via a series of transformations, occupies a middle position between painting, photography, and stage setting.

For this purpose, the artist cut one of the photographs along the outlines of the picture that dominated the installation space. In addition, he worked with his own brush on this hybrid of painting and photograph. The new print merges with the picture surface so as to abolish the difference between the photograph *of* a picture and the picture. Such interventions brought about a painted photograph or a photographic painting, thus undermining the artwork's identity. This exercise was not just idle play, but revealed the impulse to leave behind the established boundaries of any expected standard and to make a work, as indiscernible as a genre, transparent to its idea. In a later step, the artist covered up parts of the negative with paper masks, and thus in the darkroom created prints that combined photographic materials with nonexposed, white photo paper. The photograph now takes over the canvas and exchanges exposure for brush strokes. The ingenuous exercise also puts the relation of artwork and artist to the test. Picasso commented on this relation in a paradoxical performance when he posed for a photograph in front of the painted guitar player. The metaphoric guitar player here continues the old game of painting, but the living guitar player confronts him in real space.

The discovery of Picasso's photographic work has changed the familiar views of the artist, since he chose photography for reasons and aims distinct from those of drawing and painting: it served more of a self-reflexive than a creative attitude. Anne Baldassari reminds us also of his photographic still lifes that match the painted ones. Picasso began "to do constructions. He did *natures mortes* and took photographic pictures of them," to quote Gertrude Stein. Most of his later self-portraits are photographic, and they use the studio as an allegorical stage for conveying discursive messages. A telling example is the famous photograph from 1909 where he sits in the midst of his acquisitions from African and Oceanic sculpture, whose magical presence causes his inquiring glance. They were indeed irreconcilable with his own art production. Primitivism revealed an open wound in the flank of modernism, as it attested a frustrated nostalgia for art's lost power. Ultimately, it could not be a solution merely to borrow "primitive" *style*. The myth of art's origin haunted the modernists, who felt their own work devalued in the encounter with non-Western art.

The most radical departure from the authority of the single artwork happened in Picasso's old age, however, when he produced endless variants of Delacroix's *Women of Alger* or Velasquez's *Meninas*. The serial production of ever the same picture, which he chose from the history of art, never leads to the same result and thus undermines the very notion of the artwork. The liberating performance also abolished distinctions such as "preliminary study," "variation," and "copy." He freely produced arbitrary studies *after* a given work rather than studies *for* a work. This means that he reversed the usual creative process and deconstructed a museum piece by making art from art. By *remaking* Delacroix or Velasquez with his own brush, without copying them, he definitely took a *posthistorical* stance, not in the sense of the end of art but in the sense of an art beyond and without history. Thus, he undermined the visual identity of the artwork and contrasted the free gesture of painting with the physiognomy of famous pictures. His strategies in the late 1950s went unnoticed, however, or were misunderstood even by Nelson Goodman, who classified them with musical analogies.

[5]

The theater had become another escape from showing the artwork as a stereotype in a gallery. Picasso's theater period, which began in May 1917 when *Parade* was performed by the Ballets Russes, usually is treated as marginal or as an extravagant digression. But it looks different in our context and in the light of the uproar that it caused in modernist circles. His contemporaries all agreed in attributing a leading part to Picasso, who won over the ideas of the playwright (Jean Cocteau) and choreographer (Léonide Massine) and only spared the professional rights of the composer (Erik Satie). Thus, the visual artist used the stage for an unexpected performance outside his territory. The escape from the gallery to the stage was preceded by Malevich's participation in the opera *Victory Over the Sun*, performed in 1913 in St. Petersburg, and by Kandinsky's spectacle *The Yellow Sound*, where the stage represented color as mirrored by the sound of music. In the Bauhaus, the relation between art and stage became a major issue and caused a lot of controversies.

It therefore deserves special attention that Picasso, driven by a conflict with his own cubism, embarked on an unprecedented *Commedia dell'Arte* that escaped the control of the avant-garde veterans. The so-called "Manager" figures, in their strange cubist costumes, appeared like living still lives and collage canvases paradoxically walked across the stage. The big red curtain, painted in tempera and only visible during the time of Satie's overture, was easily mistaken for a specimen of Picasso's neorealism. Since then, we have understood that Picasso was one of the first to transgress the boundary lines between high and low art in that he approached mass media on a popular level. His painted harlequins are like stereotypes, as if they had been produced by mechanical tools, and thus turn against the creed of the creative artist.

The conflict with the avant-garde scene became public when Picasso, in the spring of 1924, presented his last stage piece, the ballet *Mercure*. The spectacle consisted of not only stage props and dancers but also genuine Picasso paintings, or rather, cutouts that behaved like actors and were moved around by invisible dancers acting from behind. In Picasso's words, *"poses plastiques"* replaced the actors of a piece. The result was strongly rejected by the art world, which, with the notorious exception of the surrealists, protested against Picasso's "betrayal." André Breton used this welcome opportunity to defend the freedom of an artist, who embodied the "modern unrest" (*inquietude*) in art. It was the *artwork* that Picasso seemed to have betrayed by the choice of a real stage and also by comedylike dance that set painting in motion. The joke had deeper roots, however. Picasso, who would soon start illustrating Balzac's discouraging novel *The Unknown Masterpiece*, was discussed at the time as an outdated champion of modernism who looked for an escape from his isolation among the ranks of the old avant-garde.

The surrealists, in turn, were heading to new frontiers where painters and writers joined forces and developed common projects for the first time. Such attempts culminated more than a decade later in the First International Exhibition, which the surrealists opened on January 17, 1938, in the Galerie des Beaux Arts in Paris. The participating artists and writers, sixty in number, did not deliver a studio production but introduced exhibits of an unusual type, such as improvised props and *objets trouvés*. Most of what was seen on this occasion would today qualify as site-specific. Bags with coals were hanging down from the ceiling and a carpet with wilted leaves bordered a pond with water lilies. The main area resembled a mysterious cave rather than an exhibition site. Snails were creeping over the plants, and loudspeakers roared with the terrible noise of marching Nazi troops. The exhibition space, which had become a premature installation space, abolished the distinction between art and spectacle or art and nonart. Free gestures and exotic impressions replaced the usual sight of art. The exhibition had turned against its own purpose, in that it departed from exhibiting artworks while entertaining a conceptual approach of art.

This exhibition was not merely an occasion for surrealist games; it reveals an important and general issue for my subject. It introduced modernism's permanent struggle with the idea of art against the making of artworks. Seen in this light, the split between modernism and its aftermath is in need of revision. It may be conceded that the competition between art and art theory after 1960 became much more intense and shifted the frontiers between them. The problems existed before, but now demanded a solution. The artwork, in its hybrid character as a made object that represents an idea, the idea of art, provides access to a subtext of modern art whose explosive character came into the open after the 1960s.

The philosophy of art, as Danto shaped it, reformulated the task of art theory in a time when art in turn laid claims on the domain of theory.

֍ ֍ ֍ ֍ ֍

Response

I cannot pretend that I entirely understood what I meant by "theory" when, in 1964, I wrote that to see something as art "requires something the eye cannot decry—an atmosphere of artistic theory, a knowledge of the history of art: an artworld." But I do know that by "an artworld" I did not mean what the term came to mean for those who developed the Institutional Theory of Art—though their use of "theory" was close to what I had in mind, even if I had no use for the particular definition they advanced. For me, "artworld" in that essay designated the world of artworks—everything that satisfied the criteria for being a work of art. Hence paintings and sculptures, for starters, and then certain buildings, texts, musical works. It would have been obvious to readers of "The Artworld" that the criteria would not have been *perceptual*, which is what made the artworld of 1964 philosophically so challenging, since many of the objects it included resembled to a remarkable degree many of the things it excluded. *Brillo Box* and Brillo boxes would have been a case in point, since they looked so much alike, though the former belonged to the artworld and the latter did not. Of course there were differences—*Brillo Box* was made of fabricated plywood, the Brillo boxes of corrugated cardboard. But I was fairly certain that (x)(y)[if x resembles y except that x is made of plywood and y is made of cardboard, x is art and y is not] is false. The difference between art and reality cannot be handled in that way!

And this is the point about the beds that had begun to turn up in the artworld. Some, to be sure, were components in artworks, such as the plain iron bedstead that George Segal used in one of his sculptural complexes. But many were free-standing, like the one made by Claes Oldenberg, or Robert Rauschenberg's *Bed*, which consisted in a quilt, a sheet, a pillow, all tucked into a wooden frame, but slathered over with pigment and hung on the wall, as if to display the kind of thing the word "bed" designates in English—minus of course the pigment. In the '50s, the mere presence of paint was criterion enough for art, and doubtless Rauschenberg was being ironic. But *Bed* was at once a real bed and a work of art—and since Plato's theory of art in Book X of the *Republic* required that there be a difference, Plato's theory had to be wrong. When I talked about "a knowledge of history and an artistic theory" I would have meant: a history that takes us from Plato to the artworld of 1964, and from Plato's theory of art to something that fit the artistic practice of the times better than that in Book X.

Meanwhile, though the Institutional Theory did not come into existence until after "The Artworld" was published, it was clear that I would have to reject it when it was enunciated. For since there need be no external difference between the bed that is and the bed that is not a work of art, calling one art and the other not must seem exceedingly arbitrary—and all that the Institutional Theory demanded was that something is art if a group of qualified individuals—"experts"—call it that. If that is all there is to the matter, how can they consistently call something art and something exactly like it not art? There has to be some criterion—but the criterion cannot be perceptual.

That set the scene for my analysis. But the analysis was not forthcoming in "The Artworld." I did not have a clear picture of what sort of theory was needed until I began having discussions with George Dickie about my paper and he produced his theory. He described his theory as a definition of art, and I realized that what we needed was a definition—a real definition—of art. I simply rejected his candidate. I wanted a definition of belonging to the art world. He, using "art world" in its accepted sense, defined art as what the art world says is art. My response was: when is the art world right or wrong? And for that, I thought, one needed a definition that did not beg that question.

A classical philosophical definition would provide the kind of answer I thought required to the question "What is art?" and would serve to rebut the declaration that something was not art, especially difficult to do when the differences between artworks and mere real things were for all practical purposes indiscernible. Richard Wollheim, around the same time, coined the term "minimalist" in connection with the Wittgensteinian question of what the minimal criteria are that would enable us to "pick out" objects as works of art, using Malevich's monochrome canvases and Duchamp's *Readymades* as examples. I am not sure that the terms of an adequate definition would constitute criteria, that is, "marks" with reference to which we could pick out the works of art the way we could pick out fresh fish. Examples like *Brillo Box* raised the question of whether there could be criteria, which was why I found the Wittgensteinian approach of little use, as I argue below in my response to Stanley Cavell. But that would in fact strengthen the need for a definition. Hans Belting asks, "What did it mean to speak of a 'certain theory of art'? And did such a theory apply to any art or only to that of the given moment?" The answer to the latter is that the definition must apply to art as art, irrespective of differences and times. That is why, despite my embrace of postmodernist art, mine was not a theory of postmodernist art. I have always been an essentialist, believing that a philosophical definition must apply to art everywhere and always, whatever differences there may in fact be from period to period and culture to culture. "One wonders," Belting writes, "whether there was ever an art theory valid enough to survive its own days." The artworld of the '60s was a golden age for theory, since it became clear that an artwork could look like anything at all. If one found a definition that survived that, one could be reasonably confident that it would survive whatever the future history of art might bring forth. Noel Carroll once criticized my theory of the end of art by saying that I wanted a guarantee that there would be no more counterinstances. The reverse is true: certainty that there would be no future counterinstances is what the end of art *meant*.

Be this as it may, I had no candidate in mind for such a theory in 1964, nor did I even think about the question for the next fifteen years or so. In that time, I published two volumes—*Analytical Philosophy of Knowledge* and *Analytical Philosophy of Action*—that developed aspects of the theory of representation that I had decided was the defining concept of philosophy. It was not until the late 1970s that I felt ready to take on an analytical philosophy of art—except that I did not want to use that as a title. I called it instead *The Transfiguration of the Commonplace*, a ready-made title, since I had found it in a novel by Muriel Spark. I was taken by the religious connotation of "transfiguration" since the *Brillo Box*/Brillo box distinction struck me as resembling the god/human being distinction in the case of Christ, who, to all outward appearances, was just a human being. He was a god to the eye of faith but a human being to the eye as such. He displays himself as Himself—as transfigured—in the Saint Matthew Gospel. But there is, despite Walter Benjamin's concept of "aura," no radiant halo surrounding *Brillo Box*, which will serve as a mark—a criterion—of arthood. So I had to begin with what I knew in advance is invisible.

There are two components in the theory, so far as I was able to carry the analysis in that book. Something is a work of art if it has a meaning—is about something—and if it embodies its meaning. Both of these would be invisible, so as far as the observation of the object goes, ascription to it of the status of art could be wrong. But I was interested in ontology, not epistemology. Christ, if God, would have been God even if no one accepted him as such, and he had gone to his crucifixion with his larger identity invisible. Whether these conditions were sufficient, I cannot say with certainty. But it will help here to outline briefly the difference between a work of art A and an indiscernible real thing T. A has two components—a material object O that resembles T, and a meaning M, which is related to T roughly in the way the soul relates to the body. To say that M is embodied in O requires an interpretation that connects M with various of O's properties. Not every property of O, however, is part of M. Let's consider one of Malevich's works that Belting mentions, his *Black Square* of 1915. It is a squarish black shape painted on a white square. In fact the black paint has become cracked, because of Malevich's indifference to his materials or just because of the way time has treated the pigment. It is certainly part of the material object, but is it part of the work? In my view, *craquelure* is inconsistent with the idea of suprematism, which intended that *Black Square* be regarded as a "specimen of a cosmic idea . . . meant to float freely through an imaginary space" and was meant to be looked at "with spiritual eyes," to borrow Belting's language. The work, tethered (as we are) to its material component, is subject to humiliating degradations. But seen through spiritual eyes, it flies freely and immaculately through space. So the cracks, though part of O, are not really part of M and hence have to be subtracted from our experience of *Black Square*. Jonathan Gilmore has observed that plywood is not part of the meaning of *Brillo Box* but is part of the meaning of certain of Donald Judd's "specific objects." Experiencing art requires such interpretation. "See the canvas as empty space" is an injunction through which one can begin to experience one of Malevich's suprematist paintings as he intended them to be.

Belting reads one of Duchamp's comments in *The White Box*—whether "works can be made which are not of *art*"—as "can art be made that does not consist of works?" As I read this, it is the question of whether one can make art that does not require a material component, that consists in some sort of pure idea. When Hegel spoke of the end of art, he meant, among other things, to contrast art with philosophy, which is not dependent upon the senses, the way art is. For Hegel, nothing could be art that was not sensed, and that was art's inescapable limitation. Could Duchamp have been attempting to meet Hegel's challenge by creating an art of pure ideation? Replacing works with the idea of art alone? "Physical creation was preceded and partly replaced by conceptual invention," Belting writes. It is true that Duchamp expressed an aversion to visual gratification, but that was a version of an antiaesthetic rather than antimaterial perspective. Most of his work emphatically involves materials, and is subject to the schematism I have just sketched. Consider the question of whether the notorious cracking of the glass in *Large Glass* is part of the work or merely part of the object. It seems to me that this has to be treated exactly as the *craquelure* is in *Black Square*. When Ulf Linde undertook to replicate *Large Glass,* he did not attempt to duplicate the cracks, despite which Duchamp signed the work when he visited Stockholm. And though he repudiated what he considered "retinal art," he did not repudiate the art of the past, which he said was not primarily concerned with retinal gratification, but was religious, philosophical, historical, and the like.

The need for a definition of art was made urgent by the art of the '60s, bent as so much of it was on "overcoming the gap between art and life." Belting has written a compelling essay on how many artists, within the framework of modernism, made art that was intended to dissolve the object, Tinguely's 1960 *Homage à New York* being a case in point. But you need an object to create a self-destroying work of art! So it seems to me that his examples are entirely congruent with my definition or "theory." Many artists were interested in creating art outside the commercial framework, or outside the context of the museum, or whatever. Dennis Oppenheim describes a wedge he had made inside a mountain in Oakland. "And this did two things. It first of all created an immobile, ephemeral, nonrigid form, but it also created a sculpture bound to its location. There became the question of where exactly is the object. If that hole is an object or if a hole is an object, then is it the indentation or the periphery?" It was certainly a work that could not be transported to a museum—but you need a hill in order to have that specific hole. Lawrence Wiener made a work consisting of a hole in a wall—but you could not remove the hole and take it someplace else; you could only re-create it. The plywood boxes that Robert Morris exhibited in the Green Gallery in 1964—and that I discussed in "The Artworld" that year—were destroyed afterward, but subsequently re-created. Judy Chicago's minimalist pieces, exhibited under her name as Judy Gorowitz in *Primary Structures* at the Jewish Museum in 1966, were destroyed by the artist when she began to make deliberately feminist art—but she recently re-created and exhibited them. Robert Rauschenberg erased an important drawing by De Kooning, and the erased drawing is preserved in a gold frame and shown in historical surveys of American art. Robert Barry released several gases into the desert in 1969. It was obviously difficult to retrieve the gas, but the work was exactly as material as gas itself is.

Many young artists today speak of themselves as conceptual artists, but usually this is to distinguish themselves from painters. In the early '80s there was a movement on the part of certain theorists who spoke of the

Death of Painting, and for various ideological reasons, painting came into disrepute in that period. But I can think of no one who attempts to dispense with material objects. There has been immense expansion of the materials available to artists in recent times—lard and elephant dung being two much-discussed cases. They certainly raise problems for the kind of truth-to-medium injunctions that Greenberg introduced in 1960. But my definition is hospitable to come what may. And so far as conceptuality is concerned, the other component of the definition—meaning—is perhaps as much as is needed to cover all the art of the past. So "embodied meanings"—which I used as a title for one of my books—will carry us a pretty long way. There may be a third condition—as there definitely is a fourth condition in the definition of knowledge. But I have argued, in *The Abuse of Beauty*, that there is no aesthetic condition, however historically important aesthetical qualities are and have been in the history of art.

I have but scratched the surface of Hans Belting's richly informed essay, mainly to remove what I consider misunderstandings of my philosophical intentions. With these removed as objects of criticism, we can appreciate his scholarship, without having to suppose that his wonderful discussions of Picasso, for example, entail the need for philosophical revision on my part. Philosophical clarification is another matter, and I have tried to provide that here.

7
The Sell-By Date

Daniel Herwitz

[1]

There is a certain risk in giving a philosophical reading of the very history one has lived, especially if that history seems to have culminated in one's lap, in the manner of a gift. The astonishment at being the first witness can be oceanic, suffusing the view of the entire world with a sense of millennial energy. One's story of it all becomes the central account, for history has placed one, by coincidence or destiny, at the center. From there may follow the almost irresistible belief that the rest of the world's histories can be read from one's own, as if they were the outer branches of an enormous, ancient banyan tree. Or alternately, other histories pass beyond the pale altogether.

Arthur Danto's philosophy of art is so important to the latter half of the twentieth century that I for one cannot imagine philosophizing about plastic art apart from it. His writing about the avant-gardes more than anyone else's has caused my generation to think about the putatively philosophical character of that art, about its historical explanation, and about its relevance for the philosophical definition of art. His views have been so surprising, so original, that we have felt them to be of a piece with the originality and scandal of the avant-gardes themselves: Danto is an avant-garde philosopher of the avant-gardes. Many of us have considered him *the* starting point in approaching the contemporary art world. Towering figures are figures to admire but also about whom to think critically. Arthur's generosity is such that he understands it is an homage to him when one does both. In a philosophical world sometimes preoccupied with the litigious defense of tiny positions, his is a big spirit ready to entertain ideas rather than kill them off with cleverness before they can germinate. His art criticism—written largely for *The Nation* magazine and collected in a number of volumes—is about local context; his philosophy seeks universality of scope. He seeks a philosophical definition about the general conditions according to which objects can be rightly called "art." For him this is a matter of the body of theory behind the object, not, as it were, the object itself. It is the theory that allows a "real thing" to become a work of art. This theory is historically evolving in ways that alter the kinds of things that can become art, and—related—the kinds of statements artworks can make. Beginning from Hegel's commonplace that not all things are possible at any given place and time, Danto works out how the conditions for the possibility of a kind of art—representational, expressive, etc.—are historically datable. His philosophical reading of art history is about these changes, from representational art to the present, through which kinds of art formerly beyond the pale become possible, and conversely things once possible fall away.

Arthur's most recent formulation of this view can be found, I think, in the book that came out of his Mellon Lectures at the National Gallery in the 1990s. There he formulates the claim in a way that is somewhat critical of his earlier view:

My concern in [my "The Artworld"] . . . was with works of art that so resemble ordinary objects that perception cannot seriously discriminate between them. The thesis was enunciated thus: "To see something as art requires something the eye cannot decry—an atmosphere of artistic theory, a knowledge of the history of art: an artworld." . . . I now think what I wanted to say was this: a knowledge of what other works the given work fits with, a knowledge of what other works make a given work possible. My interest was in the somewhat attenuated objects of contemporary art—the *Brillo Box*, or Robert Morris' very uninflected sculpture. . . . These objects had few interesting affinities with anything in the history of art . . . my thought in "The Artworld" was that no one unfamiliar with history or with artistic theory could see these as art, and hence it was the history and the theory of the object, more than anything palpably visible, that had to be appealed to in order to see them as art.[1]

The earlier thesis, based on a remarkably inventive use of the old philo-sophical saw about the identity of indiscernibles, proposed that what makes Warhol's *Brillo Box* art, as opposed to its supermarket cousin, is nothing the eye can discern, since both *Brillo Box* and the Brillo box in the store are (to all intents and purposes) visually the same, yet one is art, the other not. Hence the art-making property, the thing that makes *Brillo Box* art while leaving the box in the store out of this category, must be nonper-ceptual. That property is, it seemed reasonable to say, a theory. Reasonable because the histories of art had become clearly theoretical in the twentieth century, playing games with theory and highlighting its crucial role in jacking up their meanings, values, and politics,[2] and because what was happening in the philosophies of language and science at the time Danto wrote was a turn toward identifying meaning and belief with theory. W. V. O. Quine famously argued that vocables and scribbles become words and sentences on account of a web of theory held true by a speech com-munity. Since artworks on Danto's account are the kinds of things that make statements, it seemed natural to extrapolate this idea to aesthetics, and to say that just as linguistic meaning is supervenient upon perception (of utterances, marks on paper, the world), so meaning in art, and hence art itself, is supervenient upon its perceptual properties. Both are the kinds of things they are—language or art—in virtue of a web of theory held by a speech community, or in Danto's case, an art world.

Warhol's work seemed tailor-made to be a demonstration of the point. The difference, Arthur instructed readers like myself, between the two ob-jects, *Brillo* and Brillo, given the immensity of their similarities, was that the one made a statement about its relationship to the other, while the other remained essentially mute about everything. The one was proposi-tional, the other not. This was what placed the Warhol in the ballpark of art, rather than its supermarket prototype. Scribbles do not acquire mean-ings through mere perception but rather in virtue of a conceptual back-ground; Warhol's object gets its meaning from the background of theory held by the art world. The work implicitly *demonstrated* all this. Warhol laid the groundwork for Danto's own words, as if Warhol already sort of "knew it" behind the dark glasses. There is a clarity about Warhol's work that Danto alone saw in 1964. What makes it fine art is not only its one-of-a-kind status, but more than that, its complex *questioning*, its invocation of thought as well as its refusal of thought, its ambivalent game playing, its conceptual magic, its parodic hilarity. None of which applies to the super-market prototype, and all of which are located in a distinctively modernist regime of art making and reception, rooted in the history of Dada, surrealism, Duchamp, Rauchenberg, Clement Greenberg, and so forth: what Danto calls "the artworld." Were one to ascribe a similar conceptual background to the mass-produced box in the supermarket, one would be willing to call it also fine art.

That Danto could presume Warhol to have been implicitly in the same business as himself, that he could believe Warhol's work succeeded in demonstrating the essence of art for all times and places, was about as audacious as Warhol's own antics. I think of Danto as very much akin to Warhol: they share a similar modernist sensibility, playfulness, capacity for imaginative scandal. I mean the Warhol who presumed to produce works of art so close to the landscape of signage that it was only the dazzling hand of the artist himself that would spell out whatever differences, small or large, could be found between his own work and commodities and signs. Warhol's art seemed a stroke of genius for a world so permeated by the icons of film that Jackie O. could be embalmed by his silk screens in the way Egyptians once were in sarcophagi. His was a response to a commodified world in which signs and advertisements were also themselves kinds of art, including the Brillo box (the one in the store), which had been designed by an abstract expressionist painter, thus already half collapsing the distinction between industrial and fine art, between art and ad, between painting and selling. Warhol, commercial-turned-fine artist, well understood the slippage between these categories, the overlap between them.

Danto noted something important in noting that Warhol's work differs from the supermarket Brillo box in virtue of its voice, a voice only possible because of the art world behind it. But commercial art also has its forms of rhetoric, and fine art is also in its way commercial, so is there a distinction of essence between types or kinds? Suppose one wanted to discover what the essence of a man was, and decided to do it by distinguishing man from woman. What would one say, philosophically I mean, given that both are human, each is "involved" with the other, there are many "overlaps," etc.? I want to acknowledge the work of Stanley Cavell, another contributor to the present volume, by reciting the ending of the film *Adam's Rib*, concerned as it is with such a conundrum. Here it is: Pinky with a *y*, a.k.a. Adam Bonner, a.k.a. Spencer Tracy is told by his wife Pinkie with an *ie*, a.k.a. Amanda Bonner, a.k.a. Katherine Hepburn—with whom he has just been reunited after standing on the brink of divorce—"men, women, the same." "The same, huh?" Adam asks, skeptically. To which Amanda replies, "Well, maybe a little different," provoking from Adam a gleam of the Spencer Tracey Irish eye and the words, "Well, as the French say, *Vive la difference!*" When asked to translate, Adam ends the film by saying, "It means hurrah for that little difference!" and dives at Amanda with Chevalier aplomb and Yankee straightforwardness to do the unmentionable. The curtain closes and we are left at the end of the film with the question of what counts as a little difference and what a big difference, and indeed how little versus big, male versus female, *y* versus *ie*, are to be sorted out.

The question is, given the collapse of those essentialized differences between the sexes sustained only through social institutions—law and marriage—whether monosyllabic differences in the endings of pet names and other related pudenda can be demonstrated to count for big or little, to which the film supplies a skeptical answer. Most importantly, the film argues that this epistemological obscurity cannot be discussed apart from the fact of human desire. "*Vive la difference,*" Adam says, not answering the question of whether men and women are the same but displacing it, dissolving it, accepting its nagging character. What he is saying is that he cannot understand the nature of these differences apart from his desire— for her, for women, for his wife. Desire is predicated on similarities and differences but also creates them, assigns them values, makes them sustainable and livable. Or not.

I think that if Warhol is philosophical, it is because his work voices a similar love or desire about *its* partner, the Brillo box in the supermarket from which it differs by a small, almost indiscernible, increment, that of an *ie* to a *y*, microscopic, like differences in DNA. The questions that Warhol's work raises flow from its enmeshment in such supermarket products, specifically in this supermarket product (its double). *Brillo Box* flirts with the Brillo box in the supermarket. It impersonates it, tries it on (as in a garment), plays with it, enjoys doubling it. Perhaps they are of the same sex, the same gender, the same disposition, this pair of boxes. Do their differences count as small or large, tiny or stupendous, given all they share? There is surely no clear, univocal, essential answer to this question.

It will be retorted that while Warhol's work is free to entangle itself with the supermarket box, the supermarket box remains mute. It is engaged in no spirited discourse with Warhol's work, and that is the difference. Works of art are prepositional (they say and imply things); mere commodities aren't. Were one to exhibit the supermarket box in a gallery, in the manner of some conceptual artist, that might be sufficient to give it "voice," but as it happens, the thing is meant to be used—not displayed, appreciated, treated in some romping, Duchamping manner as the voice of art, the take-off on the gallery, the whatever on whatever.

True, but again not quite, for to repeat: the Brillo box was made by an abstract expressionist painter, and who is to say that it does or does not commune with abstract expressionist art? Although its purpose is consumption, its texture is not, one could argue, free of voice. Warhol's designs have become canonical for a whole design industry these days that "refers" to Warhol, whether in the design studio or on the supermarket shelf.

Now it is a feature of the way Danto sets up the problem of the identity of indiscernibles that "for all intents and purposes" Warhol's box is visually identical to its supermarket cousin. This is meant to prove that nothing perceptual spells out the reason one is art while the other is not. But it is worth noting that the playful, zany, comic, provocative voice of *Brillo Box* depends on its oversized and partly painted character. The gesture would have been provocative enough were the objects he chose to exhibit (in the manner of some conceptual artist) actually the same as those in the supermarket, say, in the manner of Duchamp's *Readymades*. Warhol chose otherwise, and this has a great deal to do with the character of desire, of flirtation, of impersonation in his work, along with its refusal to finally depart from the domain of painted objects, of those things that are *fato a mano* (made by hand). What Arthur says in the recent Mellon Lectures is quite different from what he stated in his 1964 essay, "The Artworld." In the Mellon Lectures he states that while the visually distinctive character of the Warhol work does matter, what turns it into art is what he calls a style matrix—a lineage of art work and art theory—and it is more important:

> My thought in "The Artworld" was that no one unfamiliar with history or with artistic theory could see these as art, and hence it was the history and the theory of the object, more than anything palpably visible, that had to be appealed to in order to see them as art.

The style matrix into which the art world places an object is more important than the object's palpably visual properties. . . . More significant than, bigger than, a *y* as opposed to an *ie*. No longer are visual properties excluded from having a defining role for art: they are simply less important. Now once the formulation is as vague as Property A being greater than Property B, the philosophical position seems as diluted as impossible to verify. Theory and history (the style matrices) count more than what one sees, perhaps for the Warhol, but in general . . . a lot more, a little more, almost the same, very much more? Depending on circumstance? Visual properties, now reenfranchised as essential to art, might for a given case run at 49 percent importance to theory's 51 percent. Sometimes an electoral college might have to be called in to pronounce final judgment about which wins, or there might have to be a Florida recount. Furthermore, having gone this far, why not go the whole way and say that for certain kinds of works, perceptual properties count *more than* theory, and for others, less. And soon enough one will have to ask how theory and the palpably perceptible are to be distinguished from each other. For by the lights of many, percept and concept are beyond a certain point not clearly distinguishable.

I should like to point out that even for Duchamp's *Readymades*, which really are visually indiscernible from things bought in the store (since they *are* things bought in the store), the visual properties blend with the style matrix in complex ways to establish the art. One part of the gag is just to highlight (conceptually) the importance of exhibition, of the institutions of art and the expectations of art publics, in blessing things (Duchamp would quip, absurdly) with the aura of art. Another part of the gag is to show how visual signs can take on new, poetic meanings, almost become parts of language, when exhibited under certain aspects. So a hat rack becomes the hair of Medusa, the tentacles of sex, the hard currency of feigned eroticism; a shovel stands in for a Potts (lower arm, a.k.a. snow shovel) fracture, and so on. The visual and the conceptual make music together. Which is "more important" seems a question we are epistemically unfit to answer.

This leads to a final point: Danto still leaves out the importance of institutions, systems, and practices for the constitution of art—the museum, the gallery, economy, the entanglement of art in people's lives, in their ceremonies, discourses, warmongering, nationalism, memorializations, weddings, ways of dwelling: the *world* in which the art world—that distinctive element of modern life—is set. These factors are crucially part of what produces a style matrix. Factoring them in, one returns to the thought variously posed by Richard Wollheim and Stanley Cavell, after Wittgenstein: that what makes something art is nothing less than the larger form of life that is its background. To imagine an artwork is to imagine a form of life.

[2]

If the scope of what Warhol showed pertains to all the arts, then it is an interesting question why plastic art should have hit on it. Consider film, where it would be fantastical to imagine that the medium should have arrived at this demonstration. For the film image is clearly distinguished from its sources in reality by its two-dimensional character. Film is light cast onto a flat screen, if also an uncanny double of the quiddities from which it is shot and composed. Grasping this uncanny relation of things between two and three dimensions is no more, if also no less, theoretical than grasping the difference between things in mirrors, *camera obscura*, and their sources in three-dimensional space and time. What you see in film is *a world* defined by landscape, cityscape, and human physiognomy, even if, like certain Southern Africans exposed to film for the first time, you might initially believe it the sacred world of ancestors rather than the machine translation of quotidian realities. Some shift in belief is then required to come to know what film is.

It has been fundamental to the astonishment—the philosophical wonder—of film that the recognition of metaphysical difference between things on film and things in quotidian reality has gone hand in hand with their seeming indiscernibility. When Charlie Chaplin goes berserk on the assembly line and rushes about wrenching everything in sight, including the nose of a fellow worker and the nipples of a large woman walking outside the factory, we feel that we are seeing *him* on screen, not a virtual image created out of nothing. The importance of human *physiognomy* for film art was noted as early as 1934 by Erwin Panofsky, who went so far as to say that the medium of film is physical reality itself, meaning that Chaplin's body is to the art of film as Michelangelo's marble is to his sculpture. The puzzle is therefore to explain Chaplin's presence to the viewer, since the viewer of Michelangelo's *David* can actually *touch* the marble, while no film viewer can touch Chaplin on screen—or off, for that matter.

Cavell describes the situation in these terms: the world in film is present to the viewer; however, the viewer is absent from what is happening on screen. This is an asymmetry not true of ordinary perception, where viewer and viewed are, metaphysically, in the same spatial relationship. Cary Grant may be present on screen to us, but we can in no way be present to him in the way we might have been had we met him (as I was lucky to do with Greta Garbo on a street in Midtown Manhattan in the 1960s). This relationship to things on screen is, I submit, not discerned through belonging to an art world. Cavell calls the recognition an automatism, meaning that it shares the automatic character of human perception. If the eye is in good working order, it is an apparatus that has no choice (or severely circumscribed choice) about what it sees. Open your eyes in the desert and what you see is brown earth, packed tight and strident in the shimmering sun, leading to a vista of flat, endless horizontality, with low-lying cumulous clouds. You cannot choose to see this if you are in the middle of Arizona on a clear day any more than you can choose to breathe. The act of perception is, as Kant put it, as passive as it is spontaneous. This passivity also pertains to the film image. One opens one's eyes and simply sees Chaplin rushing about. One does not choose, on account of a harmonization between the film apparatus, the editorial hand, and the human eye and mind.

It follows that what is important to making Chaplin's film *poetry*, that is, art, is just what is palpably visible about his face, his body, his movement—which is why Chaplin immediately became a hit in Calcutta, Tokyo, and Montevideo, and for all classes of people, for men and women, for children and old people. To follow Chaplin's high-speed antics and virtuoso timing requires having a human mind. It requires the capacity to follow the simple, heartfelt story, including a capacity for sympathy. These recognitional capacities are conceptual as well as perceptual. What is *not* required is belonging to a movie world, with anything like the complex theories and appeals to lineage the modernist art world has been built upon. Chaplin creates solidarity, he does not depend upon an existent community of taste and theory, membership in which may be required to appreciate and understand the recent work of, say, Jean-Luc Godard. This means that art is a more general phenomenon than that of art worlds and cannot be defined in terms of them. Art worlds are specific kinds of historical shapes: that of Parisian modernity from Manet to Godard, for example.

Now one could imagine a Danto/Warhol scandal arising in film history were that history to technologically evolve to the point where Chaplin could be virtually replicated—convincingly reinvented by computer—in new roles. Such technological means are not far off. New viewers would not, could not know whether they were watching Chaplin or his virtual double, unless apprised of the fact. Virtual reality of this kind would astonish viewers and ring significant changes in the nature of the film medium, for it would challenge the viewer's automatic perceptual belief that she is seeing real things—e.g., Chaplin's own face—shining through in the film image. The viewer's accommodation to this state of affairs would be perceptual, conceptual, and additudinal. The point would not, however, affect the centrality of the *palpably visible* in making film into poetry. Chaplin or his virtual double would still appear physiognomically; this is what would continue to make film into art.

The concept of "art" could be restricted to those art objects dependent on art worlds, like Warhol's *Brillo Box* and Duchamp's *Readymades*. That would be a way of marking the difference between Chaplin and his transmissibility and Duchamp. But is Warhol lacking in transmissibility? And for whom? To appreciate Chaplin, perhaps one can be a child; Duchamp, probably not. But there is also a sense in which a kind of appreciation of Chaplin requires belonging to the modern life he inhabits, and in which similar kinds of belonging might well and probably do allow access to Warhol's *Brillo Box* (which, by the way, children might also appreciate). The lines between art worlds and the modern life of which they are part, are too involved and too blurred for a sharp distinction of kind. The germ of truth here is that the problematic of modern art is the problematic of that distinctively modern sociological element, the art world. The condition for the possibility of Danto's theory is the modern formation of the arts he, and Warhol, and Chaplin, are all, differentially, *of.*

[3]

I wish to conclude with some remarks about this distinctive formation: the modern art world. The form of life that gave rise to the European modernists and avant-gardes was, it is well known, urban. The bourgeoisie *flâneur*ed and consumed. The institutions of production (the painter's studio, the architect's office, the craftsperson's atelier) produced, the institutions of exhibition (the museum, the gallery, the Salon des Refusés) exhibited. All were part of a larger pattern of spectacle, speed, commodification, urbanization, nationalism, and industrial capitalization that constituted Parisian—and global—modernity. This market system has proved critical for the formation and very content of modern art. The critical paintings of Edouard Manet could only have arisen because a web of museums, exhibitions, critics, bourgeois interests, and buying and selling was in place in Paris, "capital of the nineteenth century."[3] His work is about this system of gazes, sites of exhibition, modes of valuation, all of which have generated (sociohistorically) the commodity form of art. Modern art has existed in a love-hate relationship with this form, seeking to expel it in mythologies of romanticism, individual genius, Marxist struggle. These have, as often as not, contributed to art's rising price, setting demands for consistent originality while demanding constant flow of "product" with the recognizable artistic logo. Hence the Picasso phenomenon: soaring prices rooted in his achievements of genius, which impose demands of increasing conformity to "the Picasso style," which increasingly becomes marketed as an endless flow of etchings, all of which are more or less exchangeable in value. Warhol's genius was to celebrate, and expose (while also concealing) this system, to revel in his status as icon, logo, advertisement while also revealing how it homogenizes what can here be glossed as "depth" and can else-where be unfolded as idiom. At the same time, nothing is more idiomatic than Warhol, making him the P. T. Barnum of the system, the purveyor of spin as genius, the spinning of genius.

It is a basic fact of expanding markets that the they tend to generate wide variability in product types, given the desire for variation on the part of both maker/sellers and patron/buyers. This is the result of competition, and of the desire for the new (and improved, and cheaper). Modernism was dependent upon an open art market, in spite of its artists stuffed into garrets, its Salons des Refusés, and its oft-stated opposition to (or at least, indifference to) market values. Moreover, the problem of modernism was a market problem: modern artists wished to be the purveyors of value, but their capacity to set value (through talent, experimentation, theory, poli-tics, whatever) is always mitigated by the system itself, the market as a whole, the relation of consumer to producer. There is always a dialectic be-tween the intentions of the artist (her self-ideals about the genius of her achievements), and the expectations, ideals, and seductions of the con-sumer. Both are gestated in relationship (not always easy) to the institu-tions of the museum, the gallery, the critic, the university: the constructs comprising the market. This is fascinating when as hermetic a product as modern art is at stake, where the critic becomes licensed as a middleman, making the art product available to consumers by theorizing it and standing as an exemplar of passion and commitment (however that is achieved). I have no doubt that were there not a substantial gap between the demands of an increasingly open art market for product and the com-prehensibility of that product, a Clement Greenberg could never have wielded the institutional power he held. Greenberg was the equivalent of a fine impresario or a good leather salesman: the guy who brings the new stuff back from India or Brazil and proves to the market that it is worthy of demand, not merely by showing it but by *explaining* it (spinning it, spin-ning a tale of it) in such a way that the eye "follows suit" (whatever that means, however that happens). No doubt the magic of aesthetics resides here, in how the eye follows suit and attains conviction in such matters, given the theory or words of a person whose words will, twenty years later, be widely disavowed, yet whose words, and passion, stimulated the eye to do its work at the right time (back then, in the 1950s and '60s). One con-straint on market expectations is surely the natural affinity between the eye of the artist and the eye of the consumer, to whatever degree that is in place. Another is what the consumer will intellectually buy as reigning art story. Modernism has piled up a series of partly inconsistent narrative demands (for ceaseless originality, political force, total autonomy, formal sublimity, novelistic content, etc.) that conjoin in ever-surprising ways to structure expectation, value, and so on. Hence the importance of spin: of how the theorist/middleman takes the next step in presenting something (as the new example of art historical importance, the new Picasso, whatever). The role of theorization in modernist culture is an institutional one, whatever else it is (a way of claiming political authority for art that is largely irrelevant to actual politics, a way of striving, relatedly, for utopian voice, a cover-up for art without merit, a way of assigning new kinds of merit to art, etc.). Theory is a market constituent, part of what gives art its value. This is what Arthur saw, and then, I think, exaggerated, by failing to understand its distinctively modernist role as a value producer irreducible to artist, artwork, and consumer (and often at odds with one or more). In this, theory (and by using "theory" I lump together art criticism, grand narratives of modernism, philosophy, etc.) joins with the museum, the gallery, the collection, the collector, the university in being part of what comprises value.

The irony facing the modernist theorist is that he or she is in the position of authorizing the terms of art when no single element in the system is in control of how value is set (and changed). This is a terror for aesthetics, along with the fact that there is not one large-scale narrative regulating and describing modern art but many, and these are partly inconsistent.

Enter Danto, one of the finest theorists of modernism, right up there with Andre Breton, Walter Gropius, Clement Greenberg. He is perhaps the last to presume the capacity to assign general theoretical shape to modernism, and his assignment is unique because it claims that the whole point of art practice *itself* has been theoretical: to discover philosophical truth about art from *within art*—a line he takes over from Greenberg, Piet Mondrian, and others. And by "within art" I mean through visual experimentation and its resonance, circumscribed, defined, and enhanced by theory. I have elsewhere suggested[4] that Mondrian's words stand to his visual works in the same kind of relation as Danto's words do: both are languages for empowering the visual with a certain philosophical truth. That modernism demanded this is a fact about the utopian character of its times, which lent art the mantle of social and spiritual exemplar. It is a fact about the structure of the art market, which set value on the shocking and the new (to use Robert Hughes's phrase) in a way that required consumer comprehensibility while also proclaiming art to be a temple of meaning (i.e., exaggerating its meaning and value in the manner of religions). That the market got away with it is a matter of the floating significations of modernist visuality, the way it has been constructed by the times as an open signifier (abstract, metaphoric, whatever) for linguistic meaning. One might call this a Foucauldian point, about how visuality is taken by a social moment to invite and be empowered with knowledge.

Danto's story takes Andy Warhol to have revealed what makes art art: what the essence of art is. As he did so, modernism came to an end, because there was no further capacity within plastic art to pursue philosophical knowledge and its *raison d'être* ceased to be. This ending of art, this giving over of its task to philosophy, freed art and also deflated it. It freed art to do anything and everything it wanted, to relax and smell the roses, to be all things to all people or none, to claim the liberty of democratic citizens today, who can grow up to be a doctor, lawyer, drug addict, professor, even governor of the state of California (if they're Austrian). No more was art pursued by the specter of "heaviosity," to use a term introduced into the philosophical lexicon by Woody Allen. The other side was the deflation of this high purpose, this sense of being in church, this grandiose instinct for driving history forward in some fundamental way. Indeed, at its worst this ending has reduced art to anything that can be gotten away with, like the Bush administration's view of government. By this I mean art can more or less be whatever the market will bear, whatever seduces it, whatever it will "buy into." Except that there are no laws regulating (however weakly) the conduct of contemporary art, constraining market forces, apart from the obvious ones about free speech, child pornography, and so on (even there art enjoys reveling at the edge, for good, bad, or ugly reasons, depending on whom you talk to). The stakes seem to me these: will the market refuse this degradation of product, or is it precisely the generator of it? And who is in control of the process? Related, is the ceaseless variety of art production a burden or a blessing? And again: is so much of this so-called variety in art production nowadays largely homogeneous, roughly in the way so much of American diversity is reduced nowadays to the faint signs of difference combined with the loud angling for it and the sharp proclamation of it? It is Danto's honesty to come right out and make the point (having played modernist sage by giving us the story of how art came to an end) that today no one is in control of what is happening, what can happen, or how. Value is explicitly understood to be set by no single player or kind of player. Within that everything becomes possible, or little, depending on whom you talk to and what is wanted.

There are other factors that seem to me fairly distinctive of the anxious condition of the contemporary art world. These include: the combination of overproduction with department store/designer boutique homogeneity;

a belief in the joy of boundless innovation but also the sense that there has been so much innovation in plastic art that there is nothing further to do that is not playing around; and an immense deflation in plastic art on account of the postwar rise of the media, whose power of circulation and capacity to shape public opinion plastic art can never hope to rival. A great deal of plastic art is in unconscious competition with film and television, from David Salle to the blood-and-guts artists of London who simply can't cut it anatomically compared to what's seen every hour on CNN International. It was the fantasy of the avant-gardes to break through the containment of the art world and enter the stream of real life in revolutionary ways, although they usually ended up reaching nothing beyond museums, selective audiences, and the occasionally sympathetic public figure like Mussolini. This was because a high degree of background and theory was required to appreciate the avant-gardes, in short, to belong to an art world. An art world is relatively closed. And now the media fulfills the avant-garde dream of breaking out to general publics routinely, but with little or no revolutionary or even public interest. Perhaps the art world can become the object of philosophy for Arthur precisely because it is a feature of modern life that is so articulated and self-contained. That the art world is bounded, and constituted in the goal of breaking its social boundaries, seems to me crucial to its combination of energy and anxiety: for the media exists in not a closed-circuit market environment but an open one. It speaks to a massified, global public. On the other hand, plastic art continues to speak in political voices to itself: to those who make, write, look, and buy; to marginalized communities who have rallied around its symbols and assumed central places in the current art world; to collectors and critics who frequent galleries and celebrate the global circuits of exhibition.

And yet the art market is doing very well, things are selling (sometimes more, sometimes less, but selling); people are buying seriously, sometimes less so: over the Internet without having even seen the work in the flesh.

Finally, the very concept of plastic art is increasingly obscure, given the overlap between art and design on the one hand and art, media, and digital reality on the other. Perhaps Duchamp and Warhol prophesied this, but neither has been around to really see it happen.

Then is the very concept of plastic art, and along with it the ideal of a philosophical explanation of it, something past its sell-by date, like old Campbell's soup cans or Brillo boxes left over from the 1960s? It is no longer clear what would even count as a philosophical explanation, as opposed to a sociological, historical, or critical one. All of this refers to the difficulty Hegel noted about philosophizing one's own time. And yet, perhaps philosophizing one's own time is a way of driving the art world forward. Arthur Danto should be applauded for taking exactly that risk.

⊦ ⊦ ⊦ ⊦ ⊦

Response

As I have already noted in my response to Hans Belting, the title of "The Artworld" was intended to mean "The World of Art Works." Philosophers since Wittgenstein's "The World is everything that is the case" have used "world" in a somewhat poetic way, and I was thinking of The Artworld as populated by all and only artworks, much as The Animal World was made up of all and only animals. I much admired the title of Lawrence Ferlinghetti's *Pictures from the Gone World,* and I tried to think of some graphic device that would present "art" in the title as relating to "world" the way "gone" does in Ferlinghetti's title, e.g., "The *ART*world." I thought of the world of artworks as a kind of polity, in the sense that its members enjoyed certain rights and privileges, and stood in various relations to one another different from those in which things outside the art world did, or in which artworks stood to things outside their world. And I was particularly interested in the question of how something gets enfranchised as an artwork, acquiring, as I say, the rights and privileges that come with that status. The question of immediate interest for me is why *Brillo Box,* for particular instance, should enjoy those privileges—be internally compared, say, with *The Night Watch* or the Cathedral of Laon—and have all sort of protections and be worth a certain sum of money—while the ordinary Brillo boxes were excluded from these, and for aesthetic intents and purposes were worthless. As though there were some kind of injustice, or at least unfairness, since they looked so much alike, both being boxes and sharing a physiognomy. The paper, after all, was written in 1964, the year in which the Summer of Freedom took place. The idea of enfranchisement was much in the air. Years later I used "the disenfranchisement of art" as the title of a book.

Although the colloquial expression "the artworld" was certainly in my vocabulary, I thought that since my auditors at the APA meeting that year, as well as my readers, were mainly philosophers, I could count on them to think of "world" the way they were trained to think of it in discussing the External World. That, of course, did not happen. It was George Dickie who used "the artworld" in its journalistic sense, as a loosely bounded group of individuals concerned with the making, collecting, buying, selling, and judging of art—but he went well beyond that usage by adding to its responsibilities judging when and whether something was art—whether, in my imagery, something deserved entry into The Artworld as I had understood it. In a way, George really did provide an answer to the question of enfranchisement, though it was hardly what I was looking for. A few years after "The Artworld" appeared, Lars Aargaard-Mogensen asked permission to reprint it in an anthology on the Institutional Theory of Art, of which I had until then never heard. Aargaard-Mogensen then informed me that I was the founder of the theory! "The Artworld" has been thought of ever since as an early statement of views I later found myself repudiating. I mention this because Daniel Herwitz continues, in his admittedly brilliant paper, to see my views as inflected with Institutionalism.

When, years later, I did come up with the elements of a theory—of a definition—of art in *The Transfiguration of the Commonplace,* a friendly critic, Noel Carroll, pointed out that the ordinary old cardboard box satisfied it as well as its counterpart did. I could either admit this, and count the Brillo box as an artwork—or try to add a condition to the definition in order to exclude it. Egalitarian by disposition, I realized that I had inherited a prejudice under which commercial art was not really art, and that what I had thought of as The Artworld was the world of fine art—a kind of aristocracy. Philosophically, I recognized that Brillo boxes, if artworks, were poor candidates for the opposition I had been anxious to establish between artworks and real things. The criterion for "real things" would either have to be that they lacked meaning, viz., aboutness, or, if they possessed this, then they failed to embody it. The problem is more difficult than one might realize, if one reflects on what Hegel called "symbolic art," defined by the fact that between pieces of symbolic art and what they mean, there is an external relationship, so that they do not embody their designata. His examples might have been ill chosen—a pyramid might embody, to be sure at a symbolic level, the royal figure beneath it. Even the boulder that was placed over the grave of Jackson Pollock—ponderous, raw, unshaped—might be thought to embody the qualities of the artist it memorialized, that being the reason it was placed there. In any case, I'll confess that I had tacitly been thinking of The Artworld as a pretty exclusive club, keeping crass commercialism outside in the cold. Who would pay $80,000—the going rate—for *Brillo Boxes,* if you could find one? Actually, there are probably more tokens of *Brillo Boxes* around these days than there are Brillo boxes of the 1964 vintage. I know only of two—one given to the art historian, Irving Sandler, by its designer, James Harvey, and the other found in a Dumpster by the artist, Mike Bidlo. Sandler's is signed by the artist, and kept in a Plexiglas case in his living room. It already enjoyed some of the civil rights of art world membership! I think Herwitz somewhat intuits the relevance of enfranchisement when he discusses *Brillo Box* and Brillo box in terms of the screwball comedy *Adam's Rib,* which is much taken up with the issue of women's rights, and asks whether the difference between the boxes is at all like the difference between men and women. The husband, Adam, "cannot understand the nature of these differences apart from his desire."

I have actually thought about this question a great deal, and though I have not published the results, I've attempted to ground them in the differences of *styles.* One of my early sources in the philosophy of art was Borges's *Pierre Menard, Author of the Quixote.* In it, Borges set side by side two entirely congruent texts, one by Cervantes, written in Shakespeare's century, and one by the symbolist poet Pierre Menard, composed early in the twentieth century. What in particular interested me was what Borges— or, really, his Narrator—says about the *style* of the two quite indiscernible passages, letter for letter identical. Here is the passage: "truth, whose mother is history, rival of time, depository of deeds, witness of the past, exemplar and advisor to the present, and the future's counselor." After explaining how Menard's—but of course not Cervantes's—was influenced by William James, and how his language shows the influence of the Pragmatist theory of truth, Borges writes, deliciously, that "The contrast in style is also vivid. The archaic style of Menard—quite foreign, after all, suffers from a certain affectation. Not so that of his forerunner, who handles with ease the current Spanish of his time."

I found it a striking thought, when I first encountered this work, that two literary texts should be indiscernible and yet have radically different styles. At the very least, that implied that one could not ascribe a style to a text without knowing something about when it was written and what was the literary and philosophical culture of its author. Ordinarily, one would think, a literary scholar ought to be able to identify the style of something immediately—know that it was written, say, by John Milton and not by John Lennon. Borges's contrived example argues against this, and implies that stylistic ascription is a more complex skill.

I think it helps in thinking of our two boxes to recognize that difference in their styles has nothing to do with what sets them apart—their material, for example. The issue that concerns me, as it did Borges, has to do with *what makes them indiscernible.* In "Three Brillo Boxes: The Question of Style" (unpublished), I discuss the Brillo boxes of Harvey, Warhol, and Bidlo. My overall view is that until Warhol made his *Brillo Box,* the question of whether Harvey's Brillo box was art or not would never have arisen. But that leaves the question of its status as art quite unaffected.

Let me begin with Warhol's show at the Stable Gallery in 1964. Both the spaces in the gallery were stacked high with boxes bearing the logos of six different brands of American product—Brillo (of course), Kellogg's Corn Flakes, Del Monte peach halves, Heinz ketchup, and the like. Warhol's Factory produced about 300 of *Brillo Box* and I surmise a comparable number of the others, so the rooms were like stockrooms. Fred MacDarrah photographed Warhol between piles of *Brillo Box*, looking for all the world like a somewhat sullen, pasty-faced stockboy. Beyond question, *Brillo Box* was the star of the show, the piece every one remembers, mainly because it was the best design. I have more than once analyzed its rhetoric. It celebrates the product it contains. The design, in red, white, and blue, with a river of white, undulates around the box, fusing patriotism with the duty to be clean, to be sparkling, with GIANT products that work FAST. The lettering is brash and urgent. Harvey borrowed his forms from Hard Edge Abstraction, and I have found canvases by Ellsworth Kelly with just the same wave form. In the section of the stockroom that contains the soap pads, the Brillo box stands out and cries out to be opened FIRST! It is an aesthetic knockout. And it meets the definition of art to perfection: it embodies what it means to say about its content. By comparison, the other boxes are plain—connoting reliability, perhaps, or salubriousness, or whatever.

If the Brillo box is about Brillo, what is *Brillo Box* about? It is about the Brillo box, which it denotes—a commercial container, the style of which I have described. But what is its own style? It certainly has none of the visual excitement of the Brillo box, for which Harvey alone deserves credit. What does it tell us about its subject? I think—this is a conjecture of course—that it tells about Brillo boxes what it tells about the other boxes. The message is the same. They are all alike, which one would expect from someone with Warhol's egalitarian politics. As he said about hot dogs—or was it Cokes?—they are all alike and they are all good. There was something almost Maoist about Warhol, who chose repetition as a favored aesthetic: a sheet of postage stamps, a hundred Coke bottles, a wall of Campbell's soup cans, thirty *Mona Lisas*. That was certainly not Harvey's style. I wish we knew some of his other package designs, but their aim would always have been celebratory. They in effect celebrate difference, whereas Warhol celebrates sameness. Think of *Empire*—a film of the Empire State Building that lasts just over eight hours and is so monotonous that one pays attention to accidentalities of the film passing the lens of the projector—the scratches, the bubbles, the joins. He spoke of liking boredom. Wittgenstein said that it was a matter of indifference to him what he ate, as long as it was always the same. Duchamp ate the same lunch every day—spaghetti al burro, a glass of wine, a cup of coffee.

What about Bidlo's *Not Andy Warhol*, which looks just like *Brillo Box* and just like Brillo boxes? It is of course, about Warhol. The title refers to Warhol, but also to itself, insisting one of the things it refers to is not Warhol but Bidlo. It is a piece of appropriation art. Bidlo appropriated a number of artists—Picasso, Leger, Morandi, Pollock. I suppose the Picasso could be titled *Not Picasso*, the Pollock *Not Jackson Pollock*, etc. In any case, if *Not Andy Warhol* celebrates anything, it celebrates the celebrity of Warhol, which would be a condition for appropriation. Bidlo's peers would have been Sherrie Levine, Richard Prince, and Elaine Sturtevant. Warhol's peers were of course the pop artists of the mid–1960s. James Harvey's peers were the second generation of abstract expressionists, which is not, of course, the style his Brillo box expresses—but in his view, certainly, that would not be art. Package design was just his day job. To understand *Not Andy Warhol*, one would need to understand the theory of appropriation. To understand *Brillo Box,* one would have to understand the philosophy of Andy Warhol ("from A to B and back"). To understand the Brillo box, one would have had to understand not philosophy but rhetoric. *Les styles sont les hommes mêmes.* Herwitz writes that "while Warhol's work is free to entangle itself with the supermarket box, the supermarket box remains mute." No—its language is demotic. Warhol's is laconic. Bidlo's is legalistic, concerning the ownership of images.

When, in various places, I have written that in the pursuit of a definition, the important moves came from within art rather than from philosophy, I meant to emphasize that the philosophical imagination would not have produced the kinds of examples that made contemporary art as rich a field of philosophical investigation as it became in the latter third of the twentieth century. But I also think that that conceptual ferment is finished, and that even if the art world continues to make surprising things, the surprises are not of a kind to make us rethink the theory, that is to say, the definition of art. "This ending of art," Herwitz writes, "this giving over of its task to philosophy, freed art and also deflated it. It freed art to do everything and everything it wanted." The art world is, one might say, the Abbé de Theleme writ large—*Fay ce que voudras.* "No more was art pursued by the specter of 'heaviosity.'"

I feel a certain tone of disapproval, even perhaps of conservative despair, as Herwitz's paper nears its end. "At its worst this ending has reduced art to anything that can be gotten away with, like the Bush adminis-tration's view of government." I felt a certain pessimism while writing my 1984 paper, "The End of Art." I had gotten used to the idea of art as driving art history forward, as taking on that mission of progress, and I expressed a stab of regret in the concluding sentence: "It has been an immense privi-lege to have lived in history." That was twenty years after having published "The Artworld"! It expressed the somewhat tragic sense Frank Ankersmit ascribed to my view of history—the tragedy of having come out of one pe-riod into another. But this is the world—this is the art world—we live in now, and I have to say that I have come to admire it. I don't see the impulse to "get away with" something, which suspicious critics, like Hilton Kramer, express so often, or the sour picture of Warhol "laughing all the way to the bank." The last thing in the world I believe Warhol wondered was "What can I get away with?" I don't see in the art being produced in such im-mense quantity the "degradation of product" of which Herwitz speaks. There is a lot of uninspired work in the galleries. But there is so much in-genious work, so much intelligence, so much dedication, and really so much high-mindedness in the art world that, were it shared by the rest of the world, we would have entered a golden age.

We really *are* in a new age, so far as art is concerned. The life of the artist is one that increasing numbers of young people would like to live. The numbers of undergraduate fine arts majors astonishes me. The number of applicants to M.F.A. programs is beyond belief. To be sure, it is difficult to separate considerations of career from consideration of what such a life means—how to find a dealer, how to get written about. But that has been there for a long time. In his novel about Henry James, *The Master*, Colm Toibin has his hero think romantically about a young and handsome sculptor he meets in Rome. The sculptor thinks of sales, of glory, and of getting his famous conquest to write something about him. As a critic, I en-counter a lot of that. But I also find a lot of sacrifice for the sake of living the life of the artist. The embodiment of meaning is worth pursuing, even if it does not forge the uncreated consciousness of the artist's race—or gender or whatever.

Notes

1. Arthur Danto, *After the End of Art: Contemporary Art and the Pale of History* (Princeton: Princeton University Press, 1997), 165.
2. For a discussion of the role of theory in the avant-gardes, and of Danto's views in

detail, see Daniel Herwitz, *Making Theory/Constructing Art: On the Authority of the Avant-Garde* (Chicago: University of Chicago Press, 1993).

3. For a reading of Manet's work against the transformations of Paris and the flow of capital in the nineteenth century, see T. J. Clark, *The Painting of Modern Life: Paris in the Art of Manet and His Followers* (New York: Knopf, 1984).

4. Herwitz, *Making Theory/Constructing Art.*

8

Danto on Tansey

The Possibilities of Appearance

Michael Kelly

One of the principal virtues of Arthur Danto's philosophy of art is that, from its beginning in 1964, it generally has been calibrated to contemporary art, so that the substance and even tone of his philosophical writings have been responsive to, and even generated by, developments in the art world.[1] For example, his early, well-known essay on Warhol's *Brillo Box*, called "The Artworld," was written in direct response to an exhibition of that work at the Staple Gallery in New York City in 1964. According to Danto, Warhol exhibited works that no existing philosophy of art could explain, so he set out to develop his own philosophy of art, whose success is measured by whether it provides such an explanation. Over time, this essay has become the internal paradigm for all Danto's subsequent writings on art. Moreover, I believe it is a model that contemporary philosophers of art would do well to emulate.

At the same time, however, there are interests definitive of Danto's understanding of his professional commitments as a philosopher that have not always been compatible with the art world. The art world simply has different inhabitants with interests different from those of philosophers, even though Danto thinks that art and philosophy simultaneously experienced golden ages in the second half of the twentieth century.[2] This sometimes tense relationship between art and philosophy embodied in a single philosophy of art will be my focus here, especially as this relationship is revealed in Danto's art criticism, where I think the merits and potential problems of his philosophy of art are both manifest and latent. With this focus in mind, I'll discuss his interpretation of a particular artist, Mark Tansey, about whom Danto wrote an extensive monograph essay in 1992, and about whom he has written on other occasions since then.

Danto's Philosophy of Art (in Brief)

Danto has developed a distinctive philosophy of art, the centerpiece of which is an essentiaiist definition of art: something is a work of art only if it has meaning, and only if the work embodies the meaning that it has.[3] So meaning and embodiment are the two necessary, though not quite sufficient, conditions of a work of art. Inspired by this essentialist definition, Danto interprets any individual work of art by identifying its meaning and by showing how the meaning is embodied in the work.[4] This all seems straightforward enough. But what exactly is "embodied meaning"? To say that embodied meaning is *in* the work of art while unembodied meaning is something external to the work to which it refers only begs the question; for whatever embodied meaning is, we can safely assume that it is supposed to be *in* the work—or, more specifically, in the form of the work, leaving it to the philosopher/critic to show how the work's meaning explains, in turn, why it has the form it has.[5] The meaning is embodied in the form, which is, in turn, the work's content. Yet Danto does not offer any clear *theoretical* account of how we are supposed to be able to discern when meaning is embodied. Fortunately, he has had a second career as an art critic (since 1984). So one way (if not the only way) to understand what he has in mind by "embodied meaning" is to look at the examples of it that he provides in his art criticism. As we'll see, when he actually interprets individual works of art, there is a sense in which he also looks elsewhere than *in* (the form of) the works as he tries to explain their embodied meanings. The reason Danto looks elsewhere is, I think, that the embodied meanings he has in mind are universal; that is, they must, on his own account, be transcultural and transhistorical[6] or, as he says in his interpretation of the work of Cindy Sherman, must speak to all of us.[7] In short, the embodied meanings constituting something as a work of art must be universal.

The universality of embodied meaning is thus central to Danto's essentialist definition of art, and to his philosophy of art in general. Understood in this way, however, embodied meanings are artifacts of Danto's philo-

sophical interests rather than anything we should expect to find in artworks insofar as they are understood to be deeply historical. That is, the
meanings of works of art are a function of their historical context, their
historical particularity. Such particularity is not universal, so the meanings
tied to them are not universal either (at least not without some effort on
the part of the philosopher to render them so by first stripping them of any
particularity that is in conflict with universal meaning). To Danto's seemingly straightforward approach of interpreting artworks in terms of their
embodied meanings, he adds an unstated and problematic condition: that
the embodied meanings be universal. I say "unstated" because, to my
knowledge, he does not defend, identify, or even acknowledge this condition in his philosophy of art. This may not be surprising to many people,
since Danto is a philosopher and may therefore be expected to take the
claim of universality to be self-evident; philosophy's medium is the concept, and concepts are universal. Danto has said as much. But even if—or
especially because—universality is a defining interest of Danto's profession, it is incumbent upon him to justify the relevance of this interest to
our understanding of art; otherwise, it is possible not only that he will be
projecting the interests of philosophy onto art but also that in doing so he
will end up being *dis*interested in art. Such an effect would be surprising
and paradoxical indeed, because it would stem from an *interest* in art. This
effect is what I want to call iconoclasm, understood as a combination of
disinterest and distrust in art, where the distrust is a consequence of the
disinterest. Let me try to explain what I mean by discussing Danto's interpretation of Tansey's paintings.

Danto on Tansey

Danto's interest in universality is indirectly present in two ways when he
writes about Tansey's work: in the interpretation of Tansey's paintings in
relation to a reality external (and ontologically superior) to art, and in the
account of the relationship between art and philosophy as he sees that relationship embodied in Tansey's work.[8]

   Danto does not discuss universality explicitly in his essay on Tansey,[9]
nor even in his texts on the philosophy of art. But universality is definitely
an operative concept in his interpretation (and philosophy of art too)
through the concept of reality. In a word, reality backed by truth is the representative of universality in Danto's writings.

   Universality enters into Danto's interpretation of Tansey through the
contrast he draws between what seems possible in art and what is impos-

sible in reality, where the "what" is the same in both cases. The contrast first comes up when he describes Tansey's monochromatic, realist paintings as having a "flat, descriptive, didactic," photographic style that is combined with a "chiding humor" preventing them from becoming too polemical or solemn (MT 12).[10] This style, which Danto says does not draw attention to itself,[11] leads him to interpret Tansey as if he utilizes all the "tricks and tools" of illustration (MT 14) just to serve "the truth" of what the paintings "show" (MT 12). That is, the paintings (and the artist) are in the service of some universal truth, while the realism of the work is simply a means to this truth. The purpose of this "serviceable realism" (MT 17) is, according to Danto, to convince us of the truth of one of two types of events defined in contrast to reality: *what could have happened* (MT 16) or *what could not be* (MT 25). That is, in each of Tansey's paintings, an event from one of these two types is presented as if it "easily were" (MT 25), as if it truly did happen, as if it were "a matter of historical truth" (MT 16). An example of the first type would be *The Innocent Eye Test* (1981), where a cow has been guided into an art museum to view a Paulus Potter painting, *The Young Bull* (1647). Though such an event is not impossible, it is so implausible that we can be quite sure that it never happened.[12] Two examples of the second type would be the *Triumph of the New York School* (1984), in which what seem to be French military officers are depicted surrendering to what seem to be their American counterparts, and *Action Painting II* (1984), in which ten artists are shown instantaneously completing identical paintings, each of which is pictorially equivalent to a NASA rocket launch taking place right before the painters' eyes. Since the French and the Americans have never been at war with each other, the surrender Tansey depicts could never have happened; and since the launch of the rocket was itself (represented as being) only eight seconds old, there is no way the artists could have already completed their painterly equivalents of it. These are thus examples of impossible as well as implausible events.

According to Danto, Tansey is not satisfied just convincing us that these two kinds of actions are *pictorially* possible; he also *projects* the pictorially possible onto the realm of reality, where, Danto says, "our knowledge tells us there is no room" for art's possibilities (MT 25).[13] That is, the pictorially possible, defined from the start in contrast to reality, is now projected onto that same reality where, we should not be surprised to learn, it is deemed (again) to be impossible. Here is where universality—a philosophical interest—most directly enters the interpretation and becomes, in effect, the philosophical basis of any judgment of Tansey's painting. For the failure of the alleged projection of art's possibilities onto reality presupposes the *universal truth* of a reality separate from the paintings, against which they are to be judged. That is, regardless of what appears to be possible in the paintings, we need to look to this universal reality in order to judge whether what seems possible in the art world is truly possible or not. It turns out that what Tansey allegedly projects as possible is impossible. Whether this is true or not, what concerns me here is that this question has taken center stage in the interpretation of Tansey's work.

Now, while it may seem reasonable to interpret Tansey's paintings in terms of this possibility/impossibility contrast, the consequences of such an interpretation compel me to reevaluate the role of these tensions in the generation of his art. As we have seen, what appears pictorially possible in Tansey's work turns out to be impossible in reality and, since what is impossible is not real, what the paintings depict is not real. In turn, while what is real and possible is, for Danto, what is true, the unreal and impossible content of the paintings is false. That is, Tansey's paintings convey lies; put more dramatically, painting is itself a lie, as Plato long ago warned. What disturbs me here is that art is being conceived in terms of philosophical interests (and abilities) against which it can never measure up. Art appears deficient in its very conception when measured by the interests of philosophy. This is an inappropriate way for philosophy to conceive of art, or, to put the point in a way that is immanent to Danto's own philosophy of art, it means that art is being calibrated to philosophy rather than philosophy to art.

Another way to clarify how universality emerges as central in Danto's art criticism is to look at his claim that the truth of Tansey's work lies elsewhere than on the level of visual appearance. That is, his paintings are about more than what meets the eye, since what meets the eye are realistic depictions that, on closer inspection, "explode into paradoxes and conundrums, impossibilities and wonders" (MT 13). For Danto, such explosions reveal the intellectual and even moral power of art; that is, its resistance to being interpreted in visual terms alone is evidence that it has intellectual and moral power (MT 18). He thinks such power is a truth about painting, and, moreover, that it is the task (even the truth) of Tansey's paintings to illustrate it (MT 18). All the tools of his artlessly descriptive style are marshaled to convey this truth, which, on Danto's account, has biblical connotations, for the Bible, too, is lacking in "poetic embroideries" so that the truth disclosed through its language can be better served.[14]

But what truth is at issue here? It turns out, on Danto's interpretation, that what Tansey's work illustrates is an artifact of Danto's own philosophy of art, for one of his main claims is that "to see something as art requires something the eye cannot descry."[15] That is, something theoretical rather than perceptual is what allows us to recognize something as a work of art. Tansey appears to offer illustrations of the truth of this claim because we cannot make sense of his paintings in perceptual terms, that is, because their realistic appearance belies what they are really about. We have to look elsewhere to decipher their meanings and even to recognize them as works of art needing to be deciphered, for without meanings they are not art. If this is what Danto wants to say about Tansey's paintings, however, then we have a case where art is interpreted as a mere illustration of a truth that only philosophy can grasp—which introduces the second theme here, the art/philosophy relationship. Insofar as art is ontologically blind to this truth, as Danto argues, the artist is blind while the philosopher self-consciously assumes the role of the visionary, who can see without seeing. But where the artist is said by the philosopher to be blind, it may actually be the case that the philosopher is himself blind to art, or, as I would prefer to put it, reveals a disinterest and distrust in art while he articulates his conception of it, according to his philosophical interests.

There is pictorial evidence for Danto's interpretation, of course, because Tansey does "exploit the tensions between pictorial reality and reality" (MT 25). The painter's realistic style appears to invite a contrast between painting and a reality it seems to render so faithfully; and this contrast appears, in turn, to entail the possibility/impossibility dynamic described above. But we should not be taken in by appearances. While there is no disputing the fact that paintings are illusory, for they are often mistaken for a reality separate from the realm of painting and are, in fact, often deliberately made to be so mistaken, this is well known. We expect those who make and view art to know it, and we expect artists to show in their work that they are aware of this fact. By painting pictures that are realistic and illusory, Tansey may seem to be unaware of the illusory nature of his medium, which would only encourage critics, such as Danto, to point out the truth of art as illusion as they interpret his work. But what if Tansey's paintings only *appear* to be realistic and their appearance is, in fact, predicated on the recognition of art's illusory character rather than on ignorance of it?[16] What if the basic starting point of Tansey's work is the critique, in the form of pictures, of this character? And what if the pictorial strategy for communicating this critique were to create the appearance of a realistic picture that deliberately *seems* not to know itself to be illusory? In short, what if what Danto presents as his insight about Tansey's work were actually a basic condition underlying and, moreover, generating his pictures?

If that is the case, then the painter not only already knows what the philosopher-critic purports to discover, he already *practices* what the philosopher theorizes. That is, Tansey knows that art is illusory and practices it by investigating *how* it works as illusion, and, at the same time, by exploring, through pictures, whether art might be conceived separately from the logic of illusion so that its possibilities rather than impossibilities can be explored. By contrast, Danto interprets Tansey as if he were aiming at illusion, since he says elsewhere that *The Innocent Eye Test* (1981) "is a late twentieth-century equivalent [that is, illustration] of the philosophical theses [about art as illusion] we find in the writings of Ernst Gombrich and Nelson Goodman."[17] But perhaps Danto is the one stuck in the logic of illusion, while Tansey is intimating another conception of art. Danto would of course welcome such intimation, since he argues that art must embody its own philosophical essence before philosophy can articulate it. My point here, however, is that what is intimated is different from what is articulated, so art and philosophy are again not calibrated to each other in the way that Danto himself led us to believe (beginning with his "The Artworld" essay) would be the gold standard guiding aesthetics.

If this is a plausible interpretation of Tansey's work, then the philosophical effects of his work are different from what Danto imagines. First of all, as Danto does acknowledge, Tansey critiques certain Greenbergian, modernist prohibitions and pronouncements on painting.[18] In particular, Tansey's *White on White* challenges the modernist belief that color is the essence of painting. With allusion to paintings by K. Malevich and Jasper Johns with similar titles and form, Tansey shows that color alone is unable to provide a painting with any determinate form or content, despite Greenberg's confidence to the contrary, so we need to look elsewhere, beginning with figuration, understood broadly to mean human figures or almost any other figure or thing. That is, figuration is needed to give the painting some determinate form and meaning; moreover, without figuration it is not clear that we are dealing with a painting at all. The formal determinacy of *White on White*, for example, could be established by the introduction of either the Inuits or the Bedouins alone (and, in fact, by that of any single figure whatsoever, even just a dog or a camel). Tansey adds both sets of figures to suggest, I think, that his interest is in determinacy, but not in any single mode of it. That is, he is not looking to replace one dogma—about color—with another one—about a particular kind of determinacy. There is rather a pluralism of determinacy within painting: Inuits, Bedouins, or whatever figuration you prefer, or even some other way of providing determination. This is a pluralism made possible and revealed by art and not, as Danto seems to believe, one that is made possible only by the philosophy of art once it has liberated art from any worry about its essence.

The aim of the critique of modernism embodied in Tansey's work is, I think, to explore the pictorial possibilities within painting that are opened up, in principle, once the modernist prohibitions have been lifted.[19] For example, what can paintings be other than flat, non-narrative pictures seemingly reduced to color? Whatever the possibilities, Tansey need not have any interest in making them real outside painting, and for two reasons. The first is that he is fully aware of the limits of art, given its status as appearance; painting thus cannot expect (and should not project) its possibilities to be real anywhere else. To return to the example of *The Triumph of the New York School*, Tansey was clearly dealing with a historical battle within the art world rather than with any actual military battle between the French and the Americans. The second reason is that, in effect, Tansey internalizes the art/reality, possibility/impossibility tensions within painting and, in doing so, leaves any singular conception of reality or truth out of the picture, not just because they are the philosopher's interests rather than the artist's, but because they do not contribute anything to our understanding of the practice of painting. Evidence of this is the fact that the introduction of truth or reality into the conception of art only restricts the possibilities of appearance Tansey is exploring by claiming that they are *im*possible in reality, so it only makes sense that he would not endorse anything that would limit such exploration. So the pursuit of painting's possibilities naturally leads the artist away from any interest in truth or reality, at least as Danto understands them in universalist terms. In a word, Tansey pursues the *possibilities of appearance* rather than the *appearance of possibilities* (which only turn out to be *im*possibilities). If this is an accurate account of Tansey's work, then when Danto makes universality, via the concepts of reality and truth, the central interest in the interpretation of this work, he is in effect *dis*interested in the work; that is, he shows a lack of interest in the practice of Tansey's art in favor of his own philosophical interests.

The problem I am getting at here is not merely an interpretive issue (i.e., how best to interpret Tansey's art) but a philosophical one (i.e., how to explain it as art in the first place). I think Tansey's *White on White* is an excellent example to show what is at stake philosophically. Danto rightly says that without the figuration in *White on White*, we could not possibly discern the difference between the white of the (Alaskan) snow on the left of the picture and the white of the (desert) sand on the right. He then uses this point to interpret this painting as an illustration of his own philosophy

tion of art is that it leads to iconoclasm, by which I mean a combination of disinterest and distrust in art, where disinterest is an uncanny mixture of disinterestedness and lack of interest, and thus a mixture of a technical philosophical term and an everyday expression.[23]

For Kant, disinterestedness is achieved when we abstract or distance ourselves from any interest in the existence of the artwork being judged; for Danto, disinterestedness is achieved when he abstracts art from the historical conditions of its making that would prevent its meaning from being universal.[24] In Kant's case, abstraction is a *condition* for the universality of a pure aesthetic judgment of taste (of the four "moments" of such judgments, disinterestedness is the first and universality is the second; moreover, Kant claims that the second can be inferred from the first); in Danto's case, abstraction is the *effect* of the interest in universality, this time in the form of universal meaning, because it is that interest which requires the abstraction. Such disinterest, whether a condition or an effect, is a disinterest *in art* (rather than just a disinterest in interests other than universality) insofar as art is determined by the other interests from which it has been abstracted. That is, so long as art is and remains tied to the conditions of its sensuous and historical particularity (or existence, in Kant's terms), to abstract from them is to abstract from art, and therefore to be disinterested in them is to be disinterested in art. Such disinterest is akin to a lack of interest, but it is a lack that is philosophically determined and thus philosophically significant. Of course, Danto claims that the universal meaning of art is embodied in historically particular artworks, suggesting that his interest in universal meaning is compatible with art's historical and sensuous particularity after all. But his condition of embodiment is in conflict with his condition of universality, which leads Danto to abstract works of art from the historical conditions of their embodiment and thereby to end up with a *dis*embodied universal, despite his efforts to avoid just such a result. Let me try to explain briefly why I call this result iconoclasm.

The specific form of iconoclasm I have in mind is generated by Danto's conflation of his own philosophical interests in art—namely, universal meaning and essentialist definition—with what constitutes art. The problem here is not just that Danto qua philosopher has interests, which we would expect him to have, but that he inscribes these interests into the very conception of art and thereafter interprets it principally in terms of this inscription.[25] This leads to an unusual predicament where the effects of certain philosophical interests in art are disinterest and distrust in art; that is, the pursuit of the interests in universal meaning and essentialist definition results in disinterest and distrust in the very art whose meaning and definition are at issue.[26] For once Danto is committed to these interests, he becomes disinterested in the historically specific conditions of art—as was the case in his interpretation of Tansey (where he displayed a disinterest in the pictorial practice out of which the work emerged)—even though such conditions would seem to be necessary for his own criterial notion of embodiment. And, again, so long as art is determined by historical conditions,'as Danto himself seems to concede, then disinterest in these conditions is tantamount to disinterest in art itself.

Danto also distrusts these same historical conditions—and thus art—because they threaten to make it impossible for the meanings of the artworks he interprets to be universal; such distrust is most clearly reflected in his insistence that Tansey's work cannot really make the philosophical claims it seems to embody. At best, the work can reach the level of what Danto calls the "theology of painting," a Hegelian designation that makes clear that the philosophy of art is superior to art in making any philosophical claims about art. As theology, art can only illustrate what philosophy conceives about it. There is an implicit distrust of art here, I think, because Danto is concerned about separating art from philosophy as much as philosophy from art, and this concern is actually what attracts him to art that defies this separation—not just Tansey's, but Warhol's, Rauschenberg's, Sherman's, and others'—by defying the difference between art and reality (as in the case of the beds) or between art and life. As the spokesperson for reality, Danto insists on reestablishing these differences, which is a way of reasserting the authority of philosophy over art, at least regarding issues such as reality, truth, and the universality they both imply. So long as art continues to defy philosophy on these issues, philosophy will be attracted to art, so much so that philosophy's own self-conception will be shaped, in part, by its conception of art as deficient relative to philosophical interests. Such attraction is also a distrust, just as the earlier interest was also a disinterest. Moreover, such results constitute something like what Danto himself calls the philosophical disenfranchisement of art, or what I'm calling iconoclasm. That is, this combination of disinterest and distrust in art generates a philosophical form of iconoclasm, which, like the religious and political forms, has the effect, intended or not, of threatening art—in this case by manipulating the conception of it.

What I am calling iconoclasm here is the disinterest and distrust in art generated when philosophical interests are given priority over the historical conditions of art. For what interest can we have in art whose historical conditions of embodied meaning have been transcended? In fact, on Danto's own terms, how can there even be any art in which we might take an interest, for something must have embodied meaning to be art and embodiment has been undermined by his own acts of interpretive abstraction? And how can we not distrust art once, in the interest of embodiment, we recognize that it is inextricably tied to history yet also believe, in the interest of universality, that art must be abstracted from that same history? We might want to say that this would be distrust in history rather than distrust in art itself, except that there is no art without history, since there is no art without embodiment and no embodiment without history. Iconoclasm is therefore an immanent problem for Danto's philosophy of art. For when art is taken out of history, it is cut off from the very conditions that allow its meaning to be embodied and that, on his own account, therefore make it art.

To clarify further what I mean by "iconoclasm" in Danto's case, let me point—in closing—to what I see as a tension internal to his essentialist definition of art, between his embodiment condition and what I referred to in my introduction as his unstated condition that the meaning of art be universal. The tension arises because the only way we can make sense of embodiment is in terms of the historically specific practice of art, yet Danto has exhibited his disinterest in such practice by abstracting from it while pursuing his interest in universality, as he did while interpreting Tansey's work. So it seems that either the second or the third condition can be met, but not both: meaning is either universal but not embodied, or embodied but not universal. But if both conditions are not met, what becomes of the definition, since Danto himself insists that the first condition—meaning— is not enough to make something a work of art, since there are many things that have meanings but are not works of art? He needs the embodiment condition in order to have the essentialist definition of art he envisions, but he also needs the meaning to be universal for the same reason. Hence the tension. To resolve it, Danto has to choose between embodiment and universality. As we have seen, he chooses universality, thinking that it will best allow him to sustain his essentialist definition of art as embodied meaning. That is, his philosophical interest in such a definition leads him to give priority to universality over embodiment. But this leads him to jeopardize the very definition in the name of which he made his choice. The only way I can see of resolving this tension is to return to the notion of embodiment and to give it its due. This is something that I imagine would be of interest to Danto since he is, after all, the one who has made embodiment such a central notion in contemporary philosophy of art.

⽶ ⽶ ⽶ ⽶ ⽶

Response

I recently encountered a characterization of Hegel's philosophy of art in Joseph Leo Koerner's remarkable study, *The Reformation of the Image*. Hegel's, he writes, is an "aesthetics of meaning rather than an aesthetics of form." That expressed, I thought to perfection, the difference between the philosophy of art I have developed over the past forty years and the philosophy that defined the art world when I began. Indeed, I thought that artists in the '60s were striving to convey meanings, despite the prevailing formalism, and that this was true even of the artists of the '50s, despite the materialist aesthetics of Clement Greenberg. The definition provisionally advanced in *The Transfiguration of the Commonplace*—that works of art are embodied meanings—condenses this transformation in attitude and thought, and though the British aestheticians, Roger Fry and Clive Bell, made *significant* form central to their program, there is very little in their writing to suggest what they might have meant by "significant"—they seemed to have been formalists *san phrase*. The point is that the Reformation images had the power of texts, according to Koerner, which was a way of connecting them to sermons and of escaping the prohibition against images, which was usually taken to license iconoclasm in the 1550s. It is somewhat unsettling to find myself accused of iconoclasm for now holding pictures—as embodied meanings—to have something like the structure of visual texts. Michael Kelly uses "iconoclasm" in a somewhat pickwickian sense, but I would have supposed that he might be a supporter of my views, given what I take to be his own. Obviously there is some slippage between his understanding of what I do and mine.

Since it is part of the definition of art, the requirement that works of art have meaning is universal—intended to be true of artworks everywhere and always. But that, I would have thought, is consistent with every work of art having a different meaning. There is no single meaning every work of art must have. Still, their meanings, which it is the role of art criticism to identify, are universal in the sense that what a work of art means is invariant to time, place, and viewer. A portrait of Louis XIV by Hyacinth Rigaud is about Louis XIV—that is its meaning, even if should happen that that meaning somehow got lost. That happens to works of art. There are many portraits whose meanings have been lost, in the sense that no one any longer knows who was their subject. One of Rigaud's most famous portraits of the monarch shows him holding an attribute of French kings—a long scepter, pointing at the French crown—and wearing unmistakably royal robes of purple velvet and ermine. He is posed in such a way that one feels that he embodies the might of the French throne. It is meant to impress its viewers with his majesty, whether they are his subjects or not. If that is a correct reading of the portrait, it is universal in the sense that someone who does not see it that way has missed part of the work's meaning. The painting tells the viewer that this is how power looks, or at least how it looked in the late seventeenth century.

The art criticism of the work must take all this into account. It must identify the meaning and show the way it is embodied in the painting. That is what art criticism does when I write it, but not because I am a philosopher and a philosopher's mind is always centered on universal things. Rather, it is because I am writing as an art critic, and the first task art critics have is to explain to readers what works of art mean, and justify that by explaining how that meaning is embodied in just about everything in the art: the king's expression, his body language, his bodily proportion, the paraphernalia with which he is shown, his wig. What is disfiguring in art criticism such as this? What is wrong in this notion of universality? In what way is its being universal inconsistent with taking the history of the work into account? Michael Kelly's critique of my critical practice rather baffles me. If meaning of the kind I have just specified is universal, as I think it is, then there is nothing distinctive in my critical practice due to the fact that I am a philosopher as well as a critic. And if such meaning is not universal, well, Kelly's charge falls harmlessly to the ground. Either way, then, I find it hard to see the basis for his charges.

As I write this, a critical piece of mine is appearing in *The Nation*. It is about the work of the artist Lee Bontecue, and especially about the work on which her great reputation rests, which was first shown in 1960 at Leo Castelli's gallery. These pieces are made of strips of fabric, fastened with twists of wire to welded metal armatures and usually hung at eye level. The armature almost always defines a space that is not covered with fabric, and has the shape of an orifice. If the pieces rested on their backs on the floor, it would be natural to see them as volcanoes: they are, mostly, cone shaped, and the orifice would be seen as the volcano's crater, deep and black. But since they are wall pieces, with the orifice at eye level, more or less, the orifice was read as a mouth, as an eye, most often as a vagina. However it was read, the works were seen as menacing in the 1960s and are seen as menacing today, though obviously not in any literal way: there is nothing literally to be afraid of. I am not entirely sure what their meaning is, but in my essay, I lay out a range of meanings they could have, all of which convey the idea—the feeling—of menace, and I show, or try to show, how this is embodied in Bontecue's works. I know they belong to their time and place: New York, circa 1960. And I know that "menacing" was the aesthetic term of choice in most of the considerable critical literature devoted to her surprising work. Objects like Bontecue's could have been made at different times, though not always as works of art. Critics spoke of them as "cubist," a term, whether or not true of Bontecue's work, that would not have been in use before it was coined in 1912. We do in fact use such terms retroactively, speaking of Poussin's strangely slablike drawings as "cubist," the way Breton spoke of Hans Baldung Gruen as "surrealist" though the concept was not available in the sixteenth century. Would it have been true that an object like Bontecue's was cubist, had it existed in 1860? That seems to me to be an almost paradigmatically metaphysical question, of no great interest to most of us. The point is that no one in 1860 would have understood the word or used it. By contrast, I think, objects like hers would have appeared menacing even if they were used in ritual acts by headhunters in Micronesia—though they would have employed branches for armatures, or perhaps bones, rather than welded steel. Whether their being welded metal steel contributes or not to the meaning of Bontecue's work belongs to their connoisseurship. But since she used the powder formed at the end of the welding torches to dull her fabric surfaces, I guess that the use of welding has to be taken into interpretative account.

Kelly singles out for criticism my text on Cindy Sherman's *Untitled Film Stills* of the 1970s, and there he may have a point. In my presidential address for the American Philosophical Association of 1987—"Philosophy as/of/and Literature"—I advanced the idea that literature is philosophical when it is about its readers, so that in a sense, *Anna Karenina* is about whoever reads it, for it provides metaphors for everyone. My first wife, Shirley Rovetch, in important ways lived in Proust's world—she *was* Oriane, Duchesse de Guermantes, whatever the actual circumstances of her being married to a poorly paid American professor with two difficult West Side children. I was thinking that it was in virtue of a kind of metaphoric identification with its readers that great literature was great, and that we read it not just to be well-read, but that it actually enriches us to think of ourselves and our lives that way. It gives us ways of seeing one another, as it does Proust's character Charles Swann—who saw the woman he loved as the daughter of Jethro in a painting by Botticelli. And I thought this made such literature universal. I certainly felt this cut across historical and cultural boundaries, and across the boundaries of race and gender: *The Dream of the Red Chamber* was part of who I was. This was on my mind when I strove to interpret *Untitled Film Stills*. "In the particular is contained the universal," Samuel Beckett said, echoing Anton Chekhov.

The eighty or so photographs in Sherman's series are of course identified by number rather than title, but the overall impression is that they are "stills"—a genre of photographs posted outside movie theaters, as come-ons for the films shown inside. So they imply narratives, in which the starlet plays a role in love stories, adventure stories, mysteries, or the like. It was not unusual for people to believe they had actually seen the film from which a given still was taken, even though there was none. Since it is widely known that Sherman played the role of starlet in the role of a dancer, a secretary, a nurse, a young wife, a girl setting off for the city, a girl running away, a young woman in love, people sometimes thought they were in the nature of self-portraits—Cindy Sherman *as.* . . . But they were no more *of* her than *from* this or that film. Theorists liked to say that the series as a whole was about the construction of the self—that women have no given identity other than the situations into which they are thrust. I said they were as a group about The Girl—even though that was a somewhat politically incorrect designation. I thought the subject was the universal Girl, in the various situations in life in which girls find themselves. But I went further, and thought they were about their viewers, much in the way great novels are about their readers. I thought, in terms of finding one's way in life, that they were about men as well as women, old as well as young people, blacks as well as whites. And Kelly asks how such meanings can be said to be *embodied* in those photographs, observing that I have never written out a definition of embodiment. He is right to ask such questions, which are certainly a challenge.

I possess a postcard of Hyacinth Rigaud's official portrait of Louis XIV that was sent me as a Father's Day card by my younger daughter, then living in France. I thought that with the same right that Louis XV said "*L'etat, c'est moi,*" my daughter was saying, "*Le roi, c'est toi.*" You, dear Dad, are king for a day. It was, or I took it as, an affectionate critique of her father, or of any father—too powerful in the network of family politics. I thought it a pretty witty card, in truth, and have kept it ever since. Certainly Rigaud would not have been thinking that way when he painted the great portrait. But in regard to the asymmetries of power in domestic reality, it lends itself to a pretty good metaphor of the relationship in which the king stood to the people. Kings themselves use paternal metaphors this way. So what's wrong in the idea of metaphorical embodiment? We make that move all the time in interpreting paintings, or works of art in general. Recently I wrote a sustained analysis of David's *Marat Assassiné,* in which I sought to show that Marat slain, in terms of his pose, circumstance, and beauty, was like a deposition of Christ—that Marat indeed was in that painting a metaphor for Christ, and the message was that he had sacrificed himself for our benefit the way Jesus had, and that we, the viewers, were intended to worship Marat and follow him into the revolution. That is what art does, or can do. One would think Kelly would agree to that in principle, working out case after case as they present themselves. Evidently this is not so, as he contends that the dreaded universality emerges as central to my art criticism when I emphasize that "the truth of [Mark] Tansey's work lies elsewhere than on the level of visual appearance."

Some of Kelly's arguments against my readings of Tansey resemble nothing so much as Plato's caricatures of Sophists in some of the lesser dialogues like the *Euthydemus.* There Socrates takes a young boy to a Sophist in order that he be taught virtue. "You want him, then," the Sophist asks, "to be other than he is?" Of course, Socrates agrees. "You'll agree that he is alive," the Sophist says, and Socrates agrees. "Then you want him DEAD!" Shouts of laughter in the agora. Compare that with the claim that since certain of Tansey's paintings show certain things that are impossible in reality, they are false, that is, "These paintings convey LIES!" (shades of Book X). But whoever thought that the meaning of these paintings is that ours is a world of impossibilities? Tansey, sly wit that he is, is reversing Hamlet's point that there are more things on earth and heaven than are dreamed of in our philosophy by saying there are more things picturable in our painting than are possible on earth and heaven. It is possible to paint the impossible, which shows the power of art and painterly imagination. Many of Tansey's paintings are about art. The ones in question challenge a view of realism, preempted for photography in Horowitz's essay in the concept of counterfactual dependence. Whoever said painting is counterfactually dependent on reality? Or would say that if there are things in painting not in reality, the paintings in question are lies? Tell your troubles to Photoshop.

In saying this, Kelly argues that I am twisting Tansey's art to illustrate my own philosophy of art, namely, as often quoted from "The Artworld" in our conference, "To see something as art requires something the eye cannot decry." What was this? It was, of course, seeing the object in the light of our knowledge of art history and theory, neither of which present themselves to the eye the way the object does. But that is hardly the same as attributing a metaphorical content to a painting! Consider allegory. In Delacroix's *Liberty at the Barricades*, we see a handsome, angry woman holding a banner, with one breast exposed. We know from the title that she is Liberty. So we see her under an allegorical description. And we see Tansey's paintings, or the ones Kelly cites, as advancing a proposition about painting. That is an inference. But so is it an inference that the man standing in the sarcophagus in Piero's *Resurrection* has come back from death to life. Most of the world's great pictorial art show us things invisible to the eye. If that is universalism, put me down as a card-carrying subscriber.

The theory of the end of art entails that we are living in an era of radical pluralism—that anything goes. A philosophy of art must be compatible with every artistic possibility. It rules nothing out, it licenses no artistic imperatives. Unlike writers such as Greenberg or Fry, I can accept everything. As an art critic, I know, if I am philosophically correct, that my philosophy favors nothing over anything else. Once I delivered a lecture at the Sorbonne when my wife was about to open an exhibition at her gallery in Paris. A French colleague visited her show and wrote me that he was delighted, since he thought that, married to me, she would paint nothing but Brillo boxes! I attempt to follow where the art leads and find the meanings it leads me to. If the meanings are universal, that is where I go.

There is, however, one consideration concerning my critical practice that derives from the untypical circumstance that I am also a philosopher. This is that as I have no obligation to review anything that comes along, I tend as a general rule to write on art that has something philosophical about it—art that philosophizes. For that is the kind of art I feel I can write and think about in a way for which I am particularly well suited. If there were art that was purely aesthetic, by contrast, I would have no particular qualification to write about it, and very likely not a lot to say. There is a lot of art that has a philosophical component, however, more than enough to have enabled me to write a fairly regular column for *The Nation*, and for other venues, and even to compose monographs, such as the one on Mark Tansey with which Michael Kelly has concerned himself here, and which he finds somehow too philosophical, or philosophical in a wrong way. It is doubtless a defect on my part that the problem he finds with my text has not dawned on me yet. I am afraid that nothing in his critique would cause me to change a word in what I wrote. Am I to be an iconoclast in the sense of turning art into philosophy? As Circe turned men into pigs? Perhaps Circe's gesture was parafeminist, given that "Men are pigs" is not an uncommon feminist comment. But I don't think of myself as doing anything of the kind. I think that as a critic, I have a nose for paintings that already embody philosophical meanings. I don't see that as iconoclasm even in Michael Kelly's eccentric use of the expression. It would be false to the art in question to treat it any other way!

Notes

This essay is based on chapter 4 of my *Iconoclasm in Aesthetics* (New York: Cambridge University Press, 2003).

1. In his unpublished autobiographical essay, "My Life as a Philosopher," Danto says that he wanted to allow himself "to be guided by art rather than by the philosophy of art," which at the time was dominated by Wittgensteinian and institutional theories of art.

2. Also in "My Life as a Philosopher."

3. For a discussion of Danto's definition of art (both a formulation and its internal history), see *After the End of Art: Contemporary Art and the Pale of History* (Princeton: Princeton University Press, 1997).

4. See the introduction to Danto's *Madonna of the Future* (New York: Farrar, Straus & Giroux, 2000), where he describes his sense of art criticism in terms of this definition, albeit without referring to it as such. See also my interview with Danto about this book (and specifically about the relationship between his philosophy/definition of art and his art criticism) in *BOMB*, no. 92 (June 2000): 84–89.

5. Also in "My Life as a Philosopher."

6. Also in "My Life as a Philosopher."

7. *Cindy Sherman: Film Stills*.

8. That this relationship is of concern to Danto suggests to me he is implicitly worried about the relevance of the philosophical interest in universality to our understanding of particular works of art, whether Tansey's or any others. I understand Tansey's work as a challenge to the imposition of any philosophical interests onto art, whether reality, truth, universality, or, as we'll see, the thesis of the identity of indiscernibles. My interpretation is contrary to most readings of Tansey, including Danto's, where his work is taken to be an ironic celebration of philosophy, whether analytic or deconstructive.

9. Arthur Danto, *Mark Tansey: Visions and Revisions* (New York: Abrams, 1992)—hereafter MT.

10. As such, Tansey's paintings seem to be both outdated, out of time, as if they had been painted before the advent of modernism, and timely, as if they had been mechanically reproduced, which would make them very much part of the present century. While Danto interprets Tansey's choice of monochrome as part of a general strategy to give the paintings the appearance of an artless and timeless style, which directly delivers the truth of the painting's content, I think there is another reason for Tansey's choice more consistent with his other aims and achievements: all types of art and, moreover, all sorts of nonart content can be

captured in monochrome pictures, much the way black-and-white photographs can be used to reproduce images of all kinds, whether art or not. Because the use of monochrome introduces virtually any subject matter into painting, it serves as a great equalizer that defies the art/kitsch or high/low art distinctions that were essential to modernism. Thus Tansey's apparent acceptance of the modernist claim that the essence of painting is color turns out to have the effect of challenging that very claim, especially when reduced even further to just a single color per painting, since all forms of art and nonart can be rendered in monochrome.

11. In a sense, Tansey's style does draw attention to itself without aiming to do so because it is a nonstyle in a postmodernist age where drawing attention to one-self is a dominant artistic style.

12. An example of the second type would be *Pleasure of the Text* (1986), where a man standing behind a stop sign is viewing the underside of an airborne car flying perilously toward him.

13. Or, to express the same point from the opposite direction, Tansey's practice is to make what (we know) is impossible in reality seem truly possible in painting (MT 13, passim) as a way to emphasize what art *can* do rather than what it can*not* do.

14. It is also biblical in the sense that Danto says that Tansey is making a contribu-tion to the "theology of painting" (MT 12).

15. "The Artworld," in *Journal of Philosophy* 61, no. 19 (October 16, 1964): 580. The complete sentence from which I quote here is: "To see something as art requires something the eye cannot descry—an atmosphere of artistic theory, a knowledge of the history of art—an artworld."

16. "In my work, I'm searching for pictorial functions that are based on the idea that the painted picture knows itself to be metaphorical, rhetorical, transformational, fictional"—Tansey, "Notes and Comments," in MT 127–35, here 132.

17. *Beyond the Brillo Box: The Visual Arts in Posthistorical Perspective* (New York: Far-rar, Strauss & Giroux, 1992), 16.

18. For example, critiques of depth (see *Myth of Depth* [1984] or *Triumph Over Mas-tery II* [1987]), of figuration (see almost any painting), of narrative (see *On Pho-tography [Homage to Susan Sontag]* [1982]), or of color (see *White on White* [1986]), and so on.

19. As was the case with Gerhard Richter, Tansey's commitment to open up pictorial possibilities is realized, if at all, in his art; we would need to look to his pictures, especially those created after he stopped critiquing modernist and deconstruc-tive credos, to see whether these possibilities have, in fact, been realized. See chapter 2 of my *Iconoclasm in Aesthetics.*

20. Or else we have to know that the white was painted first and painted all the same, and then, after the figures are introduced, reconstruct (from know-ledge, not memory) the white in our mind as being the same, appearances notwithstanding.

21. On Danto's account, Tansey also critiques several modernist credos (e.g., Green-berg's prohibition on figuration and his apparent reduction of the essence of

painting to color and flatness) that continue to leave their mark on art, if only through postmodern artists' resistance to them.

22. Now, one might interject here that the artist and the philosopher simply have different interests when they engage either in art or in discussions of it. While this is true in general, my concern is what it means for the philosophical understanding of a particular artist's work. Tansey's practice is to make a painting in the only way he knows how: by working with the crossroads, juxtapositions, riffs, and the like that emerge in the daily practice of painting. A painting emerges only when the crossroads and the like "give one up." Whatever Danto's interest is when he interprets Tansey's painting, he must begin with what makes the painting he wants to interpret into a painting in the first place. Will that influence how he interprets it? For sure, though the painting will be underdetermined on the interpretive level, just as *White on White* is. So there will be plenty of room for the conflict of interpretations on which critics and philosophers thrive. Despite such underdetermination, however, every interpretation is indebted to the determination that makes a painting possible, for this is what makes (at least the "what" of) interpretation possible as well. If Danto overlooks these points, he has nothing left to interpret.

Philosophy thus aims to legitimate itself by arguing that art cannot be philosophical. This may seem like a mere territorial issue that, while perhaps relevant to philosophy's self-identity, is not of concern to art. Unfortunately, art cannot be so sanguine on this point, because for philosophy to achieve the security it seeks, it must inscribe its interests into art. This is, I think, what Danto inadvertently does in his essay on Tansey. Such inscription is not innocent, as if it were something we should expect one discipline to do when it engages another; for, as we have seen already, such inscription prevents philosophy from grasping the very art it seeks to understand and interpret.

To explain further that what is at issue here is philosophical rather than interpretive, I want to discuss the problem Danto seems to have with Tansey's work after 1987, beginning with *Mont Sainte-Victoire*. As if he were a Foucauldian archaeologist, Danto sees a rupture in Tansey's work around 1987. It allegedly shifts from being a series of paintings that critically illustrate the possibility/impossibility theme to being celebratory embodiments or allegories of poststructuralism, particularly deconstruction. In short, Danto thinks that in 1987, Tansey suddenly stopped ironically challenging the reigning aesthetic ideologies of his time (MT 27). If his work is interpreted in the way I have proposed, however, there is no such break. There is rather a continuity of work concerned both to critique philosophical misconceptions about art (whether modernist or postmodernist, analytic or continental) and to explore the possibilities of appearance (instead of the appearance of impossibilities). When Tansey begins to include Derrida and De Man or other poststructuralists into his work (e.g., *Derrida Queries De Man* [1990]), the effect is a critique of their tendency to view art in terms of some ontological deficiency, much the way Derrida does. One way that Tansey critiques them is by showing that their critique of representation (for being ideological as well as indeterminate) applies to deconstructivist texts themselves, for they too are representations. To demonstrate that they are indeed representations, Tansey literally makes paintings out of silk-screened photocopies of various texts and then adds figuration onto the textualized surface, as he does in *a* (see also *Close Reading* [1990] and others). Of course, it is easy to read these paintings as celebratory, as Robbe-Grillet did when he first saw *Robbe-Grillet Cleansing Every Object in Sight* (1981); but on a closer look, this painting makes an ironic comment on the impossibility of the writer's attempt to strip literature of subjectivity and meaning by reducing narratives to an act of objective scanning. The irony is that this act would have to be self-reflexive to be completed (see the duplicate, miniaturized image of Robbe-Grillet in the lower right corner of the canvas) but that is, of course, impossible. I mention this painting in particular because it was done in 1981, prior to the rupture Danto claims to identify. So this painting is rather evidence of the continuity in Tansey's paintings. For in a similar manner, when Derrida, De Man, and others are depicted in later paintings, such as *Constructing the Grand Canyon* (1990), they appear to be supervising the impossible task of denaturalizing texts (or else mining their indeterminacy)— impossible since this task would have to be denaturalized as well, but even if that were possible, it would result in something else to be denaturalized, and so on. What Danto misses in the *post*–1987 paintings is therefore their critical dimension, since he sees them only as affirmative. At the same time, what he misses in the *pre*–1987 works is their positive or constructive dimension, since he sees them only in terms of their critical edge. Danto thus fails to see that there are critical *and* positive moments generating the possibilities of appearance in Tansey's work—before and after 1987, hence there is no rupture—and, moreover, that these possibilities are in turn what make the paintings possible in the first place. So a failure to see these moments, especially as they work in tandem, is not to see the philosophical issue of what accounts for Tansey's work as art.

23. It may seem odd to accuse Danto of being an iconoclast, since a) he is an art critic as well as a philosopher; b) he is one of the few philosophers to develop a theory of art in direct response to contemporary art; c) he argues that history is central to art; and d) he has written critically about the problem of the "philosophical disenfranchisement of art," which is very similar to what I am calling iconoclasm—see his *The Philosophical Disenfranchisement of Art* (New York: Columbia University Press, 1986). But the charge is appropriate, both for reasons articulated here and for the following additional reasons. First of all, iconoclasts always have some interest in art, though only of the type (of interest as well as of art) they find acceptable, which of course it is one of the objectives of iconoclasts to determine. This is no less true of the philosophical form of iconoclasm than it is of the more common religious, political, or cultural forms. So appeal to Danto's personal or professional interest in art does not in itself exonerate him; if anything, it makes him more suspect, given my notion of iconoclasm as involving philosophical interest that actually *generates* disinterest. But more to the point here is the fact that I am analyzing iconoclasm first and foremost on the

level of theory, not on the level of actual engagement with the arts; that is, my focus is on how Danto *conceives* art, not on whether or not he is appreciatively involved with the art he so conceives.

My critique of Danto's iconoclasm is part of a longer manuscript on iconoclasm in the work of Martin Heidegger, Theodor Adorno, and Jacques Derrida. So Danto is in good company.

24. The term "disinterestedness" is of course traditionally synonymous with "impartiality," especially in connection with judgment (in legal and moral as well as aesthetic cases), but such impartiality is itself a means to achieve universality. My focus here is on the interest in universality that underlies disinterestedness rather than on the impartiality that is achieved once disinterestedness has been attained. In a word, I am concerned about the costs of such universality relative to the other interests determining art.

25. Another serious problem with this inscription is that art is deemed *deficient* relative to these philosophical interests. More specifically, art is constituted, according to Danto, by the need to define itself in essential terms; since definition is the provenance of philosophy, however, art fails to achieve this definition (the closest it comes is Warhol's *Brillo Box* in 1964). Philosophy (Danto in particular) then provides art with the essentialist definition it needs but cannot attain on its own. What should be clear here, however, is that what philosophy provides is what philosophy has determined art needs and only philosophy can provide. I think this strategy has more to do with the legitimation of the philosophy of art (in terms of the analytic criteria of what makes for good philosophy) than with art.

26. The meaning of "disinterest" is always somehow tied to that of "interest," but the relationship between these terms here is not to be understood as between two contrary terms that are taken to be mutually exclusive. If they are seen only in that contrary way, then if somebody had an interest in art, for example, she could not at the same time have a *dis*interest in it. But the terms are sometimes related in a more dialectical manner, as is the case here, where interest and disinterest are conflicting but *mutually determining* rather than mutually exclusive. Danto clearly has an active interest in art, which is evident in his philosophy of art as well as in his art criticism. But at the same time, he has a disinterest in art, or, to make the same point stronger as well as in the right order, it is *because* of the philosophical interest he has in art that he has a disinterest in it as well. For Danto displays a disinterest in art in the sense that when he is actually interested in art, his primary interest is directed to some philosophical problem, albeit as it is reflected in art, and away from the historical conditions constitutive of what art is or does. This is not to say that interest and disinterest do not conflict; on the contrary, my aim is precisely to identify and analyze their conflict, but in such a way that it is clear that when they do conflict, they are determining rather than excluding each other. And it is with such conflict in mind that it is clear why the term "disinterest" is more appropriate here than "lack of interest" (and "disinterested" more than "uninterested"), since disinterest preserves the relation to interest while "lack of interest" simply points to the absence of interest.

9
Danto, History, and the Tragedy of Human Existence

Frank R. Ankersmit

Analytical Philosophy of History, published in 1965, was Arthur Danto's first major book. The first of a trilogy, it was soon followed by *Analytical Philosophy of Knowledge,* and a few years later by *Analytical Philosophy of Action* (perhaps the best of the three). The trilogy firmly established Danto's reputation as one of the most ambitious and original younger philosophers carrying on the analytical tradition. But there is something odd about this beginning of Danto's career. What analytical philosopher in the 1960s would have planned to make his name with a book on so outlandish a topic as the philosophy of history? Danto once told me that, in his experience, analytical philosophers regard the philosophy of history in much the same way that musicologists regard military music—as a noisy pastime for less-talented amateurs in which one should certainly not indulge if one hopes to be taken seriously. So was Danto not committing a kind of intellectual suicide when presenting himself to his dainty colleagues with a book on so offensive a topic?

This may presage what I wish to do in this essay. I shall not enter upon a close discussion of Danto's philosophy of history book of forty years ago; nor will it be my aim to present a philosophy of history that might be gleaned from the whole of Danto's vast philosophical oeuvre. I shall discuss, instead, the question of the place of the philosophy of history in the philosophy of language in general and, more specifically, the assumption shared by most contemporary philosophers that the philosophy of history is merely tangential to the philosophy of language. My conclusion will be that Danto demonstrated the philosophy of history to be of far more central significance than is commonly believed by the practitioners of the philosophy of language. In order to see this, we should focus on Danto's notion of representation.

Representation

In 1985, a second edition of *Analytical Philosophy of History* was published. Three lengthy essays were added to the original text. They can be read as a reflection on the nature of historical representation and its proper place in the philosophy of language. I quote from the second and most important of them the following passage:

> The incommensurabilities between scientific and philosophical propositions reflect the incommensurability of two distinct relationships in which language stands to the world. In one relationship, language stands to reality merely in the part-whole relationship: it is amongst the things the world contains, and is merely a further element in the order of reality. In its other relationship, language stands in an external relationship to reality in its entirety, itself included when taken as included in the inventory of reality. It is external primarily when we construe it in its capacity to *represent* the world, and hence in its capacity to sustain what I have elsewhere termed semantical values, for example *"true"* and *"false."*[1]

Two ways of doing philosophy correspond to this distinction. The first includes those philosophers who prefer to model philosophical inquiry on science. For them language is just another tool in the effort to "cope with reality," as Richard Rorty would have put it; within this conception, language is epistemologically on a par with our hands, the instruments used in a scientific experiment, or the tools we use for constructing them. Danto comments that this kind of philosophy of language aims at a "naturalization of semantics." For within this approach to the traditional semantic questions, questions about the nature of truth, meaning, and reference are not essentially different from the kind of questions that are addressed in the natural sciences. The world contains electrons, molecules, plants, animals, and next to all these, such a peculiar thing as language. Though the investigation of the latter will undoubtedly have its own problems, there is no a priori reason to set them categorically apart from the kind of problems occasioned by more traditional objects of scientific research. Examples of this kind of philosophy are ordinary language philosophy as proposed by Austin, causal theories of reference as developed by Kripke, and the contemporary effort to explain the philosophical problems of consciousness in terms of neuro-physiological processes. Pragmatism had this naturalization of epistemology as its very program, and much the same is true of literary theory and of semiotics.

Within the other conception of language, the one preferred by Danto himself, language "stands in an external relationship to reality in its entirety, itself included when taken as included in the inventory of reality." That is to say, on the one hand we have the world, and on the other the language we use for speaking about the world. This implies that there is a clear demarcation line between science and philosophy: the scientist investigates the world, and the philosopher of language the problem of how language relates to the world. True, as Danto emphasizes, even within this conception of philosophy language may be seen as part of the world. But if so, this is not a return to the former conception. For then a strict distinction is made between the philosopher's own language and the language that is now situated in the world, so that the former finds itself again in this "external relationship to reality in its entirety."

Recall, next, that in the passage quoted Danto used explicitly the term "representation" when discussing the kind of philosophy of language that he prefers. This surely is no coincidence. For the notion of representation is absolutely crucial to the whole of his philosophical effort. Mark Rollins once wrote that there are two central elements in Danto's thought: the concept of representation and the method of indiscernibles.[2] So, whereas for most philosophers the term "representation" is like a coin that one never closely inspects, for Danto it is a technical term whose precise meaning we cannot afford to ignore.

Danto is an advocate of what one might call the "substitution theory of representation," first formulated, as far as I know, by Edmund Burke in his *Enquiries into the Nature of the Sublime and the Beautiful* of 1757. Contemporary advocates of the theory are Ernst Gombrich in a well-known essay entitled "Meditations on a Hobby Horse," and Kendall Walton in his *Art as Make-Believe*. Danto himself formulates the theory as follows: "a representation is something that stands in the place of something else, as our representatives in Congress stand proxy for ourselves."[3] And just like Gombrich, he conjectures that art originated from the desire to have idols function as substitutes for the gods themselves. But whereas Gombrich stops here, suggesting thereby that even today the work of art (as the heir to the prehistoric idol) is a substitute for what it represents, Danto offers a more subtle account. Unlike Gombrich, he differentiates between two stages. Initially the work of art was so much of a substitute for what it represents as to be ontologically and epistemically interchangeable with it; the idol *was* the god. (This is what we might call the "Gombrich stage.") But at a later stage, representations were relegated to an ontological and epistemic realm of their own. Only then did they come to stand in a truly semantic relationship to what they represented, instead of being in some strange way identical with it—though without ever wholly surrendering, even in this second stage, the memory of the Gombrich stage. As Danto puts it: "what we would call statues, gravures, rites, and the like, underwent a transformation from being simply part of reality . . . into things that contrasted with reality, standing outside and against it."[4] To explain it schematically: first is the thing itself, the represented; next a representation that can take its place and that is *indiscernible* from the represented; and last, a representation that has an ontological and epistemic status of its own and that is no longer indiscernible from what it represents. Nobody mistakes paintings of landscapes for landscapes themselves.

Danto then adds a comment full of the most far-reaching implications: "artworks became the sort of representation we now regard language as being, though even language—words—once formed a magical part of reality and participated in the substance of things we would now say merely form parts of their extensions."[5] Now, this is revolutionary. *For representation, as we may find it in the work of art, is presented here as the model of how language relates to the world.* This is a departure completely different from that to which we are accustomed in epistemology. One used to begin with the most simple singular true statement of the "the cat is on the mat" type, in order to proceed to more complicated uses of language. The assumption was that the simple singular statement is the most elementary unit by which to investigate how language relates to the world.

But Danto proposes aesthetic representation as more basic. Representation is more fundamental than the simple singular statement since it comprises a stage—the Gombrich stage—in which the world and its representation, or the world and the language we use for speaking about it, have not yet grown apart. Moreover, once at this most elementary stage, Danto asks a question that had never been asked before: how may representation and language succeed in acquiring semantic autonomy with regard to the represented, or to the world—an autonomy that was always naïvely and so self-evidently granted by traditional epistemology. For traditional epistemology accepts as a matter of course that the world is indifferent to what we say about it in language, and therefore ignores, or pre-supposes, the stage to which Danto commends our attention, where the represented and its representation are still closely intertwined. Danto answers the question I mentioned a moment ago about semantic autonomy by urging us to investigate the "take off," so to speak, of representation from the represented, that is, how a representation can evolve from an initial phase of still being indiscernible from what it represents to a phase where it simply *is*. Hence Danto's fascination with the Leibnizian notion of indiscernibility, and with the question of whether, under what circumstances, two things can be different in spite of sharing all their relevant features. Hence, too, his fascination with Warhol's *Brillo Box* and with the question of how one Brillo box is a mere household article while the other is a work of art. For *Brillo Box* truly is a contemporary *lieu de mémoire* of the birth of language from what was not yet language; it is a work of art reminding us of how art and representation may emancipate themselves from what is not yet art and representation. Indeed, in all these cases the issue is how semantics is born from ontological and epistemological identity.

This also explains why history should be so supremely important within the parameters of Danto's philosophy, and why he most appropriately devoted his first book to this Cinderella of contemporary philosophy that the philosophy of history unfortunately still is. One may forgive philosophers of language if they are not too deeply troubled by the problems posed by Danto's two indiscernible Brillo boxes. For most philosophers of language, art will rarely be more than a doubtful metaphor of how language relates to the world, whether one argues from art to language (as Danto does) or from language to art (as did Nelson Goodman in *The Languages of Art*). But this cannot be the case in the writing of history, which presents representations of the world (that is, of the past) no less than art. But unlike the artist, the historian does not make use of paint, marble, or wood, but of *language* for representing the world. More importantly, historians are also at pains to ensure that their narratives do justice as fully as possible to the subject matter of their narratives. Whether one would prefer to rephrase "doing justice to" in terms of "truth," "plausibility," "adequacy," "scope," or whatever alternative options one might think of is not important in the present context. What is important, however, is that historical writing is the closest textual or narrative analogue to the true statement. This is why one can only be amazed by the complete neglect of history by philosophers of language. Surely, nobody could deny the practical and theoretical significance of what we can say about the world in terms of the true statement or in terms of scientific theories—and all that has been discovered about this by philosophers of language and of science belongs to the greatest triumphs of twentieth-century philosophy. But we need not only think of historical writing, for articles in newspapers, the kind of reports used in court or in politics, and even the kind of stories that we tell each other or ourselves in daily life show how deep this use of language penetrates into the heart of all human existence. In sum, the philosophy of language has remained an unfinished torso due to such a strange and complete disregard of the problems the historian professionally has to face. Danto's main achievement as a philosopher of history has been, in my view, to remind us of this.

Danto on Historical Representation

Let us now turn to the issue of historical representation, specifically, the issue of the relationship between a representation and what it represents (and hence, between the historian's language or text and the past).

As might be expected from what was said above, Danto rejects traditional empiricist and epistemological accounts of how historical language relates to the world. For the empiricist, the inventory of the world is indifferent to the categories and schemes we adopt for speaking and thinking about it. Trees and electrons exist whether the concepts "tree" and "electron" are in use or not. The objects are simply there, in the world, and when we have experience of them we can arrange our conceptual dictionary accordingly. But, as Danto argues, representations are different, since, in a certain sense, the represented has no existence without its representation; indeed, in a way, representation even precedes the represented. In order to make clear what Danto has in mind and to avoid any unwarranted idealist interpretation of his intentions, I refer to an example given by Danto himself. He asks, can one speak of the United States of America before, say, 1776? In one sense, yes, of course, since the mountains, rivers, and prairies of this marvelous country are supremely indifferent to the name people decided to give to it. But in another sense, no, insofar as the country only came into being when people started to use the name United States of America. And so it is with representation in general—and certainly with historical representation: the represented only acquires its contours thanks to the representations we have of it.[6] We can only speak of "the Renaissance" after representations of it are given to us precisely because no such era exists until it is represented as such. The same is true for political representation. A democratic nation only comes into being after it has unfolded itself in a represented electorate and its representatives. Without representation there is no nation. This, then, is how renaissances and democratic states differ from trees or electrons.

Next, epistemology. There are two dimensions to Danto's rejection of epistemology for historical representation. First, he rejects the "very idea of conceptual schemes"—to use Davidson's terminology. It may surprise us to find Danto's critique of epistemology already in his philosophy of history book of 1965, since at the time, epistemology was still the only game in town. Danto dismisses here epistemological worries about the reliability of historical knowledge. Most often these worries originate in the indisputable fact that we cannot have direct access to the past since it no longer exists. On this Danto comments:

> This is in some way an odd kind of lamentation. Our incapacity, which is granted, to observe the past, is not a defect in history itself, but a deficiency which it is the precise purpose of history to overcome. It is not, comparably, a deficiency in medical science that people fall ill, but rather, the deficiency in human existence in which illness consists is precisely what we have medical science *for*: we would not need it if we were always sound. That cities lie at a spatial distance from one another is not to be regarded as a defect in our systems of transportation: it is a deficiency, if one may style it thus, which systems of transportation are precisely designed to overcome.[7]

This powerful and most ingenious argument makes clear why, at least for history and for historical representation, epistemology is useless. For it suggests that epistemology aimed to do what can only be done by historians themselves, that is, to bridge the gap between the present and the past. If we worry about whether or not to believe a historical account, we should listen to the arguments that historians have for their views and not to epistemological speculation—and that is the end of it. Historical representation is "instant epistemology," so to speak: it does for individual historical problems what epistemology attempts to do for knowledge in general by means of its conceptual schemes. But precisely because of this, epistemology can only be expected to raise a cloud of dust, with the result that nobody can see anymore—to paraphrase the Bishop of Cloyne.

This brings me to a second dimension of Danto's attitude toward epistemology. As the idea of historical representation as "instant epistemology" already suggests, there is a continuity between what the historian and the epistemologist have always believed themselves to be doing. More generally, the historian or artist thinking about how to represent (part of) the world is in fact doing what is the essence of the philosopher's job, namely, finding out about the epistemological problem of how language of history or "the language of art" relates to the world. Needless to add, this is one of the main arguments of *The Transfiguration of the Commonplace*. Danto argues there that art has become, since Warhol, the continuation of philosophy with other, and probably more effective, means, as Clausewitz would have put it.

If little is to be expected from empiricism and from epistemology to clarify the relationship between historical writing and the past, we should look elsewhere. Obviously, this will require a closer look at (historical) representation. Now, recall that in representation everything begins with an initial "Gombrich stage" in which the represented and its representation are still "indiscernible." When asking ourselves what this "indiscernibility" might mean for the writing of history, we had best consider what Danto writes about the so-called Ideal Chronicler:

> I now want to insert an Ideal Chronicler into my picture. He knows whatever happens the moment it happens, even in other minds. He is also to have the gift of instantaneous transcription: everything that happens across the whole forward rim of the Past is set down by him, as it happens, the way it happens. The resultant running account I shall term the Ideal Chronicle. Once the event E is safely in the past, its full description is in the Ideal Chronicle. We may now think of the various parts of the Ideal Chronicle as accounts to which historians endeavor to approximate their own accounts.[8]

The past itself and its Ideal Chronicle might be said to be indiscernible, since *ex hypothesi* the past contains nothing that is not in the Ideal Chronicle. Of course, they are not indiscernible insofar as the past is not a text; but just as translation aims to preserve meaning while moving from one language to the other, so one might say that the Ideal Chronicle respects indiscernibility when moving from the represented past to its historical representation. A duplication of the past itself would not do, for we can say that things are *identical* with themselves, but not that they are *representations* of themselves. In this way it seems reasonable to agree with the claim that the Ideal Chronicle is a representation that is indiscernible from the past reality it represents. So far, so good.

But Danto then introduces a theme that came to play an ever more important role in his later philosophy. He points out that there is a category
of highly important descriptions that no historian could ever do without,
and that is nevertheless forever outside the reach of the Ideal Chronicler.
This is the category of so-called narrative sentences, which Danto defines
as follows:

> Their most general characteristic is that they refer to at least two time-
> separated events though they only *describe* (are only *about*) the earliest
> event to which they refer. . . . Narrative sentences offer an occasion for dis-
> cussing, in a systematic way, a great many of the philosophical problems
> which history raises and which it is the task of the *philosophy* of history to
> try to solve.[9]

An example of a narrative sentence is "The Thirty Years' War began in
1618." This sentence is, obviously, only "about" the outbreak of the war in
1618; it describes only this event. But it does so by implicitly referring also
to the year 1648, for the sentence could only be uttered *after* that year, that
is, after it could be known that the war would last for thirty long and bloody
years. Because this narrative sentence could not be in the Ideal Chronicle,
Danto infers that a complete description of some event, or part of the past,
can never be given at the time of the event itself. Many meaningful and informative descriptions can be given only at a time later than the event in
question.

Four consequences follow from this. First, the difference between the
sentence "A war began in 1618" (which is in the Ideal Chronicle) and the
narrative sentence "The Thirty Years' War began in 1618" (which is not)
cannot be related to any historical content. It is a difference in *perspective*,
in whether we look at the past from the perspective of the past itself or
from that of a later period. Hence, though the past and its representation
can be said to be indiscernible at the level of the former sentence (which is
in the Ideal Chronicle), they are discernible at the level of the latter narrative sentence (which is not in the Ideal Chronicle). Recall that for Danto,
all the real semantic problems of our use of language arise when language
comes to stand in an external relationship to the world. So this gives us a
formal determination of the task of the philosophy of history: it should
focus on the change of perspective that determines what can and what can
no longer be part of the Ideal Chronicle.

Second, only in objects' moving from "indiscernibility" to "discern-
ibility" do the philosophical problems that really count come into being.

The "method of indiscernibles" almost automatically focuses attention on what will truly be essential for a discipline such as historical writing. Most contemporary philosophy of history is strangely unmethodical, focusing on what happens to catch the eye of a particular philosopher engaged in some other project. For example, the well-known "covering-law debate" was, in fact, a spin-off of the "unity of science" thesis. This thesis urged philosophers to fit the writing of history into the conceptual framework of the sciences—and the "covering-law model" was an attempt to do so. A little later, hermeneuticists hijacked history in an effort to make it land at the airport of Heideggerian existentialism. A little later again, literary theory was wheeled in to be the instrument for analyzing the historical text. But all this is a way of doing the philosophy of history without focusing on what is central to history itself.

Third, Danto's approach provides the means to see what is inadequate to the more traditional variants of historical theory. Thus, though Danto still writes with sympathy about the covering-law model in the 1965 book, we need only recognize the immense gap separating representation from explanation by general laws in order to relegate this model to the museum of obsolete curiosities—as Danto was soon to do himself after its publication. Much the same is true of Hayden White's proposal to investigate the writing of history with the instruments of literary theory. For this approach restricts our gaze to the historical text, and thus disregards the issue of the relationship between the representation and what it represents.

Fourth, hermeneutics will have to go as well. Think of Collingwoodian hermeneutics, according to which the historian should "re-enact the past in his own mind." It is obvious that this is a conception of the writing of history that reduces it to the Ideal Chronicle. No room is left for the *ex post facto* perspective that Danto identifies as the heart of the writing of history:

> The reason an event is mentioned in a narrative is typically different from the reason the event happened: different, in brief, from historical explanation. This is so obvious it would hardly bear mention were it not for the practice of some of the great philosophers of history to use the one sort of reason in place of the other, projecting onto the fabric of history the structures which belong instead to its narrative representation.[10]

At both levels a different logic obtains: the reasons agents may have for doing certain things—at the level of *their* representations of the world—

will undoubtedly differ from the reasons historians may have for including or omitting something from their narrative—at the level of narrative representation. "Stories are not lived, but told," as Louis O. Mink's famous slogan goes—or, as Danto puts it himself, "ends of stories belong to stories, not to reality."[11] The implication is that there could not possibly be the kind of continuity between the past itself and the historian's narrative about it postulated by hermeneutic theorists such as Collingwood, Paul Ricoeur, David Carr, and Jörn Rüsen.[12]

Danto's Hegelianism

Danto's greatest achievement as a philosopher of history is, in my view, his theory that the perspectivism of narrative sentences compels us to recognize the metaphorical nature of historical representation. The central idea here is that representation objectifies how people in the past related to their world in a way that they were incapable of. Representation achieves this peculiar opposition between ourselves and the people of the past because representations are, as Danto puts it, both "within and without reality at once." They are "inside" the world because they are part of the makeup of our world. But they are "outside" the world as well because they originate in a perspective we have on it, and having perspectives on the world places us outside it. How we represent the world can never be part of our representations themselves; we see the world *through* our representations of it, but do not see them. "I represent the world, not my representation of the world," as Danto puts it.[13] This results in a peculiar asymmetry in how we relate to our own and others' beliefs: whereas we perceive those of others as being part of a network of their representations of the world, we think of our own as being directly related to what they are beliefs about. We experience them as being transparent with regard to what they are about, whereas we experience those of others as part of a system of representing the world. As Danto writes: "To put it with a certain dash of paradox, we do not occupy our own interiors. We live rather naively in the world."[14] The explanation for this is that when I speak about my beliefs, I make a claim about the world, whereas when I speak about the beliefs of others, I speak not of their world but of whether they hold these beliefs or not:

> I cannot say without contradiction that I believe that s but that s is false, but I can say of another person that he believes that s but it is false. When

I refer to another man's beliefs I am referring to him, whereas he, when expressing his beliefs, is not referring to himself but to the world. The beliefs in question are transparent to the believer; he reads the world through them without reading them. But his beliefs are opaque to others: they do not read the world through these beliefs; they as it were, read the beliefs. My beliefs in this respect are invisible to me until something makes them visible and I can see them from the outside.[15]

This is what history and historical representation are all about: what used to be naïve, natural, unreflected, and part of how the world simply is suddenly, when seen from the historian's perspective, takes on the appearance of the historically contingent, of how a certain civilization or people in a certain historical period saw their world.

This insight is elaborated down to its last and most breathtaking consequences in Danto's later philosophy. First, Danto relates it to what he describes as the *intensionality* of representational language. The link between the two will be obvious if we take into account how he defines intensional contexts: "intensional contexts are such because the sentences in whose formation they enter are about specific sentences—or about specific representations—and not about whatever those sentences or representations would be about were they to occur outside those contexts."[16] That is to say, the truth of sentences in intensional contexts is not decided exclusively by what they say about the world but also by how they are formulated, and hence by the sentence as such. For example, the intensional sentence "A believes that the water boils" cannot be exchanged for "A believes that the temperature of the water is above 100 degrees Celsius," since A may not know that water boils at 100 degrees Celsius. Taking into account this property of intensional contexts, it will be obvious that narrative sentences and historical representations are intensional. They describe the past in a way of which no omniscient observer in the past itself would have been capable. The sentence "A believes that in 1618 a war began" could not be exchanged for the sentence "A believes that in 1618 the Thirty Years' War began," if only because many people, more particularly all people living between 1618 and 1648, could not know that the war that broke out in 1618 would last for thirty years. Furthermore, the linguistic turn has taught us that the intensional character of historical writing is right at the heart of the discipline.[17] For historians continuously devise new vocabularies, in terms of which they propose to conceive of the past, that were unknown to the people in the past themselves. So intensionality is far from being a merely accidental property of historical writing; on the contrary, because of its perspectivism, historical representation is necessarily intensional.

Here we can observe a surprising overlap with Hayden White's view that all historical writing is guided by one or more of the four major tropes. To see this, note that intensionality is a prominent property of metaphor as well. Danto considers Romeo's metaphor "Juliet is the sun" and then reminds us that in this metaphor the phrase "the sun" can certainly not be exchanged for the phrase "the body of hot gases at the center of the solar system."[18] So the message a metaphor wishes to convey depends on how the metaphor is formulated, and the words used for expressing it cannot be exchanged for words having the same reference. And though Danto does not make the point himself, the same argument can be given for the historian's text. For just like the user of a metaphor, historians deliberately choose the text that they submit in order to portray the past, and the fact that they propose *this* text or representation is tacitly meant to exclude all alternative texts that could be written. This is where texts and representations differ from statements: statements are not exclusivist; the exclusion of other statements is not part of their meaning. But aggressiveness against other representations is part of the meaning of individual representations.

So, before presenting their texts to their readers, historians carefully ponder the pros and cons of alternative texts—those written by other historians, or alternative versions of their own final text. Though all the texts are about the *same* past, though all of them have the same referent,[19] for a particular historian *this* text is most appropriate for accounting for (some part of) the past. In this way, historians find themselves in the same position as Romeo: both are fascinated by some object, either Juliet or (part of) the past, and both then ask themselves what chunk of language could best represent it. What is presented is inextricably linked with the way it is presented: "thus a metaphor presents its subject and presents the way in which it does present it. And it is true if the subject can be presented that way, though it may be false or flat if presented in a different form."[20] So both metaphor and historical representation have in common the concern of how best to couple language and the world. This is where Danto's and White's conceptions of narrative and of historical representation are in unexpected agreement. (White does not stop there, going on to say that historical representation may also be synecdochical, metonymical, or ironic, but one may well doubt whether much is gained with this addition.

Does it not confuse the issues of the relationship of the represented and its representation with empirical observations about the literary properties of historical texts?)

However, the most amazing implication of Danto's claim about the intensionality of historical representation is what it implies about truth. If historical truth, the truth of historical representation, is intensional as Danto understands this term, it follows that in history truth always is *ex post facto*, since truth is indissolubly linked to historical representation and historical representation to historical perspective. But perhaps this is an unsatisfactory way of stating the situation, because it doesn't do justice to the tragic character of historical truth, to the fact that we can only recognize ourselves in what we are no longer. Since history and historical truth can show us only what we are no longer, it cannot show us what we are. The paradox is that truth should not be associated with either the past or the present, but with the temporal standpoint from which we have, so to speak, taken our leave from the past as a world that is now, in the true sense of the words, *historical and past*. Paradoxically, truth is not the privilege of the insider but of the outsider. Just as for Hegel the owls of Minerva can only fly at dusk when a form of life has grown old and the transition to a new world has announced itself, so for Danto historical truth is backward-looking. This is expressed in a marvelous way when he ponders what happens when a civilization moves from one stage in its life to a later one:

> And something of the same sort is true for the historical period considered as an entity. It is a period solely from the perspective of the historian, who sees it from without; for those who lived in the period it would be just the way life was lived. And asked, afterwards, what it was like to have lived then, they may answer from the outside, from the historian's perspective. From the inside there is no answer to be given; it was simply the way things were. So when the members of a period can give an answer in terms satisfactory to the historian, the period will have exposed its outward surface and in a sense be over, as a period.[21]

In these beautiful lines Danto expresses the tragic character of historical truth: as soon as it can be formulated, we have moved to a world beyond it. But this does not mean that this historical truth has now become irrelevant: on the contrary, we define ourselves and the present in terms of what has been superseded by the course of history. To put it into one formula: *we are what we are no longer*—and in this way the past persists in us, precisely because *this* is the past that has been superseded by *us*. We define ourselves, our identity, in terms of what we have left behind. This is the framework of our relationship to the past—within which we should admire and embrace the wisdom expressed in Hegel's philosophy of history, and thank Danto for reminding us of it.

Conclusion: History and the Tragedy of Human Existence

The major achievement of Danto's philosophy of history is, in my view, his conception of historical representation, and especially the Hegelian idea that flows from this conception, that in history truth is always *ex post facto* and not to be found in the past itself. Danto has elevated this idea in his *Transfiguration* into an insight into the tragedy of human existence. We desperately long for truth about ourselves, but if it is revealed to us we have, at that very moment, moved beyond the place where it could still be *our* truth. Danto softens this tragedy in our relationship to truth into an elegy; there is no quasi-existentialist pathos, no despair, nor even nostalgia in his account of how we relate to a truth that can only manifest itself in what has become for us a past in which we can find our home no longer. He does not attempt to compensate for the tragedy of historical truth by the seductive prospect of a comic Hegelian reconciliation of thought with the world.

Danto's serenity about this tragic disunion of truth and life certainly has much to do with the fact that art has been the main inspiration for his historical thought. For will the artist not prefer life to truth, will he or she not see the work of art as a symbolization and even as the celebration of the relationship between the two? The priority of life to truth will be both necessary and self-evident to the artist. But this must be different for the historian. Historians investigate the past in the hope that the truth about it will serve life, and the present. This is what has inspired all of Western historical writing since the birth of historicism, now some two hundred years ago—and this is how Nietzsche so movingly defined the assignment of the historian, following his friend and master Jakob Burckhardt.

Though the historian's assignment is more modest than that of the artist, it is not without its specific grandeur. For precisely in its position between truth and life lies a secret that may clarify the nature of both, and of which, perhaps, only history can make us aware. For what lies, in the end, between truth and life? What is the nature of this domain beyond truth where life is not yet? Is this not, as I would venture to suggest, the domain of experience—that is, of a variant of experience in which we have an openness to the world, in which we are willing to risk everything we have and everything we are? For this is at stake when we move, in Danto's account, from one period in history to a later one, and when the past and a former identity define ourselves in terms of what we are no longer. This experience of the past is absolutely essential, the place where the structures of historical consciousness defining how we relate to the past originate.[22]

⑂ ⑂ ⑂ ⑂ ⑂

Response

The ingenuity of Frank Ankersmit's piece is that it addresses my 1965 *Analytical Philosophy of History* as itself subject to the ideas it sets forth, especially the idea of what I introduced as "narrative sentences"—sentences that are about something that happens at a certain time, but refer to something else that takes place at a later time. The most important descriptions of historical events are not necessarily those that could have been known at the time they took place, since they have among their truth conditions later events, entirely unknowable to those contemporary with the original event, for whatever reasons the future is unknowable. Historical descriptions are really re-descriptions of events from perspectives that only the future can have revealed. The assassination of the Archduke Franz Ferdinand in Sarajevo was shocking to those who read about it in the newspapers, but its importance, invisible at the time, is now historical boilerplate: it began World War I. That was not something the assassin meant to do—not what anybody had in mind. But the assassination set off a string of decisions that took Europe into a war that changed everything. The world at the end of the war was unimaginably different from the world that was taken for granted when the archduke was killed. Ankersmit describes my book from the perspective of a philosophy of language that grew out of it, but was not something readers of the book would have gotten from it in 1965. It was not something intended by its author—me. It could not be reached by an act of *Verstehen*—an imaginative identification with the interior life of its author—since my mind might as well have been a tabula rasa, so far as that philosophy was concerned. If my situation in writing the book is at all typical, the method of *Verstehen*, what philosophers at the time would have called "historical understanding," is of decidedly limited value. As I understood and understand it, historical understanding is grasping what happened from a perspective that no one can have occupied at the time, since it is available only through seeing the past from the vantage point of a future unknowable when the past was present.

Ankersmit rightly draws attention to the concept of historical representation that is certainly laid out in the book, but that I would have been unable to make explicit until twenty years later, when the book was resissued with three later essays under the title *Narration and Knowledge,* by which time the concept of representation had become central to the way I saw and did philosophy. My main ambition in writing *Analytical Philosophy of History* had been to overcome certain skepticisms with regard to knowing about the past by demonstrating that what was taken by skeptics to show that historical knowledge is blocked through the fact that we cannot observe the past was irrelevant, since the main interest of the past for us could not, just because of the logic of narrative sentences, have been available to those who could observe the past directly. So it was primarily an exercise in historical epistemology. In terms of the polemical situation at the time, I was eager to show that the descriptions of events that counted as history could not be fitted into historical explanations as they had been analyzed by C. G. Hempel, since they would have been unknowable at the time the events took place. Hence history did not fit the model of science to which Hempel and other like-minded philosophers of science subscribed. History was an autonomous discipline—and although this characteristic was peripheral to my way of thinking then, it is really one of the humanities. This incidentally gave my book an importance in Europe that it never had in the United States, where, as Ankersmit correctly observes, the philosophy of history remained of peripheral significance. But German historians have told that the impulse of university administrators was to subsume history under the rubric of a social science, which would have made it in time as barren as the social sciences have become in consequence of trying to accommodate them to a Positivistic picture of science that made observation criterial to validity. Here was a book by an analytical philosopher that argued that this was the wrong way to go! And what was nice was that the book also had an argument against the idea of *Verstehen*—the basic operation to which defenders of the so-called *Geisteswissenschaften* typically appealed.

I have the most vivid memory of writing down those thoughts about the two relationships in which language stands to the world late in the summer of 1965. In one relationship, language is part of the world; in the other, it stands over and against the world as a representation. In that sketch, written in a friend's apartment in San Francisco, I said that the domain of philosophy is the space between language and the world. The concept certainly derived from Wittgenstein's *Tractatus,* which I loved as a piece of writing. There is language, as a set of propositions, and there is the world, as a set of facts that are pictured, one by one, by the propositions. What language cannot picture, on Wittgenstein's view, is the space between propositions and facts. No wonder, I thought, that he had difficulty in dealing with philosophy! If the space between language and the world is philosophy's domain, well, there are no philosophical facts in the world, and there are no philosophical propositions either, in a language that pictures the world fact by fact. Linguistics deals with language as part of the world—just the way Wittgenstein attempted to deal with it in the *Investigations,* as an instrument for facilitating forms of life. Instrumentalism has no room, however, for representations, and at that point I felt that my path in philosophy was set. I was going to write about representations systematically, and explore not the world but how we represent it and how we must be what I came to think of as *ens representans.* I mention this episode, however, because when I wrote my sketch—which became the preface to *Analytical Philosophy of Knowledge*—*Analytical Philosophy of History* was already in print. What Ankersmit has done, in making the idea of representation pivotal in his essay, is to describe my book on history in terms of the ideas that came to me afterward. Perhaps they are already there, somehow, but they would, as I say, have been invisible to me at the time I wrote it. What I would have been able to say, later, is that given the fact that narrative sentences are so central to the way we represent the world, we are, as *ens representens,* through and through historical. That is the deep reason that history is one of the humanities.

Ankersmit grasps this perfectly:

> We need not only think of historical writing, for articles in newspapers, the kinds of reports used in court or in politics, and even the kinds of stories we tell each other or ourselves in daily life show how deep this use of language penetrates into the heart of human existence.

In brief, we do not begin the acquisition of our knowledge of the world with the kind of knowledge that "The cat is on the mat" illustrates, but with "Once upon a time there was a cat." A teacher in the Philadelphia ghetto told me of trying to get his students to photograph their world, and that one student, who had been rebellious and difficult, finally took a camera and brought back some images of street corners and doorways. The teacher was deeply encouraged, and hoping to encourage the student himself, began to point out how to make better photographs by learning something about composition. The student was disgusted with this, and he explained his pictures this way. "That doorway was where my friend Dana got raped. That corner is where we used to score drugs." And so on. He was not showing the world his neighborhood of squalid doorways and scary street corners. He was showing the world as he lived it, as a site of stories that meant something in his life. Years later, my friend Karlheinz Ludeking drove me around Berlin—his city. There was the Reichstag and the Kurfurstendam, of course—but also where he lived as a student; where he and his wife, Christiane, first met; the restaurant where their wedding was held—places whose meaning for him would be invisible to everyone except those who had had thoe meanings explained to them. In showing these places to me, he was in effect making me part of his world. It was an act of deep friendship. Stanley Cavell, in his contribution, mentions the ending of one of Antonioni's films, *La Notte,* which shows an exceptionally long scene of an intersection in Milano at night, with traffic moving along the street and the stoplight going on and off. It is a piece of urban geography, but what we who have seen the film know is that what is significant is that the man and woman in the film have made a date to meet there—and Antonioni has given us enough time to know they will never show up. These kinds of meanings are invisible and unphotographable, at least directly. They are like events until they have been narratively redescribed. "The philosophy of language is an unfinished torso," Anksermit puts it poetically, "due to such a strange and complete disregard of the problems the historian professionally has to face."

I hit on the idea of narrative sentences at a time when analytical philosophers were identifying different kinds of sentences—observation sentences, reduction sentences, and the like—and at first they seemed a kind of joke. Like "The automobile has not yet been invented," said, maybe, in 1790. But I began to notice how frequently they were used in poetry, as in Yeats's *Leda and the Swan,* where he describes the rape of Leda in these terms: "A shudder in the loins engendered there / The burning wall, the broken tower, / and Agamemnon dead." I spent an entire summer writing "Narrative Sentences," which was accepted and published in *History and Theory.* Aside from responses from those to whom I sent offprints, I heard nothing; and when the magazine listed some of the important papers it had published as an incentive to subscribe, my piece was not mentioned. At that point I realized it would be lost if I did not publish a book. In those days it was unusual for analytical philosophers to publish books, unless they were collections of papers. But I enjoyed the experience of working out a whole subject at book length, and though the response to the book was not entirely thrilling, at least it was noticed, though the philosophy of history itself, so far as it was noticed, was mainly taken up with Hempel's theory of historical explanation, which was a product of the Unity of Science movement, and William Dray's book on historical understanding, which had the Ordinary Language movement behind it. I thought my book transcended the terms of that controversy, which is another way of saying that it fit nowhere.

Once I began to develop the idea of representation, as described above, I conceived the project of writing a large, systematic work in five volumes—an analytical philosophy of representation. The number five was suggested to me by the five volumes of George Santayana's *The Life of Reason,* which, according to Ernest Nagel, Morris Raphael Cohen had used as his text in a course at City College called "Philosophy of Civilization." I decided to count *Analytical Philosophy of History* as the first volume, as it was after all about how we represent ourselves in history. I had begun to think of the theory of knowledge and the theory of action as mirror images, with basic actions and basic sentences playing corresponding roles in each. Basic sentences would be what we would represent the world with if we did not have the cognitive wherewithal to frame narrative sentences, which explains why classical epistemology is so barren, just as Ankersmit observes. So the *Analytical Philosophy of Knowledge* and *Analytical Philosophy of Action* came next. They did not constitute a trilogy, as Ankersmit quite excusably supposes, but a truncated quintology. I did not want to call the fourth volume *Analytical Philosophy of Art*, since there was already a subject by that name, in which I had no interest whatever. The book I wrote was instead titled *The Transfiguration of the Commonplace*—a declaration of sorts that I was now in a new place. I never attempted to write the fifth and final volume, which was on human beings as *ens representans*, because it brought in issues on the philosophy of mind with which I did not wish to engage but for which I knew my book would be criticized bitterly as not paying sufficient attention to "the literature." The closest I ever came to fitting everything together was my overview of philosophy (which was subversive since it was *my* philosophy that the book was about), *Connections to the World.*

I wonder whether what Ankersmit speaks of as the tragedy of being in history is not somehow an artifact of modernism, in that it involved living beyond a historical period in which we were at home, into one in which we are, as it were, in historical exile—a period when we exist but do not belong. This goes beyond the concept of narrativity, I think, since I believe that perceiving the world narratively defines our humanity wherever in history humans happen to be. I mean I can imagine Odysseus in his older age showing strangers around Ithaca, pointing out, like the ghetto youth described above, sites where various of the episodes in his homecoming took place, narrativizing the island. Nestor was the paradigmatic old man of the age of Agamemnon, no longer able to run as fast as he once did or fight with the heavy weapons he could now barely lift—but he was never historically displaced, never out of date. In *Analytical Philosophy of History,* I discuss the thought of Thucydides, that the future must resemble the past, so that in describing the present war in detail, he is, as it were, mapping future wars for the benefit of those who must fight them. The rate of historical change was slow enough in the ancient world that there was not the experience, common enough in modern times, of living into a period when everything had changed and men, women, and children no longer acted they way they used to.

At the beginning of his essay, "On the Use and Abuse of History," Nietzsche gives us an amusing portrait of animal consciousness: "They know not the meaning of yesterday or today; they graze and ruminate, move or rest, from morning to night, from day to day, taken up with their little loves and hates and the mercy of the moment, feeling neither melancholy nor satiety." Humankind cannot, he goes on to say, regard animal being without a twinge of regret—"for even in the pride of [our] humanity [we] look enviously on the beast's happiness." There are two correlative questions to which the difference between the beast and us gives rise: why can the beast not remember, and why can we not forget? We envy the beast because it "forgets at once and sees every moment really die, sink into night and mist, extinguished forever." The beast, in brief, "lives *unhistorically.*" It follows that to be human is to live *historically*—that history is the mode of our being, a dimension of our ontology. Remembering and forgetting are intertwined with our essence. But this is not enough, as I see it. To exist historically is to be aware of how the past is other than the present, and how we cannot really live the way we did when it was present—not because we are older, but because the world has changed in ways that unfit those who were at home in it ever to be entirely at home in the present. This is forcibly the case with the recent history of art. Obviously it is possible to make adjustments. But there is really a viscosity in human life that prevents us from adjusting fast enough. I tried to cover this in "The Problem of Other Periods," which was republished in *Narration and Knowledge.* A period has an inside and an outside—an *en soi,* to borrow Sartre's language, and a *pour autrui.* It is one thing to live a period, and another to know about it through historical research. The dimension of tragedy comes with historical displacement, and the sense that we can't go home again. For a truly historical being, to be once again at home in the past, it would be required to forget the future. Personally, I am not given to nostalgia. Especially as a philosopher of art, I am really grateful to have lived though the changes I have experienced, into a period I could never have imagined, say, in the 1960s. But I can sympathize with those to whom historical adjustment has been difficult.

Notes

1. Arthur C. Danto, *Narration and Knowledge: Including the Integral Text of* Analytical Philosophy of History (New York: Columbia University Press, 1985), 305, 306.
2. Mark Rollins, Introduction, in Arthur C. Danto, *Danto and His Critics* (Cambridge, MA: Blackwell, 1993), 1.
3. Arthur C. Danto, *The Transfiguration of the Commonplace: A Philosophy of Art* (Cambridge, MA: Harvard University Press, 1981), 19.
4. Ibid. 77.
5. Ibid.
6. For a very similar argument, see H. G. Gadamer, *Wahrheit und Methode* (Tübingen: Mohr, 1960), 128–37.
7. Arthur C. Danto, *Analytical Philosophy of History* (Cambridge, England: Cambridge University Press, 1965), 94, 95.
8. Danto, *Narration and Knowledge*, 149.
9. Danto, *Analytical Philosophy of History*, 143.
10. Danto, *Narration and Knowledge*, 356, 257.
11. Danto, *Beyond the Brillo Box: The Visual Arts in Post-Historical Perspective* (New York: Farrar, Straus & Giroux, 1992), 241. This seems to be contradicted by Danto's confession on the same page that he considers himself to be "a narrativist *de re.*"
12. David Carr, *Time, Narrative, and History* (Bloomington: Indiana University Press, 1986); Paul Ricoeur, *Temps et Récit*, 3 vols. (Paris: Seuil, 1983–1985); Hayden White, *Metahistory: The Historical Imagination in Nineteenth-Century Europe* (Baltimore: Johns Hopkins University Press, 1973); Louis O. Mink, *Historical Understanding* (Ithaca, NY: Cornell University Press, 1987); R. G. Collingwood, *The Idea of History*, ed. with intro. by Jan van der Dussen, rev. ed. (Oxford: Oxford University Press, 1994); Jörn Rüsen, *Historische Vernunft: Grundzüge einer Historik I* (Göttingen: Vandenhoeck & Ruprecht, 1983).
13. Danto, *The Transfiguration of the Commonplace*, 206.
14. Danto, *Narration and Knowledge*, 339.
15. Danto, *The Transfiguration of the Commonplace*, 206.
16. Ibid. 187.

17. See for this my *Historical Representation* (Stanford: Stanford University Press, 2001), chapter 1.

18. Danto, *The Transfiguration of the Commonplace*, 189.

19. Elsewhere I have argued, though, that different texts could not have the same referent because of the fact that to one representation corresponds one represented only. See my *Historical Representation*, chapter 1.

20. Danto, *The Transfiguration of the Commonplace*, 189.

21. Ibid. 207. For a specimen of Danto's own writing perfectly exemplifying this insight into the nature of history, and matching the quoted passage in both profundity and literary beauty, see Danto's account of the demise of logical positivism in *After the End of Art: Contemporary Art and the Pale of History* (Princeton: Princeton University Press, 1997), 142. The irony, the powerful metaphors, the succinctness and exceptional force of this passage prove that no contemporary philosopher may claim to surpass the stylistic excellence of Danto's prose. One cannot fail to ask what continental philosopher could write a passage like this one.

22. As I attempt to make clear in my *Historical Experience* (Stanford: Stanford University Press, forthcoming).

10
History and the Sciences
Philip Kitcher and Daniel Immerwahr

[1]

The history of philosophical reflection on history is largely dominated by attempts to determine the relation between history and the sciences. In the twentieth century, the two most prominent attempts were those of C. G. Hempel, in "The Function of General Laws in History,"[1] and of Arthur Danto in *Analytical Philosophy of History*.[2] Hempel's article aimed to resolve a long-standing controversy about the relationship between history and the *Naturwissenschaften* (a debate that had raged particularly fiercely in the late nineteenth and early twentieth centuries, although there had been important earlier eruptions[3]), by deploying a philosophical reconstruction of the natural sciences that he and his colleagues were in the process of developing.[4] Danto's penetrating study of issues in the philosophy of history appeared when the account of the sciences offered by Hempel and others had begun to be challenged, and Danto was quite conscious of the fact that some of the emerging perspectives on the sciences might enable philosophers of history to accommodate many of the complaints that historians and historiographers had leveled against Hempel's approach.[5] Specifically, by developing an account of historical explanation that made narratives (rather than general laws) central, Danto simultaneously brought the analytical philosophy of history far closer to historical practice and connected historical understanding to the emphasis on causation as central to an explanation that increasingly figured in critical responses to Hempel's famous "covering-law model."

Since 1964, even since 1985, philosophical views about science—or better, philosophical views about the sciences—have changed again. At the beginning of the twenty-first century it may no longer be possible to talk of a consensus about the character of the sciences. Yet because so much of the contemporary discussion in the philosophy of history seems to take for granted views about the natural sciences that virtually no philosopher of science writing today would accept, it seems worth returning to the old question of the relation between history and the sciences with a more up-to-date philosophical perspective. We'll approach the issue against the backdrop of a view of the sciences that one of us has developed elsewhere;[6] if the account proves unconvincing at particular points, we hope that philosophers of science who hold different views will be inspired to address the status of history using their own preferred accounts.

[2]

To assert the kinship of history and the sciences might be to claim any of several different things. The most prominent, however, are to maintain a kinship of method, a common aim, or similar achievements—or, of course, any combination of these.[7] Superficially, there are major differences between the methods employed by historians and those used by stereotypical natural scientists; historians aren't noted for their propensity to perform experiments—rather, they trudge off to archives, assemble documents (and other remains of the past), and scrutinize them. To the extent that philosophers have sought community of method throughout the natural sciences, however, they haven't hoped to discover it at this level of description; it's a commonplace that there are areas of scientific inquiry in which investigators make observations rather than performing experiments (particularly in astronomy and in the study of animal behavior); and, as we might expect, "historical sciences" like paleontology and historical geology reveal researchers who use the rock strata very much in the way that historians use their archival sources.[8]

One principal theme in the suggestion that the natural sciences share a common method has been the idea of a theory of confirmation that applies irrespective of subject matter. However natural scientists obtain their data, it's supposed that there are general standards for assessing the degree to which the data support the hypotheses the investigators entertain. Proposals about these standards are controversial, and some philosophers have been skeptical of the notion that context-independent standards can be precisely formulated.[9] Insofar as one focuses on the particular claims that historians often defend in their writings—"When Parliament began to 'tell stories to the *People*' in the Grand Remonstrance of 1641, the members had no intention of deposing their king,"[10] "Joan of Arc merely checked the English advance by reviving Dauphinist morale, and the Regent managed to halt the counteroffensive. It was not the Maid who ended English rule in France"[11]—we think that there's no reason to hold that the standards for assessing evidence are any different in history than in the natural sciences, or indeed, in the social sciences, literary attribution, musicology, the reconstruction of artworks, criminal detection, plumbing, salesmanship, or whatever. If a satisfactory formal theory of confirmation can be given for the natural sciences in all their forms, we see no reason to think it wouldn't work equally well for all kinds of inquiry, including the marshaling of evidence for specific historical theses; if no such theory is available, it will remain possible to identify the kinship between historical inferences and arguments and those that are advanced in many areas of scientific inquiry.

We shall not elaborate on these points because we think that the interesting issues about the relation of history and the sciences concern aims and achievements, not standards of evidence. Those issues arise in two ways, depending on the guiding conception of the ultimate aims of the sciences. If, as many writers tacitly or explicitly assume, the natural sciences aim at truth, the controversy can be formulated in terms of whether truth is an aim of history.[12] Alternatively, if the starting point is the familiar suggestion that the aims of the natural sciences are explanation, prediction, and control, the dispute emerges rather differently. With a small number of exceptions, most writers about history will agree that historians rarely aim to predict or control, so that the kinship between history and the sciences will be debated in terms of the aspiration to provide explanations in history that are akin to those offered by natural scientists. This, of course, is the classic way Hempel raised the question, and, from 1942 to the present, many scholars have taken the issue of the relation between history and the sciences to be a question about the character of historical explanation.[13]

There are thus several theses that we think it worthwhile to present explicitly:

Veritism about the sciences. The natural sciences aim at, and sometimes achieve, truths about various aspects of nature.

Bernardism about the sciences.[14] The natural sciences aim to provide explanation, prediction, and control.

Veritism about history. History aims at, and sometimes achieves, truths about various aspects of the past.

Impracticality of history. History rarely, if ever, aims at prediction and control.

Explanationism about history. History aims to provide explanations.

Strong explanationism about history. The principal aim of history is to provide explanations.

We think most of these theses deserve considerable scrutiny.[15]

[3]

One exception is the uncontroversial *impracticality of history*; despite the prevalence of slogans advertising the importance of learning from history, we take it that their plausibility rests on the thought that a historical account of some past events can provide the basis for a hypothesis in some area of social science, a hypothesis that can then be applied to a new context.[16] If the *impracticality* thesis is in place, then it's not hard to understand how those who believe in the kinship between history and the sciences are led toward—if not all the way to—*strong explanationism about history*.

Start with *Bernardism about the sciences*. If history shares an aim with the sciences, then it must be that history aims at explanation and/or prediction and/or control. By *impracticality of history*, explanation is the only candidate. Hence we arrive at *explanationism*. But suppose *strong explanationism about history* were false. Then the provision of historical explanations wouldn't be the most central or prominent aim of history, so there would have to be some *nonscientific* ends of equal or greater importance. Hence an account of history that assimilated it to the sciences would be inadequate. Conclusion: to assert a kinship between history and the sciences, you need something like *strong explanationism about history*.

As Hempel saw, *strong explanationism* isn't enough. To demonstrate the kinship, you also have to scotch doubts about differences between the explanations provided by scientists and those offered by historians. So a familiar dialectic begins. Hempel presented a general model of explanation, according to which explanations are arguments whose conclusion describes the phenomenon to be explained and among whose premises is at least one general law. Faced with the obvious objection that historians rarely[17] state (or are in a position to state) general laws, Hempel suggested that they don't offer complete explanations, only explanation sketches. As Danto saw, there's some tension in the proposal that scientists achieve their aims but the principal aims of history are almost always unattainable—at least if one wants to emphasize the kinship between history and the sciences.[18] Hence *the* task of the analytical philosophy of history came to be showing how historians achieved a distinctive form of explanation, narrative explanation, and that this was quite respectable. Exposing "the structure of narratives" became a cottage industry—and the wheels still hum.

We suggest that Hempel's particular account of science infected the whole discussion at quite an early stage. This was a matter not only of adherence to the covering-law model of explanation but also of the unquestioned deployment of the categories of *Bernardism* and the paradigms on which Hempel and his co-workers concentrated their attention. We'll start with the theses *explanationism about history* and *strong explanationism about history*.

It seems clear to us that there are some historical works that do attempt to provide explanations. Historians have offered rival explanations for the fall of the Roman Empire (in 410, 476, or 1514!), the outbreak of the Civil War in England, the growth of the abolitionist movement in North America, and the origins and course of World War I.[19] In some instances, the historian focuses on a particular event—a change of government, a battle, the official acceptance of some doctrine—and tries to show why that event occurred; in other instances, the project involves linking a sequence, or a complex web, of events and explaining why all these events occurred.[20] Philosophical reflections on history have been largely directed toward works of these types—at the cost, we think, of overlooking other kinds of historical venture.

In *Montaillou*, Emmanuel Le Roy Ladurie does something very different. He uses the records of the Inquisition, which tracked down the Cathars (proponents of the Albigensian heresy) in the early decades of the fourteenth century in the villages of the French slope of the Pyrenees. (Montaillou is a mountain village that sheltered an unusually large number of Cathars and Cathar sympathizers.) Le Roy Ladurie is not principally interested in explaining why (or how) the tireless inquisitor Jacques Fournier succeeded in routing out the heretics, or anything similar. His aim is to take us into the world and the lives of the Pyreneean community, constructing the kind of ethnographic account that an anthropologist might give for some distant group. Summing up his conclusions about the conflicts between local clans in Montaillou, he introduces an obvious, but useful image:

> The study of Montaillou shows on a minute scale what took place in the structure of society as a whole. Montaillou is only a drop in the ocean. Thanks to the microscope provided by the Fournier Register, we can see the protozoa swimming about in it.[21]

One of the most prominent "protozoa" under Le Roy Ladurie's "microscope" is a likeable shepherd, Pierre Maury, to whose actions and attitudes he devotes more than sixty pages. Here is a typical passage:

> Pierre Maury had his leisure moments. When necessary he got his friends to look after his sheep for him while he went down to the neighboring town, to take, or to collect, money (iii.166). Or he might absent himself for purely personal reasons, without any problems of time-keeping or supervision, to go and visit friends, mistresses (unless they came up directly to see him in his *cabane*) or fellow-sponsors, friends acquired at baptisms recently or long ago.[22]

Nothing much is explained here, but this passage, in combination with plenty more like it, provides a picture of how Pierre Maury lived. We learn what it was like to be a Pyreneean shepherd, with heretical leanings, at a particular time. (Or, attending to Le Roy Ladurie's claim about the relation between Montaillou and the broader society, we learn what it was like to be a French peasant at a particular time.)

Similar points could be made with respect to other influential microhistories. Natalie Zemon Davis's *The Return of Martin Guerre* is, as she says, concerned to bring forth not only the actions of her subjects but also "the world they would have seen and the reactions they might have had."[23] Unlike Le Roy Ladurie's *Montaillou*, Davis's book tells a story—indeed, a compelling story.[24] A Basque peasant, Martin Guerre, goes off adventuring, leaving his home and his wife, Bertrande de Rols. Years later, another peasant, Armand du Tilh, comes to the town, claiming to be Martin. Because he looks like Martin and has learned many things about him, he is hesitantly accepted as Martin—even by Bertrande, who surely knows the difference. Armand plays his role successfully for a few years, until his trial, at which he is being prosecuted (unsuccessfully) for fraud, is interrupted by the entrance of the real Martin Guerre.

Davis is clearly interested in explaining a number of things, including why Armand decided to impersonate another man and why Bertrande accepted the impersonation. Giving these explanations depends on doing something else, which we take to be Davis's overarching aim: to enable a contemporary reader to understand what it was like to live in a particular sixteenth-century French culture. Davis doesn't simply list the reasons that might have moved Bertrande;; she tries to make us view the world through Bertrande's eyes. Here is part of her account:

> What Bertrande had with the new Martin was her dream come true, a man she could live with in peace and friendship (to cite sixteenth century values) and in passion. It was an invented marriage, not arranged like that of her own of eighteen years earlier or contracted in a customary way like that of her mother and Pierre Guerre. It started off with a lie but, as Bertrande described it later, they passed their time "like true married people, eating, drinking, and sleeping together." . . . In the marriage bed of the beautiful Bertrande things now went well.[25] Within three years, two daughters were born to them. . . .
>
> The evidence for the relationship between the new Martin and Bertrande comes not from this peaceful period of three years, but from the time when the invented marriage was called into doubt. Yet it everywhere attests to his having fallen in love with the wife for whom he had rehearsed and her having become deeply attached to the husband who had taken her by surprise. When he is released from prison in the midst of later quarrels, she gives him a white shirt, washes his feet, and receives him back into her bed. When others try to kill him, she puts her body between him and the blows. Before the court he addresses her "gently"; he puts his life in her hands by saying that if she swears that he is not her husband he will submit to a thousand deaths.[26]

The power of this passage is to make Bertrande, and her apparently odd behavior, comprehensible to us. Davis does this not simply by laying out Bertrande's reasons for accepting Armande but by making her emotions immediate to us—by presenting the couple as tender lovers. After we read this account, Bertrande no longer seems alien, because Davis has given us a way to assimilate her experiences to our own.

And that, of course, is the principal point. The *entrée* to the world of sixteenth-century French peasants isn't a means to answering the burning question why Bertrande de Rols accepted the false Martin, but rather the end at which Davis is aiming. Skillful historian that she is, Davis has combined her introduction to a past culture with a particularly poignant story, so that readers want answers to questions that can only be addressed by entering the culture. Those in the grip of *strong explanationism* might insist that the aim of *The Return of Martin Guerre* is to answer explanation-seeking questions—like Why did Bertrande accept Armand as Martin?—but this is to overlook the enormous difference between such questions and the usual paradigms, questions like Why did Constantine declare that Christianity was to be the official religion of the Empire?, "Why did Napoleon lose at Waterloo?, and so forth. By Davis's own lights, Bertrande wasn't a Historically Important Person who did Historically Consequential Things;[27] she is interesting because she is a gateway through which we can enter a strange and intriguing world.

We've already emphasized the similarity between the historical works we've been reviewing and projects in ethnography, and it's easy at this point to take a wrong turn by invoking an influential theory of what such ethnographies do. Many historians and anthropologists have been inspired by Clifford Geertz's famous essay "Deep Play: Notes on the Balinese Cockfight," and by his deployment of the Rylean notion of "thick description." It's become fashionable to suggest that historians—or really up-to-date historians—aren't in the business of giving explanations or causal analyses, but rather give accounts of the "meaning" of cultural institutions and practices.[28] We intend neither to lurch from *strong explanationism* to its contrary nor to acquiesce in a tendentious theoretical description of the kinship between illuminating ethnography (of which we take Geertz's account of the Balinese cockfight to be an outstanding example) and the microhistories of Le Roy Ladurie and Davis. The relations between Geertz's account and some notion of "meaning" for cultural items (as well as the relations between Geertz's account and causal analysis) require more extensive treatment than we can offer here. For our purposes, it's enough to identify important historical works that serve as *prima facie* counterexamples to *strong explanationism*, and to be able to specify the kinds of questions that they address. (Of the latter, more shortly.)

The microhistories surely can be described as providing materials for explanation in the sense(s) typically employed in discussions of the aims of history, but to describe them in this way would be to miss their point. The authors give so much detail not so that we can answer a plethora of why questions (formulated about individuals about whom we have no antecedent interest) but so that something can be evoked in the reader, so that there can be a psychological change through which Pierre Maury, Bertrande, and Menocchio cease to be remote deviant peasants and become

206 PHILIP KITCHER AND DANIEL IMMERWAHR

fellow humans, who, for all their apparent strangeness, are more like ourselves than we had thought. We don't want to assimilate this evocation to
explanation, let alone to make it the central feature of "historical explanation," but we do want to recognize its importance as a mode of historical
knowledge.[29] *Strong explanationism* seems to have left philosophers the
unfortunate choice between denying important historical aims and accomplishments and adopting an implausible view of explanation as the
achievement of empathy.

It's important to recognize that the features we've discerned in the microhistories are also present in a much wider spectrum of historical writings. Military history has traditionally been seen as a clear example of a
genre in which authors attempt to offer explanations—indeed, critics of
explanationism are quite reasonably challenged to account for the large
number of works devoted to the origins and resolution of battles and
wars. Even in military history, however, we can find historians whose concerns are similar to those of Le Roy Ladurie and Davis. John Keegan's celebrated book *The Face of Battle* has much to tell us about why Agincourt,
Waterloo, and the Somme went the ways they did: Keegan provides rich
accounts of the outcomes of these three battles. Nevertheless, that is not
all—and, we believe, not primarily—what he intended to do. At the end of
the first paragraph, Keegan tells us, "I have never been in a battle. And I
grow increasingly convinced that I have very little idea of what a battle can
be like."[30]

The investigation he undertook, on which his book was based, was motivated by his sense of his own ignorance of the very points he felt he
should be conveying to his students, all of whom were cadets at Britain's
elite Royal Military Academy at Sandhurst; Keegan felt difficulty in answering "what, for a young man training to be a professional soldier, is the
central question: what is it like to be in a battle?"[31]

One way to approach that question is to describe the circumstances of
the individual participants in major historical battles in ways that enable
readers to relate the soldiers' predicaments to their own experiences—to
describe in some detail the gear that would have been worn, the equipment carried, the ways various types of encounters would have gone, the
sounds that would have been heard, the limitations on visibility, the effects
of incidents that occurred, and so forth. Here is Keegan's description of
the crucial failure of a French charge at Waterloo.

The men at the front could see their officers, see the enemy, form some
rational estimate of the danger they were in and of what they ought to do

about it. The men in the middle and the rear could see nothing of the battle but the debris of earlier attacks which had failed—discarded weapons and the bodies of the dead and wounded lying on the ground, perhaps under their very feet. From the front came back to them sudden crashes of musketry, eddies of smoke, unidentifiable shouts and, most important, tremors of movement, edging them rearward and forcing them, crowd-like, in upon each other.[32]

This passage contributes to two quite different historical projects. Keegan is interested in explaining a particular incident, late in the day at Waterloo, when the Imperial Guard, charging the British position, were met with sudden and unexpected fire and, as was recorded by soldiers on both sides, those in the center and rear of the columns (soldiers who were in less danger than those in front of them) turned and retreated. He also wants to convey to readers who have never had military experience what it was like to advance in a column at the end of a long battle, and he does so by connecting the predicament of the soldiers who fled to experiences most of us have had. We may not know exactly, or even approximately, what it was like to be a French soldier in that charge, but, because we have been in crowds that suddenly pitched us in unanticipated directions, Keegan's description provides a much better appreciation than we would otherwise have had.

It would be easy to multiply examples. Keith Thomas's magisterial study of the ways religion, magic, and the emerging science catered to a broad variety of human needs during the sixteenth and seventeenth centuries could be viewed as explaining the trend indicated in his title, the "decline of magic."[33] But Thomas is concerned to display the rich variety of magical practices and the diversity of ways the church attempted to assimilate them. Paul Cohen's illuminating approach to the Boxer Rebellion, *History in Three Keys*, explicitly commits itself to a difference among three styles of approaching the same events, the first offering an explanation of what occurred, the second attempting to reconstruct the world of the Boxers, and the third examining the various ways the rebellion has been interpreted to illuminate later political programs.[34] Small wonder that many historians have resisted analytical philosophy of history, feeling that the complex texts they most admire are somehow reduced or eviscerated by philosophical analyses. Moreover, as we'll argue in a moment, they've been right to object to the model of scientific explanation that has almost invariably been wheeled out when philosophers try to identify the links between history and the sciences. But the rot goes deeper.

The trouble lies with *strong explanationism*. In terms of the views of explanation typically presupposed in discussions of history, the types of studies just reviewed count as a decisive refutation of *strong explanationism,* and they inspire us to go further in the liberalizing direction marked out by Danto, modifying the emphasis on causation and on the centrality of narrative. As we proceed, the centrality of explanation to history will appear in a new light.

[4]

Claims about explanation in history can be read in several ways, of which we'll distinguish three.

> *The Strict Interpretation.* Explanations are arguments in which general laws figure in the premises.
> *The Orthodox Interpretation.* Explanations are answers to why questions.
> *The Liberal Interpretation.* Explanations are answers to questions of many different types (how questions, what questions, when questions, and so forth, as well as why questions).

The most vigorous program for assimilating history to the natural sciences, the Hempelian program, attempts to defend *strong explanationism* under the *strict interpretation*. Sensitive readers of historical texts notice that those texts rarely succeed in giving the right kinds of arguments and appear to contain a lot of interesting material of a different kind. So they reject the *strict interpretation* in favor of the *orthodox interpretation,* contending that historians have a special way of answering why questions through the construction of narratives, and that the important philosophical project is to understand the structure—or logic—of narratives. We agree that historians sometimes construct narratives and that these narratives answer certain kinds of questions (whether they are best construed as why questions is a topic we'll take up below). But we think *strong explanationism* is doomed even on the *orthodox interpretation*. Friends of the latter sometimes recognize that achieving some type of empathetic understanding of historical actors is a goal of many historical works—but they distort the point by relentlessly insisting that this has something to do with answering why questions. Our claim is that re-creating past experience, enabling a modern reader to have access to a past world, answering questions of the form What was it like to be . . . ? is valuable for its own sake. (We recognize that addressing such issues may sometimes be a prelude to answering why questions; our point is that it need not serve in this way). Paul Cohen's separation of his first two approaches to the Boxer Rebellion is exemplary in this respect.

Adopting the *liberal interpretation* would appear to attenuate the connection between history and the natural sciences, and, indeed, that would be so if one continued to insist on the *strict interpretation* or the *orthodox interpretation* in reading *Bernardism about the sciences*. We propose, however, to adopt a *liberal interpretation* consistently, for explanation in the sciences as well as for explanation in history. As we'll emphasize below, the natural sciences aim at lots of different things, and the questions they answer are heterogeneous. So the possibility of kinship between the aims and achievements of history and the aims and achievements of various areas of natural science is not foreclosed by our rejection of *strong explanationism* when construed by way of either the *strict* or the *orthodox* interpretation.

Although we believe that the rejection of the covering-law model of explanation, with the shift to the *orthodox interpretation* and the advocacy of narrative as a mode of historical explanation, doesn't go far enough, we agree that it was correct to abandon Hempel's account. Indeed, the covering-law model has been under severe attack as a model of scientific explanation for three decades or more, and it will be helpful for later discussions to examine why its fortunes have waned.[35] Hempel's lucid analysis of explanation encountered four major difficulties, two of which are pertinent to its failure with respect to history.[36] These are the insufficiency of Hempel's conditions on explanation and the incompleteness of his discussions of how explanations relate to context.

Setting aside details that are irrelevant for our purposes, Hempel is committed to the view that any deductively valid argument among whose premises is a general law explains its conclusion. It's not hard to think of many different counterexamples, but two general types are especially forceful. Asymmetries of explanation arise when a pair of arguments differs only in the fact that each is obtained by switching a premise and a conclusion in the other, where each set of premises contains a general law, and one, but not the other, strikes us as explanatory. So, to cite a standard example, one can explain why a flagpole casts a shadow of a certain length by appeal to the height, the elevation of the sun, and the law that light travels in straight lines; but, although one can derive the height of the flagpole from the length of the shadow, the elevation of the sun, and the principle of rectilinear propagation of light, that derivation is not explanatory.[37] Irrelevancies in explanation result from the possibility of stating general laws that don't identify a factor that is explanatorily crucial. A standard example concerns a man who takes birth control pills; even though it's a matter of scientific law that ingesting those pills prevents pregnancy, we can't explain the man's failure to become pregnant by appealing to the law and the fact of his peculiar medication.[38]

In the context of historical explanation, the same general problem was identified by J. H. Hexter, who saw that Hempel's model permitted trivial derivations of no explanatory value. Hexter noted that one can't explain the presence of the Giants in the 1951 World Series by deducing the conclusion "The Giants played in the 1951 World Series" from premises asserting that the Giants won more games than any other National League Team that year and that whenever a National League Team wins more games than any other National League Team it goes to the World Series.[39] Now one might quibble about whether the generalization he cites should count as a general law (after all, it refers to a particular social entity, the National League), but it wouldn't be hard to develop Hexter's example to avoid any such objection.[40] Indeed, once one appreciates the problems posed by explanatory asymmetry and irrelevance, it becomes clear that nonexplanatory derivations that fit the Hempelian model are legion. Hexter saw this very clearly—he concludes that his Hempelian argument about the Giants' victory doesn't "tell the questioner what he wants to know"[41]—and, insightfully, he goes further, claiming that the philosophical discussion of history has been distorted: "the notion that the sole appropriate response of the historian to his commitment to communicate what he knows is something designated 'explanation' is wildly arbitrary."[42]

Given the deficiencies of the covering-law model in stating sufficient conditions on scientific—or historical—explanation, philosophers have sought to isolate what is problematic about the nonexplanatory derivations. Although no current model of explanation enjoys the widespread acceptance that Hempel's account once had, the most popular suggestion has been that explanations have to identify causally relevant factors.[43] Invoking the notion of causation was anathema to Hempel and his colleagues, for whom much of the point of an analysis of explanation consisted in demonstrating that one didn't need to appeal to any (suspect) causal concept.[44] For our purposes, however, questions about whether causal concepts need analysis (and, if so, how the analysis is to be done) are secondary; once the specification of causes is seen as crucial to scientific explanation, there seems to be a much more straightforward connection between history and the natural sciences. Causal explanation is common to human affairs, to evolutionary and developmental biology, to geological studies that trace the emergence of mountain ranges and other large topographical features, and to cosmological investigations of the formation of atoms, nebulae, stars, and planets.[45]

At this stage, it's useful to take up the second major difficulty with the Hempelian approach to explanation, the lack of any detailed account of how explanations are responsive to contextual variables. Hexter's example of the Giants' success in 1951 is pertinent here—we might imagine *some* contexts in which the Hempelian argument serves to explain to someone why the Giants went to the World Series (consider someone who is very ignorant about this kind of competition, for whom it's a genuine option that a team might go on to the final phase if they won more than a particular percentage of the games, or defeated a particular opponent, or scored the most runs); but the contexts that readily come to mind are ones in which the Hempelian account doesn't provide what a person asking the explanation-seeking question wants to know. Further, it isn't obvious that insisting that genuine explanations specify causes helps to resolve the trouble, for one might argue, with some plausibility, that Hexter's derivation actually satisfies the causal constraint. The trouble, quite evidently, is that there are causes and causes; some are remote, some are very close to their effects; some strike us as unimportant or uninteresting, others are salient. The essential context-dependency of specifying causes was brought out very clearly by N. R. Hanson, and we'll amend a famous example of his.[46]

Why did the Princess of Wales die? We don't know the details, but there was surely a moment shortly before the fatal crash at which the wheels of the car were set on a trajectory that would inevitably lead the vehicle into a high-velocity collision with unyielding concrete. So there's some mechanical story that specifies an event that caused the crash, and another mechanical-physiological story that specifies the damage produced in Lady Diana's body. Imagine that you are given these accounts in any amount of detail. Have you been offered an answer to the question?

We think not—at least not if the context in which the request for explanation was posed was relatively normal. We can envisage accounts at many different levels of analysis, some that appeal to blood-alcohol levels and unfastened seat belts, others that focus on the paparazzi and their intrusions into Diana's life, yet others that concentrate on her unhappy marriage and the attitude of the Windsor family. No one of these will answer to every normal context of requesting explanation, although for each there's a range of mundane contexts in which it would be appropriate. It's not enough, then, to replace Hempel's covering-law model with the suggestion that explanations specify causes. The right sorts of causes must be picked out, and they must be given their due—and what "right" and "due" mean depends on the context in which the why question is posed.

Hexter's discussion of the 1951 World Series comes close to making this point. He presents a graph, showing the number of games by which the Giants trailed the Dodgers from August 13, when they were thirteen games behind, to the dead heat at the end of the season, the three-game playoff, with the third game run deficit inning by inning (with, of course, the dramatic Bobby Thomson home run represented by a final upward spike).[47] Hexter suggests that we can use the graph to understand why some proposed explanations succeed, proposing, in effect, that the points of sudden change mark the places at which causes are especially to be sought. In our judgment, this isn't quite right: we can envisage circumstances under which it would be precisely the points at which the Giants maintained ground (or didn't lose too much) that corresponded to the important causal foci—imagine that August and September 1951 were marked by outbreaks of intestinal flu that laid many baseball players low, and that the Giants held their own even when barely able to field a team. So we draw a somewhat different conclusion: historical explanations seek particular kinds of causal information, and there's no context-independent way to specify the kinds that are salient.

But we don't believe that matters are any different in the natural sciences, particularly those whose modes of explanation are closest to history. Consider the process that begins with the fertilization of an egg and culminates in a mature organism. The causal history behind the presence of a particular trait can have the same complexity as that behind the death of Princess Diana—perhaps there was a particular allelic combination that gave rise to a protein that might have been modified in the presence of a cytoplasmic constituent that wasn't available, and the subsequent receipt of molecules from the ambient environment triggered an increase in the rate of cell division in a specific developmental field, and so on and so forth in a cascade of effects. Just as we could devise in the case of the car crash (or in the case of the Giants' success) any number of causal stories that focus on factors inapposite in any normal context, so too with the embryological example; by analogy with the causal-mechanical account of the fatal collision, we can select some late developmental stage and show that available intracellular energy doesn't suffice to break the bonds of appropriately chosen constituent molecules. Moreover, as we imagined a variety of narratives that emphasized different factors—the alcohol, the paparazzi, the Windsors' disapproval—so too we might concentrate on the organism's genotype, on the details of maternal inheritance that led to a missing cytoplasmic constituent, the signals from the environment, or the increased rate of cell division.

Our examination of *strong explanationism* thus leads us to two conclusions, one that militates against the assimilation of history to the natural sciences and one that favors the assimilationist program. The negative point is that, on both the *strict interpretation* and the *orthodox interpretation*, *strong explanationism* must be rejected; as Hexter saw, historians are not simply in the business of giving explanations, conceived as answers to why questions (or how-did-it-come-about questions).[48] The positive point is that Hempel's account of explanation for the natural sciences must give way to a much looser causal-contextual view that allows for affinities between scientific explanations and historical explanations. It looks, then, as though part of what historians aim at and achieve might prove similar to what (some) natural scientists aim at and achieve; and as though the extent of the similarity might vary quite widely depending on which historians and which scientists are considered. As we suggested above, while this is to endorse Danto's claims about *one sort* of history and *one sort* of science, it is also to embrace a pluralistic view of both types of inquiry that liberalizes his position.

We think that this conclusion is along the right lines, but that it needs refinement. We'll try to improve it by taking up some of the other theses we promised we'd scrutinize.

[5]

A different way of specifying the aims and achievements of the sciences is to invoke the idea of the pursuit of truth and advocate *veritism about the sciences*. Just as there are different ways of interpreting *strong explanationism*, depending on the concept of explanation chosen, so too with *veritism* and the notion of truth. We'll approach the issues by adopting a relatively modest version of the correspondence theory of truth.[49] We hold that there's a relation of reference between the singular terms of our language and mind-independent entities and between the predicates of our language and sets of mind-independent entities, and that a sentence is true by virtue of corresponding to the way the world is, as the entities referred to by its singular terms stand in the right relationship to the sets referred to by its constituent predicates—where the right relationships are those characterized by Tarski.[50] There are influential arguments to the effect that, on this interpretation, *veritism about the sciences* can't be sustained—or that it can only be upheld for certain kinds of scientific claims (those that are concerned only with observable entities).[51] Since one of us has argued at some length that *veritism* can be defended against these challenges, we'll simply take *veritism about the sciences* (on our modest correspondentist interpretation) for granted in what follows.[52]

Some historians and philosophers of history have resisted *veritism about history*, at least when that thesis is articulated via a correspondence approach to truth. We want to start by identifying some *veritist* themes that are quite innocuous.

In his celebrated *The Age of Constantine the Great*, the nineteenth-century historian Jacob Burckhardt tells his readers about the birth of the future emperor: "[the Alemanni] were defeated at Windisch by the General Constantius Chlorus under Aurelian (274), and indeed on the same day that his son Constantine was born."[53] Even though this is the second clause of a two-part sentence, it is quite complex. One way to expose its logical structure would be as follows: there is an event e, such that e is in 274 and e is a battle and e is a defeat of the Alemanni by Constantinus Chlorus, and Constantinus Chlorus is at the time of e a general under Aurelian and e is at Windisch and on the same day as e there is an event f, which is a birth, and a son is born to Constantinus Chlorus in f and that son is Constantine. It's easy to recognize that there are plenty of ways in which Burckhardt's claim might turn out to be false. Indeed, we'd agree with the judgment that *certainty* about any conjunction like this involving happenings in the distant past is too much to hope for. *Veritism*, however, isn't about certainty but about truth. We judge that Burckhardt aimed to tell the truth, in the modest correspondence sense, that he assembled evidence to this end, and that, given the evidence, there's good reason to think he attained it. For consider the terms that figure in our reconstruction of the sentence: there are singular terms—"Alemanni," "Windisch," "Constantine," and so forth—and predicates—"is a battle," "is on the same day as," "is a birth," "is a general under." According to the modest correspondence theory, the singular terms refer to entities that are independent of the psychological life of Burckhardt or his contemporary reader, to a tribe, a place, and a person; similarly, the predicates have in their extensions events, ordered pairs of events, events, and ordered pairs of people, respectively. There is nothing obscure or metaphysically dubious in this account of the truth of Burckhardt's sentence. Nor is it mysterious how a chain of informants might provide evidence for each of the constituent claims. There are, of course, interesting issues about how historians should satisfy themselves that their conclusions are backed by a reliable sequence of informants—it might even turn out that the resolution of those issues might raise suspicions about some part of

Burckhardt's judgment—but the general possibility of finding out (say) that Constantinus Chlorus defeated the Alemanni at Windisch shouldn't be dismissed. Hence, as long as we focus on sentences like the one quoted, *veritism about history* seems unproblematic.

Where then does trouble come in? Although Burckhardt's sentence is logically complex, it has a certain type of conceptual transparency. What we mean by this is that the language, particularly the predicates, it contains don't seem to embody either a classificatory scheme that might easily be rejected or a categorization that depends on subjective judgment. It's possible that our descendants might reject such categories as "battle," or "being on the same day as," but the possibilities seem too remote to buttress a charge that the historian can't aim at or achieve truth because the classificatory scheme presupposed in the representation of historical events is always laden with the values and prejudices of the writer's time and circumstances. We can bring out the contrast by considering the account that one of Burckhardt's predecessors gives of the character of the Empress Theodora. Gibbon's description is full of references to acts of "prostitution" (a category that covers both her alleged affairs and her public performances on the stage) and her "licentiousness" (which, if we ignore the real possibility of Gibbonian irony, might be viewed as expressing a moralistic disapproval of female sexual desire). Here is a relatively short sentence:

> Her chastity, from the moment of her union with Justinian, is founded on the silence of her implacable enemies; and although the daughter of Acacius might be satiated with love, yet some applause is due to the firmness of a mind which could sacrifice pleasure and habit to the stronger sense either of duty or interest.[54]

We imagine opponents of *veritism* protesting that Gibbon's sentence isn't true, that it embodies categories that he was entitled to use but we are entitled to reject, and that similar infection permeates all historical writing. (The infection is just much harder to recognize in a sentence like the one previously quoted from Burckhardt.)

We agree that no contemporary historian should be tempted to use Gibbon's sentence (despite its elegance) in a description of Theodora—it would be right to say that some of his words are not ours.[55] That, however, shouldn't be confused with the issue at hand, the truth of Gibbon's claim. Here it may help to consider parallel examples in the sciences. Gibbon's rough contemporaries Joseph Priestley and Georges Cuvier used terminology we'd reject: Priestley identified the properties of a gas he called "dephlogisticated air," noting that it supports combustion and respiration better than ordinary air, and Cuvier presented his admiring audiences with new fossil species (assuming a fixed, monotypical notion of species). We reject the language they employed, abandoning Priestley's term "dephlogisticated air" and attaching a different concept to Cuvier's "species," but this doesn't prevent us from recognizing that Priestley says true things about oxygen (the gas he sometimes refers to using "dephlogisticated air") and that Cuvier correctly separates different fossil species.[56] At least part of Gibbon's sentence can be retrieved in a similar way. When he talks of Theodora's "chastity" after her marriage to Justinian, we recognize that he means to refer to her sexual fidelity. Thus the first part of his sentence might be recast as the claim that after marrying Justinian, Theodora didn't have sexual relations with anyone else, together with the suggestion that the lack of rumors about her behavior (in a context in which she had many detractors) serves as evidence for this. Once this has been done, Gibbon's claim seems no more problematic than Burckhardt's.

Let's now look at an alternative way in which conceptual transparency might fail. Consider a passage we've already quoted from Desmond Seward's *The Hundred Years War*: "Joan of Arc merely checked the English advance by reviving Dauphinist morale, and the Regent managed to halt the counter-offensive. It was not the Maid who ended English rule in France." One might worry that this claim presupposes a subjective interpretation of how causal categories are to be applied, that Seward has focused only on the relative short-term consequences of Joan's actions and failed to appreciate her influence on events that took place after her death. In articulating his view, he notes that Joan's initial successes (the relief of Orléans, the march through English-Burgundian territory to Rheims, and the coronation of the Dauphin) were followed by a period in which Bedford, the Regent, had a number of victories, a period that ended with Joan's capture, trial, and execution. Seward thus emphasizes the fact that something more, beyond the revived morale of the French, was needed to drive the English out of France—he points to the ineptness of Cardinal Beaufort's military policy (especially after Bedford's death), the Franco-Burgundian alliance, and improvements in artillery technology (particularly associated with Maître Jean Bureau).[57] Enthusiasts for Joan (and for traditional celebrations of her) might suggest that her influence was decisive—without her there would have been no possibility of driving the English out. The sophisticated historian, reviewing this clash of judgments, may declare that there's no fact of the matter. History is just indeterminate as to whether Joan ended English rule in France.

We agree that there are several different ways of elaborating such causal notions as "ending English rule," but we believe that, once the meanings have been fixed, it's possible to talk about the objective truth (or falsehood) of historical statements. To a first approximation, the traditionalist insists that, without Joan's intervention, the English would have continued to dominate northern France (and Guyenne): if we imagine a world very like the actual one, in which Joan doesn't intervene (she doesn't hear the voices, or she is turned away from the Dauphin's camp), then the English presence remains. Likewise, a rough way to gloss Seward's claim is that many continuations of the course of events at Joan's death would have led to the preservation of English rule: in worlds like the actual one in which Beaufort is less powerful (or more clear-headed) or Burgundy stays allied to England or Maître Bureau doesn't achieve his technological advances. Historians are sometimes suspicious of counterfactual claims, but we concur with those authors who believe that counterfactual explorations are embedded in historical practice.[58] We don't believe that it's easy to give a full theory of historical counterfactuals that will reveal how they are objectively true and false,[59] but we can defuse the argument for maintaining that counterfactual judgments must be subjective that appeals to such clashes as that between Seward and the traditionalist. For in this and kindred cases, the disambiguation of the causal claims exposes the fact that both might be correct; we see no difficulty in supposing that Joan-less worlds would have seen continued English domination, and that worlds with Joan but without (say) Bureau would have unfolded to the same end.

We offer a further consideration against the worry that counterfactual claims are mere flights of the historian's fancy. In some instances, the counterfactual judgment mirrors the decision making of a historical protagonist: Joan was moved to go to the Dauphin because she thought that her intervention was needed to save Orléans; Maître Bureau worked with his brother on improving artillery because he thought it would make a difference to the French success. Setting aside the heavenly voices of the one and the commercial interests of the other, we can endorse the idea that both had a clear understanding of the possible futures. When historical agents consider their options, they may sometimes be myopic or deceived, but where we retrospectively find no basis for impugning their judgments, we'd expect their most central decisions to involve suppositions and counterfactuals that are objectively correct.[60]

We've been arguing for a particular elaboration of *veritism about history*, and it will be worth presenting it explicitly.

> *Veritism about historical statements.* History aims at, and sometimes achieves, true statements about some aspects of the past, even when the statements in question may be couched in categories that later historians might reject or when those statements contain causal concepts.

Even if (as we hope) we've been successful in defending this thesis, it may seem beside the point. For although aiming at true statements might be part of the historian's enterprise—what accounts for the long hours in the archives—there's plenty of room to doubt that it's the whole, or even a major part. If that were all there were to doing history properly, then it would be easy: all one would have to do would be to find some hitherto un-worked piece of archival material—the journal of a nineteenth-century Shropshire pig farmer, say—establish the reliability of the source, and then proceed to regale the learned (and maybe unlearned) world with true statements about the past ("On April 18 1836, there were intermittent showers on Wenlock Edge . . ."). Opponents of *veritism* probably have little patience with our efforts to support *veritism about historical statements*, be-cause they consider the historian's task as producing histories, and al-though histories contain statements (and although historians want those constituent statements to be true), the collection of statements doesn't ex-haust the history. Indeed, opponents will continue by suggesting that the interesting thesis of *veritism about history* is the claim that the aim of his-tory is to produce true histories (as opposed to disjointed collections of facts), and although *veritism about historical statements* is a necessary condi-tion for that thesis, it falls far short of being sufficient.

This objection contains several important insights, which deserve careful articulation. We'll begin, however, with a cautionary point. Truth is primarily an attribute of sentences or statements; there may be derivative notions of truth that apply to thoughts or to visual representations. Any notion of truth that is supposed to apply to a complex of statements—a historical work, a narrative, or a history—must be carefully explained in terms of the core notion of truth, that is, truth as a property of individual representations (paradigmatically statements). Casual invocation of truth for complex texts (histories, narratives), and direct denials that such texts are true are both misguided.[61] We need first to understand how a concept of truth might be supposed to apply here.

At this point it will be useful to explore a parallel source of confusion in the philosophy of science. One influential line of argument against realist approaches to the aims and achievements of the sciences, the "pessimistic induction on the history of science," begins from the judgment that past science is full of theories that once appeared extremely successful and that we now reject. The conclusion we're invited to draw is that none of the current theories, however successful they may appear, is true. Indeed, to suggest that we ever achieve true theories may be a serious deception, and if true theories inevitably lie beyond our reach, true theorizing can't be our aim.[62]

But what does it mean to say that a theory is true? According to a once popular notion of scientific theory, there's an easy answer: a scientific theory is a collection of statements, consisting of a set of principles and their deductive consequences; the theory is true if the conjunction of the principles (the axioms of the theory) is true. Now although philosophers have reconstructed a few parts of science in this way—most notably in theoretical physics—it has become increasingly evident that there are vast areas of the natural sciences that the axiomatic conception of scientific theories fits badly, if at all.[63] Even where it is applicable, however, the axiomatic conception and its coordinate notion of truth lead to an interesting reappraisal of the "pessimistic induction." To show that a successful theory is false, all that is needed is to find some false constituent statement—one fault infects the whole. Realists can thus reply that all that has been shown is that the theories we've so far developed aren't *completely* true. More exactly, they can defend *veritism about scientific statements*—the sciences aim at, and sometimes achieve, true statements.

And here, of course, the impatient antiveritist protests. To say that the sciences aim at true statements is far too weak. Truth is cheap. Without large government grants (or private funds) you can discover vast numbers of truths about nature: look around! There are indefinitely many languages you could use to announce indefinitely many truths about the immediate vicinity. If *veritism about the sciences* simply retreats from the claim about seeking true theories, maintaining *veritism about scientific statements* instead, then it has trivialized the scientific enterprise.

The negative point is correct. The bare substitution of *veritism about scientific statements* is inadequate. But it's a mistake to think that the old idiom of "true theories" was satisfactory, or to suppose that theories are the be-all and end-all of good science. Instead we propose to adopt

Veritism about significant scientific statements. The sciences aim at, and sometimes achieve, significant true statements about aspects of nature.

Similarly, we maintain

> *Veritism about significant historical statements.* History aims at, and some-
> times achieves, significant true statements about aspects of the past.

Neither of our theses is worth much, of course, until we've said something
about the notion(s) of significance involved.

For the case of the sciences, we summarize an approach one of us has
developed elsewhere.[64] Significant statements are answers to significant
questions. To say that a question is significant is not to say that it's posed
to us by nature,[65] but that people in a particular context find it to be worth
addressing. There are general sorts of considerations that make a question
worth addressing. Sometimes we need to know how to predict an outcome
in order to achieve our ends; sometimes we need to know something in
order to intervene successfully in nature; sometimes we are simply cu-
rious about some aspect of the natural world. Here is the point at which
Bernardism and *veritism* connect. When the connection is made, however,
it's important not to suppose that all instances of disinterested curiosity—
all cases in which the significance of a question is epistemic rather than
practical—involve why questions. Both in the sciences and in history, there
are many different kinds of questions to which we'd like answers.

Consider the following sample. What are the constituents of eukaryote
cells?, Will the universe continue to expand indefinitely?, Is there intelli-
gent life elsewhere in the universe?, When did human language evolve?,
How many species of australopithecines were there, and how are they related?, To what extent can one form a range of silicon compounds that ri-
vals the diversity of carbon compounds?, What is the natural host organism
for the Ebola virus?, Can nonhuman animals count?. We suggest that
these questions are significant, that they are significant independently of
any practical use we might make of answers to them,[66] that we aren't interested in them because answers would constitute a law or a theory,[67] and
that none of them is naturally reformulated as a why question. Scientific
significance is much more heterogeneous and messy than traditional philosophical accounts have recognized. We can defend *Bernardism* only if
we're prepared to view explanations as answers to significant questions,
which fall into a wide variety of types—in short, only if we're prepared to
adopt the *liberal interpretation.*

Historians too are concerned with a wide range of questions. We've already noted that the point of some historical works is to answer questions
of the form What was it like to be . . . ? Yet even in the case of historical

texts that might seem to be directed towards causal explanation of some outcome, it would be wrong to insist that a single why question is the focal point. It's tempting to think that a history of the Hundred Years War is effectively an explanation why the English were driven out of France, but the primary concern is surely to inform the reader about what happened in a particular region at a particular time. Many histories are far more interested in the route than in the terminus. A striking example is Robert Hughes's brilliant evocation of "the system," the settling of Australia by convicts (and the law enforcement officers who disciplined them).[68] It would be a travesty to confine Hughes's account to a single why question, or even a small set of why questions—for example, Why was the system abandoned?. His rich treatment answers a wide range of questions—Who were these convicts?, What were their lives like?, What opportunities were available for them?, How harshly were they disciplined in Australia?, How did they graduate from the system?, and many others. We're given what many histories provide, a picture of a place and a social group during a particular period, a "portrait of an age."

At this point, we can return to the impatient critic, and to the insight that there's more to a history than a collection of statements. What the critic sees is that a serious historical work structures the constituent statements, and that the criterion for good structuring is not correspondence to reality. A familiar way of developing the point is to refer to the structure as a "narrative" and then to debate whether narratives are answers to why questions or whether they should be understood by deploying categories from literary criticism (or theory).[69] Precisely because we understand histories as answering a range of significant questions, we adopt the neutral term "structure." What makes for a good structure, we suggest, is the provision of answers to significant questions. Thus an unstructured list of true statements fails as history because it doesn't answer any significant question (beyond whatever significant questions would have been answered by the constituent statements). In the work of a gifted historian, however, the combination of the statements provides answers to a much broader set of significant questions. Thus, for example, the individual details of Hughes's *The Fatal Shore* compose a portrait of early Australian life.

There are forms of historical structure that are very close to, even identical with, structures that inform scientific works. One kind of significant scientific question concerns the ways aspects of nature have come to be as they are; thus there are important works of science that develop accounts of how the universe began, how it evolved, how the earth's surface came to be as it is, how the continents reached their present positions, how life evolved, how hominids originated and radiated, how different human groups became differentially successful.[70] Equally, for groups of human beings, both large and small, there are historical texts that tell structurally similar stories, histories of particular nations or institutions or local communities. Second, as we've already noted, some scientific investigations are concerned to identify the causes of complicated phenomena—to explain, for example, the distribution of the biota in a particular region of the globe—and their proposals are structurally similar to those offered by some historians, interested in such things as the causes of World War I or the schism between Catholicism and the Orthodox Church.

Yet historians, particularly the most creative of them, raise new kinds of significant question. They expose features of our own lives we overlook or take for granted, by showing how people lived when those features were absent. They illustrate possibilities we had not considered by taking us into past societies or situations. The historian's selection of true statements about the past may bring into new relations things with which we are familiar or expand the world of our mundane experience. Tapping into our curiosity about the character of our own lives and the possibilities of human experience, they may make us interested in people or periods that we had not previously seen as significant, such as Bertrande de Rols or the late eighteenth century in Botany Bay.

So, while our *veritist* theses bring out the commonality between history and the sciences, we think it right to emphasize the ways historians can generate new significant questions by drawing on our curiosity about the possible forms of human life. Once again, we reach a mixed conclusion. History shares with the sciences the aim of reaching significant truth. It differs from the natural sciences in having special opportunities for generating new significant questions.[71] Historical works that address the types of significant question addressed in the natural sciences will foster the impression that there's no significant difference. Some historical works that raise radically different kinds of significant question will contravene that impression. And many texts will present a mixed picture. We now want to close with some brief reflections on the links between history and anthropology and between history and literature.

[6]

Here's an obvious counter to the assimilation of history to the sciences: style matters in history, but not in science. Is that correct?

In general, we suggest, rhetoric should be judged by its ability to promote the function the text is supposed to serve. It's a mistake to think that rhetorical considerations don't matter in science: on the contrary, scientific presentations adopt a very particular style, designed for the cognitive ends that are to be attained.[72] Yet it seems that the original point can be restated; there are great historical works that are rightly prized for their literary merits, while in correspondingly major scientific texts any suspicion of a literary flourish is sacrificed to the rigid demands of the conventions of scientific rhetoric.[73] Doesn't this suggest that the cognitive functions are different?

Everything depends on the kinds of questions that historians and scientists are trying to answer. As we've suggested, there are species of history that are very close in aim to the historical sciences—histories that relate what happened in a given time period or that are focused on answering a single why question (or a cluster of related why questions). In these instances, the cognitive ends to be served are the perspicuous presentation of a sequence of events or of an ensemble of causes. The style of the historian should be adapted to those ends, enabling the reader to appreciate the elements of the sequence or the comparative importance of the causes. There's no significant difference whether the topic is the medieval papacy or the evolution of the vertebrates. Here we think that stylistic considerations bear in the same ways on the historical work and on the scientific presentation.

Pure cases are probably quite rare. Most histories, we believe, are interested in answering a broader range of questions, and among those they'll attempt to address are issues about what a particular past situation was like. In doing that, of course, they'll need to make the past vivid, to present the telling detail in ways that prompt an imaginative response on the reader's part. We alluded earlier to the similarity between this sort of historical writing and the construction of a good ethnography. Because the aims of this type of history are like those of some anthropologists, it's entirely appropriate that texts that offer a "portrait of an age" should be held to the standards of ethnographic writing—which typically diverge from those of the natural sciences. What succeeds in delineating the precise relations among a complex of causes may not work at all for conveying the lives of past people.

Insofar as both history and anthropology aim to introduce possible ways of living of which readers hadn't been aware, by highlighting individual situations and characters, they share goals with works of literature.

It should therefore be unsurprising that some historical writing has a literary flavor. This is not simply a matter of outmoded, preprofessional history—the familiar point that Gibbon is worth reading just for the glories of his style; the passage quoted above from Natalie Zemon Davis wouldn't disgrace a work of fiction, and we could make similar claims for many of the historians we have cited.

These observations of important differences between some historical writings and works in natural science—grounded in the kinds of cognitive aims we've tried to survey in previous sections—lead us to two closing questions. The first concerns the place of literary analysis in the understanding of the practice of history. Since we agree that some historical enterprises may have similar aims to those of literary works, we believe that the tools used to elucidate the latter may prove valuable with respect to the former (and conversely). We can thus welcome studies that identify the literary tropes in historical writing. We are sympathetic to the pioneering ventures of Hayden White, provided that such efforts distinguish the various kinds of cognitive functions served in historical writing and do not operate with the presupposition that all historical texts are structured by narratives.[74] We should not forget the ways historical works aim to provide true answers to questions about the past or think that historical understanding can *only* be discussed using the language of literary criticism (or theory). Just as our view of the practice of history makes room for the expression of modifications of some of Hempel's ideas, so too we'd make room for a transformed version of White's literary analyses, focused on precisely those parts of historical practice where the connections in aim with literature are closest. Here, too, we view ourselves as liberalizing Danto's project: once we admit a number of different modes of structuring historical texts, the connections between different modes and literary analysis may be quite variable.[75]

Our second question raises the need for truth in history. We've written so far as if the truth of the constituent statements of a historical work were a *sine qua non*: we could be given lots of truths about the past without having a good history, but, it's seemed, we can't have good history in the absence of lots of truths about the past. It seems possible, however, that a historical work might get the big picture right and have most—even all— of the details wrong. Perhaps there are histories that are groundbreaking in bringing to bear kinds of descriptions that others have overlooked, introducing categories that are crucial to understanding the causes of events or bring into focus the lives of past people, and yet, for all that, the deployment of these categories is inaccurate. So, for example, it may well be true that there was the kind of shift in understandings of madness that Foucault claims, even though he has picked out the wrong historical episodes and the wrong agents for documenting it.[76] More radically, a historian might deliberately choose to introduce into a historical discussion conjectures for which there's no evidence or even statements known to be false.[77] Doing so might make the past more vivid or open up for the reader possibilities that had previously not been appreciated. If these are proper goals of historical writing, shouldn't we allow that constituent truth isn't a necessary condition of good history? Hence, we can envisage areas of historical study for which *veritism* isn't an appropriate aim.

We've emphasized throughout that there are many varieties of history, some that are close to the (historical) natural sciences, some that border on anthropology, some that border on works of literature. Far from restricting historical writing, we'd encourage the development of many different genres, including those that cross the boundaries between history and fiction. Moreover, we'd recall that the natural sciences often fictionalize, introducing ideal entities for purposes of shedding light on the behavior of messier and more complicated things. There's no reason to deny historians the same license. Indeed, insofar as we relax *veritism* for one group, in the interests of significance, we should relax it for the other as well.

But, of course, scientists are usually quite clear where they are pretending, noting explicitly that the pivot isn't frictionless and that the breeding population doesn't satisfy the conditions of the Hardy–Weinberg law. If historians choose to take up the exciting challenge of writing the kind of fictional history exemplified by Schama's *Dead Certainties*, then we have no objection, only words of encouragement, as long as they honor the same demand, making it clear to their readers just where they have embellished the account.[78] Otherwise we may be deceived into thinking that we have history "as it actually was." and that the work answers questions to which it wasn't properly directed. In his attempt to draw firm boundaries between history and fiction, the eminent historian Eric Hobsbawm claims that "If history is an imaginative art, it is one which does not invent but arranges *objets trouvés*."[79] Whether or not they receive the label "history," we allow for collages that touch up the objects a bit, provided that the artist acknowledges the handiwork.

How then do we sum up the relation between history and the sciences? Are they akin or are they different? We suggest that the questions invite oversimplified answers—and thus foster unprofitable controversy. A harmless, but not very informative, response would be to point out that the enterprises we group among the sciences are diverse, that the practice of history is also diverse, and that some things we count as history are similar to some of the things we categorize as sciences in their aims, achievements, and methods. A better answer is to provide a picture of both kinds of diversity and to identify the points of similarity and difference among specific historical studies, specific parts of natural science, specific work in anthropology, and specific types of literature. We've been trying to clear the ground for providing that better answer.

‖‖ ‖‖ ‖‖ ‖‖ ‖‖

Response

It would be instructive to write a narrative of the philosophy of science, beginning with the Unity of Science movement that C. G. Hempel's various contributions to the theory of explanation exemplify—including "The Function of General Laws in History," which may have seemed a footnote but proved to be one of the movement's crown jewels—to Philip Kitcher and Daniel Immerwahr's "History and the Sciences." I suppose my *Analytical Philosophy of History* belongs in the narrative, since, as Kitcher and Immerwahr observe, it "appeared when the account of the sciences offered by Hempel and others had begun to be challenged"—but I think the appearance of my book has to be explained along with the challenges. I cannot imagine that it in any way contributed to the break-up of logical empiricism, if only for the reasons that Frank Ankersmit mentions in his contribution to this volume, that the philosophy of history remained a pretty marginal discipline in analytical philosophy. In a way Kitcher and Immerwahr sketch the narrative in the footnotes to their valuable paper, but for me the interesting question is what is the historical explanation of the work of Tom Kuhn and N. R. Hanson (who had been my classmate at Columbia, and a close friend). Both of them were deeply influenced by Wittgenstein—Kuhn through Stanley Cavell—and the story may begin with whatever it was that caused Wittgenstein to jettison the project of the *Tractatus* and begin those diffident, inconclusive, intimate little conversations with himself—with *Du*—in the *Investigations*. But what explains *that*?

Logical empiricism was a living reality when I wrote *Analytical Philosophy of History* in the early '60, and Hempel's paper defined the territory into which it ventured. I had already published what became my central chapter—"Narrative Sentences"—and I knew already that there were descriptions under which events could not be explained, namely those that had as a truth condition events that took place after—and perhaps long after—the so-called *explanandum* was part of history. The events that explained the birth of Isaac Newton in Woolthorpe in 1642 could hardly explain that event under the description—perfectly acceptable in a history of science—that the author of *Principia Mathematica* was born in Woolthorpe in 1642. Defenders of the covering-law model may have been willing to say that as long as there is some description under which a given event could be so explained, the model was more or less safe. But one could hardly hope that this captured what made these events historically important. The birth of Isaac Newton was mainly important to his parents in 1642, but the birth of the author of *Principia Mathematica* became an event important to humankind, just because the masterpiece was itself such an important achievement. And what entered into the historical explanation of the book involved the history of physics in a way that explanation of the birth of the author would not. Still, I felt constrained to show that narrative explanations could be modeled on Hempelian explanations, and hence that the covering-law model might be preserved. In showing this, I felt my book maintained its credibility with regard to the readership that was important to me, namely the logical empiricists and of course Hempel himself, of whom I was extremely fond as a person. He was a man of exceptional generosity and curiosity.

Even so, the main thought that narrative sentences opened up for me was that in order to know what made an event *historically* important—or what Kitcher and Immerwahr call "significant"—would require knowing the interests of future generations. In *Analytical Philosophy of History* I invented what I termed "The Ideal Chronicle," in which whatever happened was inscribed immediately—in which whatever took place was entered in terms of what could have been observed at the time it happened. So in a way the whole of history is there so far as it could have been known under "observation sentences." But which events were important? That, as I say, depended upon future interests, which there would be no way of predicting. When Artemesia Gentileschi painted a marvelous *Susanna and the Elders* at the age of 16, the event was of considerable interest to her father, the painter Orazio Gentileschi, since having a talented daughter in the household was a significant addition to his workshop. She became part of the history of Carravaggism, but who was interested in that other than specialists? Her paintings were in storerooms of most museums that owned one, rarely on their walls—until the advent of twentieth-century feminism, when women art historians, prodded by Linda Nochlin's essay

"Why Are There No Great Woman Artists?" began to canvass the history of art and discovered that Artemisia was a considerable artist, and the history of Carravaggism had to be restructured. When human interests, various as they are, define importance, determine the relevant descriptions of the pasts, the hope that history will become a science as science was conceived of under logical empiricism becomes pretty fragile. The great merit of Kitcher and Immerwahr's paper lies in the way it shows how that fragility vanishes when science itself is recast in twenty-first-century terms.

In the end, the reputation of my book was less a matter of whatever respectability it attained among the logical empiricists than of how it was perceived by continental philosophers. Jürgen Habermas published an early book that discussed the social sciences as Hempel and as I had written about history, and when he and I met, he said that my book had carried analytical philosophy to a point at which it had turned into hermeneutics. I had a somewhat uncertain grasp of hermeneutics, then as now, but I took this as a considerable compliment. And in an important way, it connected with my own agenda at the time. *Analytical Philosophy of History* was published in 1965. In that same year, I also published *Nietzsche as Philosopher*. The agenda of that book was to overcome the same sort of gap that Habermas felt the other book did: I was eager to show that Nietzsche had greatly contributed to philosophy in just the same way that logical empiricism understood philosophy. He had deep and original things to say about language and about logic. He was one of us, rather than the blankly alternative philosopher his enthusiasts held him to be. I mention this here because it is another example of the erasing of boundaries that, as I see it, twenty-first-century philosophy of science, as practiced by Kitcher and Immerwahr, is attempting.

I'll return to this in a moment, but I want first to bring forward another fragment of my philosophical activity in those years, namely the philosophy of art. In 1964, I published probably my most influential paper, "The Artworld," which was prompted by the appearance of works of art that entirely resembled objects that were not considered works of art at the time. My paradigm of this was of course Andy Warhol's *Brillo Box*, which to all intents and purposes looked just like the commonplace objects in supermarket stockrooms. And my question was what made the one a work of art and the other what I termed a "mere real thing." I knew—or perhaps merely intuited—that observation of differences, such as they were, was not going to explain the ontological difference between works of art and mere real things, but the best I could do at the time was to propose that the two had disjoint classes of causes, or better, that to see the one as a work of art, one had to know something of the recent history of art and something of the theory that was current in art world discourse. My point was that something is a work of art in virtue of a theory, and in a general way I was beginning to think of the history of art as having the structure of a conversation, in which something like historical implicature connects things up, the way Paul Grice was saying that conversations hold together by means of implicatures, the rules for which he attempted to work out. Interestingly, this kind of case turns up in *Analytical Philosophy of History*. I imagined two narratives, each titled *The Battle of Iwo Jima*, word for word identical—except that one was written after the Battle of Iwo Jima took place, whereas the other was written in the early nineteenth century. Nothing observable need distinguish a piece of historical from a piece of fictional narrative. There is no point in repeating here the analysis I developed for explaining the difference, but the idea of using indiscernible counterparts became an important philosophical method for me, and which I came to think actually defined a problem as philosophical.

But what interested me as I learned more and more about the art history of the '60s was the fact that many of the avant-garde art movements of the time were engaged with the project of overcoming the gap between art and life. This had begun in the 1950s, actually, in the work of Robert Rauschenberg, and one of its high moments was the 1952 performance of John Cage's *4'33"* in which the sounds one heard within that interval of time was the piece—the sound of a motorcycle outside, of people coughing, or rustling their programs. Cage was interested in overcoming the gap between the sounds of everyday life and musical sounds, narrowly conceived. His students formed a movement called Fluxus, in which again the issue was to break down barriers—to make art that was indiscernible from life. And as the decade evolved, this was the project of pop art, minimalism, conceptual art, and artworks came to look like ordinary things—rows of bricks, a single lit fluorescent bulb, a pile of hemp in a corner, a module of a prefabricated house, a stack of railway ties, an array of neckties.

What has this to do with the thought with which this response to "History and the Sciences" began—the narrative of the philosophy of science, beginning with logical empiricism and ending with Kitcher and Immerwahr's essay? What interests me is what explains that narrative. Philosophy is no more immune to historical explanation than art or life is. What happens in philosophy is not exclusively a matter internal to philosophy. Philosophers are inflected in what they do by what happens in the world outside philosophy. My overall view is that a certain liberalization began to surface in the '60s, though its causes would have to be sought earlier than that. As I see it, Western civilization was entering a new period, which I think of as the end of modernism and the beginning of something that as yet lacks a historical designation, but which we find ourselves having to deal with everywhere in life.

In 1960, the art critic Clement Greenberg published a powerful essay titled "Modernist Painting," in which he compared modernism in art with a form of self-criticism exemplified in the philosophy of Kant, whom he complimented in consequence as the first modernist. Self-critique in the arts, as Greenberg viewed it, consisted in purifying the medium unique to any art of whatever was extrinsic to it. In an example with which Greenberg's thought has been identified, flatness is what is unique to the medium of painting, which must accordingly be purged of illusionism of any kind, and depth given over by right to sculpture. His basic thought was that each art must discover the principles unique to it, and then abide by those. Painters sought purity in painting, and "truth to the medium" became a critical principle throughout the arts. Modernism so characterized was coming to its end when Greenberg published this famous essay—as Hegel wrote, "The Owl of Minerva takes flight only with the falling of the dusk." By the time a period reveals itself, it is largely over with.

I have a sense—perhaps this is sentimentality—that cultural changes first show up in art. Just when it seemed that a classification of the arts based on differences in the media had become canonical, everything began to blur. The arts all began to interpenetrate one another, media became mixed, and it became difficult to tell the difference between artworks and mere real things. This became conspicuous in the work of Marcel Duchamp, whose *Readymades were* mere real things. Boundaries began to dissolve. As the '60s unfolded, the boundaries between the races were attacked. Blacks were enfranchised. By the end of the decade, the boundaries between the sexes began to crumple. The ideas of each race having its "place," as in aApartheid, and of women knowing their place lost appeal. Everything in principle became open to everyone. Everyone was an artist, Josef Beuys said in the '70s. Anything can be a work of art, Warhol said.

I think the *Tractatus* was an exemplary piece of modernist philosophy, logical atomism being another, with its partition of the world into different orders of fact, each with is own logic. I think the entire idea of philosophy as logical construction is modernist through and through. The idea of pure philosophy belongs to the same mentality as pure painting. The *Investigations* was a postmodernist work, and I think *Analytical Philosophy of History* was transitional, on its way into postmodernism. I think Kitcher and Immerwahr are advancing a postmodernist philosophy of science, drawing as they do, parallels between history and science, finding ways to overcome that boundary.

If I am right about a new period of history beginning in the 1960s, then a fascinating problem in historical explanation is how to account for this change. Periods have a certain reality. They are not just arbitrary ways of dividing history up, but involve almost seismic changes in the way those who belong to them think about the world. What explains the shift that Hegel notes from what he calls the classical period of art to the romantic? The gods in classical art exemplify different attributes—power, wisdom, eroticism. But they do not have what one might call interior lives. In romantic art, interiority, by contract, is the defining attribute. The explanation has to do with the advent of Christianity, the need to represent the theological virtues—faith, hope, charity—and especially suffering and love. Art, religion, philosophy in the romantic era differ profoundly from what they were in the classical era, and those differences penetrate the way people view themselves and the world. The shift from Enlightenment to Romanticism at the turn of the nineteenth century, and the shift from that into modernism around the 1860s, are similar deep changes. Whatever the case, entire populations were transformed, and it has been exciting to experience the irresistible shift into postmodernity. It is deeply affecting to see that the philosophy of science is itself part of its time.

Notes

We are delighted to dedicate this essay to Arthur Danto. Thanks to Isaac Levi for his constructive suggestions on an earlier version, and to the editors for their advice about the penultimate draft.

1. Originally published in *The Journal of Philosophy* in 1942. We'll refer to the reprinting by Hempel in his *Aspects of Scientific Explanation* (New York: Free Press, 1965).

2. Cambridge: Cambridge University Press, 1964. The book was reprinted, with additional material, under the title *Narration and Knowledge* (New York: Columbia University Press, 1985). We'll refer to the later edition.

3. Wilhelm Dilthey and Benedetto Croce are the most prominent advocates of the difference between history (as a *Geisteswissenschaft*) and the natural sciences, and Hempel's article is naturally read as responding to them—despite the fact that he doesn't mention them and takes, as his official target, a related view advanced by Maurice Mandelbaum. We think that the controversy about the scientific status of history goes back at least to the Enlightenment.

4. Essentially the view that has become known as "logical empiricism," articulated by Hempel, Rudolf Carnap, Hans Reichenbach, Ernest Nagel, and Karl Popper; although there were important differences among these philosophers, all shared

the following views: scientific theories are deductive systems; scientific laws are generalizations, some strictly universal, others statistical; scientific explanation consists in producing arguments that use general laws to derive a description of the phenomenon to be explained. It is worth noting explicitly that, despite the prominence of Hempel's work in discussions of historical explanation, much more detailed (and more nuanced) proposals about historical explanation and the role of general laws were offered by Nagel and by Morton White.

5. *Narration and Knowledge,* xi; Danto refers to the impact of the work of N. R. Hanson and, particularly, of Thomas Kuhn. We agree that Hanson, and especially Kuhn, forced a rethinking of many points that logical empiricism had taken for granted.

6. See Philip Kitcher, *Science, Truth, and Democracy* (New York: Oxford University Press, 2001); some parts of the picture are articulated in more detail in an earlier book, *The Advancement of Science* (New York: Oxford University Press, 1993), but, where there are differences, the views of the later book are to be preferred.

7. Of course, claims about aims typically constrain theses about achievements and about methods, so one shouldn't assume that all these elements can vary independently.

8. It's no accident that we talk of the "fossil record" and the "rock record." And, of course, one of Darwin's most extensive defenses of his views draws an extended analogy between the sequence of organisms whose remains have been preserved and an incomplete, tattered, and defaced library (*Origin of Species,* chapter IX [closing paragraph]).

9. Kuhn articulates this kind of skepticism, not only in *The Structure of Scientific Revolutions* (Chicago: University of Chicago Press, 1962) but also in "Objectivity, Value Judgment, and Theory Choice" (in *The Essential Tension* [Chicago: University of Chicago Press, 1977]). For a thorough survey of the leading contender for an account of scientific confirmation, see John Earman, *Bayes or Bust?* (Cambridge, MA.: MIT Press, 1992).

10. Edmund S. Morgan, *Inventing the People* (New York: Norton, 1988), 55.

11. Desmond Seward, *The Hundred Years War* (New York: Penguin, 1999), 213.

12. Here one may compare Robert F. Berkhofer Jr., *Beyond the Great Story* (Cambridge, MA.: Harvard University Press, 1995), and Joyce Appleby, Lynn Hunt, and Margaret Jacob, *Telling the Truth About History* (New York: Norton, 1994).

13. Partly because of Danto's important book, partly because of historians' concerns about styles of history ("narrative" versus "analytic"), this has shaded into a discussion of the character of historical narratives. (See, for example, Geoffrey Roberts, *The History and Narrative Reader* [London: Routledge, 2001], which collects many of the classic contributions.) As we'll try to make clear, we think that these disputes have been stymied because of failure to probe the broader questions about the aims of the sciences and of history.

14. This thesis is named for Claude Bernard, whose study of experimental physiology and medicine is one of the classic sources of the view that the sciences aim at explanation, prediction, and control.

15. As Isaac Levi pointed out to us, this list would be rejected by many philosophers in the pragmatist tradition, who would set up the issues very differently. We take the point, and regard our list as emblematic of a version of logical empiricism that is antithetical to pragmatist themes and modes of formulation—a version more evident in Carnap and Hempel than in Nagel. We also believe that the view of the sciences and of history's relations to the sciences that we elaborate below is far more akin to the pragmatist approach to scientific inquiry.

16. Perhaps this is too quick, in that there are instances in which history might be credited as the ultimate source of claims advanced by economists or political scientists who make predictions—as, for example, when they suggest that economies planned by powerful authoritarian governments have a high probability of leading to disastrous consequences for the citizenry. Moreover, as with the lines between history and other disciplines, the distinction between history and economics (or that between history and political science) may be blurred. Even if these caveats about the *impracticality* thesis are correct, they will not affect the main conclusion we draw from it. For it would be hard to dispute the idea that any social scientific predictions drawn from history are obtained through the historical explanations that have been given, and this would leave intact the primacy of explanation as a goal.

17. There are important exceptions. Historians sometimes draw on generalizations about the transmission of infectious agents or about the effects of various kinds of missiles; for examples, see W. S. McNeill, *Plagues and Peoples* (New York: Doubleday, 1976), and John Keegan, *The Face of Battle* (London: Penguin, 1978).

18. *Narration and Knowledge*, 203 ff.

19. We offer a handful of representative texts: Edward Gibbon, *The Decline and Fall of the Roman Empire*; Michael Grant, *The Fall of the Roman Empire* (Radnor, PA: Annenberg School Press, 1976); Lawrence Stone, *The Causes of the English Revolution* (New York: Harper and Row, 1972); David Brion Davies, *The History of Slavery in Western Culture* (New York: Oxford University Press, 1966); Lyn MacDonald, *1914* (London: M. Joseph, 1987); John Keegan, *The First World War*; and Niall Ferguson, *The Pity of War* (New York: Basic Books, 1999).

20. Thus one of the differences among historians who try to explain the origins of the First World War I consists in their specification of the congeries of events that are to count as the beginning of that war; this difference in *explananda* doesn't occur when the task is to explain something like Constantine's declaration that Christianity was to be the official religion of the Empire.

21. *Montaillou* (New York: Vintage, 1979), 276.

22. Ibid. 174. A *cabane* is a mountain hut, typically occupied by several shepherds and constituting a social unit; the reference to sponsoring indicates Pierre's involvement in Cathar religious practices; the parenthetical numerical reference is to the published version of Fournier's inquisitorial register.

23. Natalie Zemon Davis, *The Return of Martin Guerre* (Cambridge, MA.: Harvard University Press, 1983), 5.

24. As witnessed by the fact that it became a moderately successful film.

25. The real Martin had apparently been impotent; Davis, *Return of Martin Guerre*, 19; things went better after Martin's return—see 124.

26. Davis, *Return of Martin Guerre*, 44–46. See also 55, 61, 79–80, and 92.

27. Another famous microhistory, Carlo Ginzburg's *The Cheese and the Worms* (Baltimore: Johns Hopkins University Press, 1980), underscores the point we make here. Ginzburg takes us into the world of peasants in the Friuli region of Italy by focusing on a miller, Menocchio, who was tortured and executed for his heretical beliefs. Ginzburg isn't trying to persuade us that a person previously deemed unimportant has great significance. The aim is to show us how the world appeared to people who normally get left out of histories. The same purpose could have been achieved by concentrating on a different peasant, perhaps Marcato, who came from the same town and was also executed. What distinguishes Menocchio is that we happen to know something about him. But, as the last sentence of *The Cheese and the Worms* tells us, "About this Marcato, or Marco—and so many others like him who lived and died without a trace—we know nothing" (128).

28. See Berkhofer, *Beyond the Great Story*, 31–33.

29. There are other distinctive psychological changes that histories might endeavor to induce. Sometimes historians attempt to provoke a moral reaction by explaining how some contemporary institution has been deliberately designed to exclude a particular class of individuals or to detract from their welfare; a prime example is Mike Davis, *City of Quartz* (London: Verso, 1990), which shows how various aspects of Los Angeles were set up to make life hard for the indigent. Of course, there's a long tradition of histories "to a moral purpose," as well as an extensive critique of their propriety—perhaps most famously encapsulated in Ranke's dictum; we won't attempt to resolve the thorny issues here.

30. Keegan, *The Face of Battle*, 13.

31. Keegan, *The Face of Battle*, 16; it's entertaining to think that, had he read Thomas Nagel's famous essay, Keegan might have entitled his book *What Is It Like to Be in Battle?* Other military historians have approached the same question, particularly in the case of World War I; see for example the books of Lyn MacDonald—especially *Somme* (London: M. Joseph, 1983), *They Called It Paschendaele* (London: M. Joseph, 1978), and *The Roses of No Man's Land* (London: M. Joseph, 1980).

32. Keegan, *The Face of Battle*, 174.

33. Keith Thomas, *Religion and the Decline of Magic* (Oxford: Oxford University Press, 1970).

34. Paul Cohen, *History in Three Keys* (New York: Columbia University Press, 1999).

35. For more detail on this issue, see the opening sections of Philip Kitcher, "Explanatory Unification and the Causal Structure of the World," and the later parts of Wesley Salmon, "Four Decades of Scientific Explanation," both in P. Kitcher and W. Salmon, eds., *Scientific Explanation* (Minnesota Studies in the Philosophy of Science Volume XIII, Minneapolis: University of Minnesota Press, 1989).

36. The two problems we won't consider are the intractability of the problem of specifying the notion of scientific law and the counterintuitive consequences of Hempel's model of probabilistic explanation. Both troubles are presented very clearly in Salmon, "Four Decades of Scientific Explanation."

37. The example was originally devised by Sylvain Bromberger in the early 1960s.

38. This example was introduced by Wesley Salmon in "Statistical Explanation and Statistical Relevance"; Salmon notes that an earlier example of the same type was formulated by Henry Kyburg.

39. See Hexter, "The Rhetoric of History," reprinted in his *Doing History* (Bloomington: Indiana University Press, 1971), 30. Hexter formulates the point a bit more carefully than we've done here.

40. Here's a recipe for doing so: one can give a Hempelian argument for a conclusion asserting that the Giants won any specific victory (say, their thirty-seventh) by using physical laws to derive the trajectory of the winning hit; now add the true conditional statement that if the Giants won that game they would win the pennant.

41. Hexter, *Doing History*, 31.

42. Hexter, *Doing History*, 29; see also 71, where Hexter adopts what we've called the *liberal interpretation*.

43. See, for example, Wesley Salmon, *Scientific Explanation and the Causal Structure of the World* (Princeton: Princeton University Press, 1984); Paul Humphreys, *The Chances of Explanation* (Princeton: Princeton University Press, 1990).

44. Logical empiricism was mindful of Humean strictures about causation. Some of those who have identified the need for a causal constraint—Salmon, for example—have accepted the thought that invocation of an *unexplicated* notion of causation is illegitimate. Interestingly, the approach that Salmon has adopted, which sees causation in terms of the transmission of conserved quantities, seems very hard to apply in the context of historical explanation.

45. It should be noted that causal-historical explanation is prominent in some areas of the sciences (like the ones we've listed); that a different type of causal explanation (causal-mechanical explanation) is widespread in others, as for example in biochemistry and solid-state physics; and that there are some parts of theoretical science in which it's something of a strain to think in causal terms (the theory of the chemical bond, sex-ratio theory). See Wesley Salmon, "Scientific Explanation: Causation *and* Unification" (chapter 4 in Salmon, *Causality and Explanation* [New York: Oxford University Press, 1998]).

46. See N. R. Hanson, *Patterns of Discovery* (Cambridge: Cambridge University Press, 1958), 54. We should note that the context-dependency of explanation has been thoroughly analyzed by Bas van Fraassen (*The Scientific Image* [Oxford: Oxford University Press, 1980], chapter 5), who offers a pragmatic theory of explanation. One of us has criticized Van Fraassen's theory on the grounds that it trivializes the notion of explanation (P. Kitcher and W. Salmon, "Van Fraassen on Explanation," *Journal of Philosophy* 84 [1987]: 315–30), but the objection would now be modified; as we'll argue below, what counts as the right sort of causal relation to

invoke in answering an explanation-seeking why question is contextually determined, and Van Fraassen was insightful in pointing this out.

47. Hexter, *Doing History*, 35 (fgure 1). We are grateful to David Sidorsky for pointing
    out to us that Hexter's account does not mention the controversy about whether
    the Giants were stealing the Dodgers' signs.

48. Hexter rightly appreciates the greater naturalness of "How did it come about that
    . . . ?" rather than "Why?" in historical studies. See *Doing History* 30.

49. The modesty comes in two ways. First, we don't suppose that there are special
    entities—facts—to which true sentences correspond. Second, we don't assume
    that the core notion of reference can be specified in a physicalist vocabulary (as,
    for example, Hartry Field's "Tarski's Theory of Truth," *Journal of Philosophy* 69
    [1972]: 347–75 proposes). For further exploration of the position, see Philip
    Kitcher, "On the Explanatory Power of Correspondence Truth," *Philosophy and
    Phenomenological Research* 64 (2002):, 346–64.

50. See "On the Concept of Truth for Formalized Languages" (in A. Tarski, *Logic, Se-
    mantics, Metamathematics* [Oxford: Oxford University Press, 1956])—or any pre-
    sentation of the semantics for first-order logic in a logic text. Effectively, our pro-
    posal adds to Tarski's well-known account only the idea that the reference relation
    connects linguistic items with mind-independent entities.

51. For a general skepticism about *veritism* as we've interpreted it, see Richard Rorty,
    Consequences of Pragmatism (Minneapolis: University of Minnesota Press, 1982);
    Hilary Putnam, *Reason, Truth, and History* (Cambridge: Cambridge University
    Press, 1981); Nelson Goodman, *Ways of Worldmaking* (Indianapolis: Hackett,
    1978); more local versions are advanced by Bas van Fraassen, *The Scientific Image*
    (Oxford: Oxford University Press, 1980) and Larry Laudan, *Science and Values*
    (Berkeley: University of California Press, 1984). See also Arthur Fine, *The Shaky
    Game* (Chicago: University of Chicago Press, 1986).

52. or the defense, see Kitcher, *The Advancement of Science* (chapter 5); *Science, Truth,
    and Democracy* (chapter 2); and especially "Real Realism: The Galilean Strategy"
    (*Philosophical Review* 110 [2001]: 151–97).

53. *The Age of Constantine the Great* (Berkeley: University of California Press, 1949),
    71–72.

54. For Gibbon's description of Theodora, see chapter XL, part 1, of *The Decline and
    Fall of the Roman Empire*. The quoted sentence is from page 56 of volume 5 of the
    Oxford English Classics edition (1827).

55. Famously, Oscar Wilde replied to the prosecutor who asked if his works consti-
    tuted blasphemy, "That is not one of my words."

56. For detailed defense of the claim about Priestley, see Philip Kitcher, "Theories,
    Theorists, and Theoretical Change," *Philosophical Review* 87 (1978): 519–47.

57. Seward, *The Hundred Years War*, 221–62.

58. See the introduction to Niall Ferguson, ed., *Virtual History* (London: Picador,
    1997), especially 87, and also Geoffrey Hawthorn, *Plausible Worlds* (Cambridge:
    Cambridge University Press, 1991).

59. The most prominent philosophical account is that of David Lewis (*Counterfactu-
    als* [Oxford: Blackwell, 1974]), which deploys a notion of similarity across possi-

ble worlds. An obvious worry is that similarity depends on a choice of respects and degrees, and that such judgments are irremediably subjective.

60. For a similar assessment see Niall Ferguson's introduction to his *Virtual History*.

61. The philosopher of history who is clearest on this point is F. R. Ankersmit; see his *Narrative Logic* (Boston: Martinus Nijhoff, 1983).

62. The most fully developed version of this argument appears in Larry Laudan's "A Confutation of Convergent Realism" (*Philosophy of Science* 48 [1981]: 19–49); this essay is essentially reprinted as chapter 5 of his *Science and Values* (Berkeley: University of California Press, 1984).

63. Some challenges have developed the "semantic conception of theories," according to which theories are families of models; for an accessible presentation, see Ronald Giere, *Explaining Science* (Chicago: University of Chicago Press, 1988), chapters 3–4. Others have emphasized the apparently nonaxiomatic structure of evolutionary biology, molecular biology, the geological sciences, and so forth; see Philip Kitcher, *The Advancement of Science*, chapters 2–3. Another source of trouble emerges from the powerful account of "normal science" offered in the early chapters of Kuhn's *The Structure of Scientific Revolutions*.

64. Philip Kitcher, *Science, Truth, and Democracy*, chapter 6.

65. Here it seems to us that Rorty's skepticism about nature's agenda is insightful; see the introduction to *Consequences of Pragmatism*.

66. One might worry that the issue of the natural host for the Ebola virus is a practical question. Indeed, knowing the answer might enable us to prevent future outbreaks of Ebola. Nevertheless, even if we had a sure-fire vaccine for this disease— and were thus unconcerned about passage of the virus to human populations— we'd still be interested in knowing where the virus originally came from.

67. In some instances, of course, we might achieve an answer by developing a general theory; but even in such cases we'd be interested in the answer whether it came as a consequence of theory or not.

68. Robert Hughes, *The Fatal Shore* (New York: Knopf, 1986).

69. For this debate, see Geoffrey Roberts, *The History and Narrative Reader* (New York: Routledge, 2001). The approach to historical narratives in literary terms was pioneered by Hayden White in *Metahistory* (Baltimore: Johns Hopkins University Press, 1973). We'll briefly discuss the approaches of Ankersmit and White in the final section below.

70. For the first and last, see Steven Weinberg, *The First Three Minutes* (New York: Basic Books, 1977) and Jared Diamond, *Guns, Germs, and Steel* (New York: Norton, 1997), respectively. There are vast numbers of books on the history of life and on hominid evolution.

71. Plainly, the sciences often generate new questions that have practical significance for us. The difference we're trying to characterize here is that, because of our background curiosity about the possible forms of human life, history has a particular way of generating new issues for us.

72. See Philip Kitcher, "Persuasion" (in Marcello Pera and William Shea, eds., *Persuading Science: The Art of Scientific Rhetoric* [Sagamore Beach, MA: Science His-

tory Publications, 1991], 3–27), and "The Cognitive Function of Scientific Rhetoric" (in Henry Krips, J. E. McGuire, and Trevor Melia, eds., *Science and Rhetoric* [Pittsburgh: University of Pittsburgh Press, 1993]).

73. The general point can be appreciated by comparing the major works of great scientists with the books in which they summarize their views for a general audience. But there are important exceptions: the famous laconic last sentence of the Watson–Crick paper announcing the structure of DNA, some of Stephen Jay Gould's professional articles in paleontology, and, reverting to an earlier time, Darwin's *Origin*.

74. See White, *Metahistory*. White is quite explicit in claiming that all historical texts are structured by narratives, so the position we are recommending requires some adjustment of his views.

75. A consequence of this liberalization may be the severing of some links among Danto's "analytical philosophy" projects. As the editors pointed out to us, the emphasis on narrative and on causal explanation in history fits very well with Danto's explorations of action.

76. Michel Foucault, *Madness and Civilization* (New York: Pantheon, 1965). Although we allude here to a common criticism of Foucault, to the effect that he's wrong about the facts of the history of attitudes to insanity, we don't want to take a stand in this controversy.

77. See Simon Schama, *Dead Certainties* (New York: Knopf, 1991).

78. Schama himself is quite scrupulous in this regard.

79. Eric Hobsbawm, *On History* (New York: Norton, 1997), 272; the passage is from the essay "Identity History Is Not Enough."